TACTICS ON
BASS

Other Freshwater Angling Books by the Author

Tactics on Bass

Ray Ovington

Charles Scribner's Sons · New York

Copyright © 1983 Ray Ovington

Library of Congress Cataloging in Publication Data

Ovington, Ray.
  Tactics on bass.

  Includes index.
  1. Bass fishing.   I. Title.
SH681.O83   1983   799.1'758   82–42663
ISBN 0–684–17860–5

1 3 5 7 9 11 13 15 17 19   F/C   20 18 16 14 12 10 8 6 4 2

Printed in the United States of America.

CONTENTS

PREFACE AND ACKNOWLEDGMENTS

Tactics on Bass is not just another theory book—it is a series of guided fishing trips to some great waters all over the map. Like *Tactics on Trout,* published in 1969, *Tactics on Bass,* my thirty-fourth book, is a departure from the usual fishing book in content and objective. Both books on tactics accent the approach to specific waters and the presentation of standard-type lures, rigs, and baits. In order to do this in proper perspective and in enough detail, specific diagrams and illustrations of age-old tricks (and possibly some new ones) literally take you fishing with me. In this way you can see the various types of lake and shoreline waters and water conditions, and how to read them and fish them.

Ever notice how many people, when explaining something that is complicated, will tend to talk with their hands or reach for a napkin, menu, corner of newspaper or whatever, then draw a rough diagram of what they are trying to convey? That's what I've done here by providing simple diagrams and step-by-step instructions, sketches of flies and lures and rigs, ways to fish the water, plus some detailed sketch diagrams of the water situations discussed in each chapter. The objective is to keep it simple and plain. I hope to have conveyed in the book's illustrations the same thing we could have accomplished by sitting across the table from each other having a cup of coffee and scratching on the back of a menu.

Many fishing situations might appear obvious when first seen in print, but you could be surprised at how you might have overlooked great possibilities or bypassed opportunities to catch a big one. Also, when you go fishing on your own in the future, the situations we have fished here together will come to mind and act as prompters for the selection of lures and techniques. So gather your tackle and join me for some great fishing tactics on the water. We may not catch a bass every time we cast, but we'll have fun trying.

As well as the guides in the background for this book, there are many other people who have contributed to that background whom I would like to thank:

Angus Cameron, who toiled through my last volume, *Tactics on Trout,* and edited my very first book, *How to Take Trout,* back in 1950 when he was editor-in-chief of Little, Brown.

Lowell Pratt, editor of the famed *Barnes Sports Library* and later with several publishers, including Thomas Nelson's Sons (for whom we published the Young Sportsman's Library) and later with his own firm for which I was editor-in-chief of the Compact Outdoorsman's Library. Lowell has been a great inspiration.

Lee Wood, possibly the greatest newspaper editor of all time, for many years kept a sharp eye on my daily column, "Outdoors," for the *New York World Telegram and Sun,* for he is an astute angler.

Jim Deren, of the Angler's Roost in New York City, spawned my desire to write about my fishing and hunting experiences.

Dick Wolff, one-time tackle salesman for William Mills and Sons, New York, and long-time vice-president of the Garcia Corporation, has been a constant friend and advisor, as has Arthur Mills, the great angling authority who showed me the absolute tops in custom-made split-bamboo rods for bass bugging.

Actually, it all started because I had a father who, though a dedicated businessman, took much time off to wet my feet in angling waters all over the world.

Figure 1.   A "blank," featureless lake surface.

INTRODUCTION

As you can readily see, this is a pretty scene of a lake, selected from memory because it is so typical of most lakes in the northern and central states. Note, however, that I have left a completely blank and featureless water surface. This is the usual sight that the average angler sees when he first approaches a body of water. Many bass fishermen die of old age without much more understanding of the waters they fish than what you see right here. Their bass fishing is often a game of chance. Perhaps, after many years of trying to beat the odds, they are able to come up with some very generalized theories and catch some fish, but there is a lot more to bass fishing (or any encounter with nature and its creatures) than that tiny segment of life that meets the casual eye.

It has become evident to me that to be successful on a strange bit of water a guide is necessary, particularly if the trip is to be a short one. The guide can show where to fish, when to fish, what lure to use at a specific time, and how it should be presented and fished. Without him and his hard-earned secrets, the stranger is starting out as the guide did when he was a local boy. It has taken that guide a lifetime to acquire all the knowledge of a particular lake that he is eager to share in a few short engagements with you. You simply haven't got all that time to spend on one lake or in one area, having at most a few days or weeks. For you to set out alone from a dock to catch some bass, Lady Luck would have to be your guide; in fact, she'd almost have to do the fishing for you.

If you have experienced what I've just said, you can recognize that it takes time and experience, even with an accomplished guide, to become a consistently good bass fisherman. Even the best guides and well-known experts are forced to admit to failure some of the time. If you are neither, you always have the excuse that nature was unkind to you today.

If I were to leave you unattended in the situations described in this book, without a guide, after having fished here with me, I would not expect you to come in every time with the limit of bass or even one fish. Nevertheless, I propose to act as your guide throughout the fishing we'll do together in this book. I can't show you all the tricks in the very first situation, but many of the points we encounter and put into action in the fifteenth situation, for example, can be used in the first, and so on. The composite experience you'll build up in these pages will cover almost every typical situation that you'll find on the average bass lake and stream in the United States and southern Canadian provinces.

Fishing like this may open your eyes as they may never have been opened before. You'll become aware, for instance, that random casting of various lures here and there is a highly unprofitable way to spend your time. You'll learn to stop, even if only for a few seconds, to sense the water, feel the conditions, and see beyond the nature signs, to be aware of the situation of the moment, even though there is no sign of even a chub or minnow surfacing. Seeing in this way will tend to make you aware that you are almost blind and will inspire the deeper effort of seeing with all your senses. Nature isn't just trees, bushes, grass, rocks, gravel, sand, mud, and water—it is *life*, and a steady *living* going on. There are no mysteries under that water, all proceeds according to plan for the bass, dictated by the ecosystem in which he lives and the present weather and water conditions. All he does is what comes naturally. To clear the "mystery" we must lift the veil of our own ignorance and eliminate our own concepts about what's under the shimmering surface, of which we know practically nothing.

Knowing what to look for, what to see, then what to do are the primary skills you can gain with me as your guide for the moments we fish together here, but you'll need a real guide on unfamiliar water. If no guide is available, what you have been able to learn here will stand you in good stead. Much of what is presented in this book has been learned from countless guides who literally took me by the hand and made me see, look, and sense the water, then showed me how to fish it, so there are many guides between these covers to help you.

GUIDES

Before we put the tackle in the car and head for the lake, I'd like to mention a few things about "handling" a guide and about methods of "casing" a lake.

Guides are people. Some sportsmen consider them servants, since they have paid their money and made their demands. But let me advise that when you first say hello, do so in a way that instantly draws on the friendliness of your guide. Young or old, guides are used to city slickers coming to the country with all the know-how of a just-graduated college boy and his thousand dollars' worth of tackle. They can spot a "know it all" almost before the introductions. If you can "merge" with your guide and encourage his friendship at the start, he'll likely get you to fishing and to where the fish are a lot more readily. There are many guides who will make their "sport" work awfully hard for the first few days of the trip, simply to break down the ego of the client. If the angler comes through with spirit and with some of the ego knocked out of him in good time, the guide may show him his pet spots where the big ones lie. It is common knowledge that many guides prefer to save the best fishing spots for the last, so that the customer goes away pleased.

The other aspect of the guide–sport relationship is that a true man-to-man understanding and lasting friendship can be brought about merely by the common interest of enjoying fishing together. So don't go at the guide as though he were a servant, nor try to impress him with how much you know. Try to find out what he knows and you'll have more fun and catch more fish. If in the course of a day you have a legitimate request to fish a certain type of water in a way the guide does not suggest, make this known to him—but do it in an asking way, and you'll likely receive a good reason why your idea is as good as his, better than it, or not as good. Don't demand, or you'll turn him into a servant and he'll be just that.

CASING A LAKE

If you will be fishing a given lake tomorrow, say, without a guide, I'd like to outline here a few basic principles about casing a lake, or sizing it up for its possibilities.

All you really know about this unfamiliar bit of water at the moment is that it is supposed to contain bass. You've heard about it from friends, read about it, or merely surmise that it has a suitable fish population, since it is in the type of country for lakes that have the reputation of containing bass. There is a blue spot on your road map with a name for the lake. There is a road around most of the lake, and you can see even from the generalized map that there are shoreline indentions, a couple of feed-in streams, an inlet and outlet, and an island in the middle. First, if you can, drive the circumference in your car to get a look at it. Find the sharp coves and sharp points of land, note the deep land drop-offs that will indicate deep spots, the shallows and, if possible, locate the midlake shallows and grass flats, pad flats, and so on.

Stop in at the general store in the area and get to talking. Visit the local bar, even if you don't drink the hard stuff. By all means, visit the local sporting goods store in the neighborhood and buy some lures that are recommended. Infiltrate! Be a little humble . . . one of the locals just might take you fishing!

If by an orderly and well-planned means you have previously gotten a detailed map of the lake, you can discuss this with whomever. If you are smart, a geodetic survey map of the lake and its environs will be in your hand. Chances are that the local talent has never seen one; their maps are in their heads. Armed with this conversation piece, you have something to offer them, and then you are really on your way. Incidentally, the state conservation departments and the lumber companies usually have maps of their lands, with sufficient lake and stream indications to give you at least a head start. You might even call the game warden or the forest ranger, but find out whatever you can *before* you go fishing.

There is one more important thing—the principle of how a lake *works*.

Water temperature is a great deal more important to a bass than the temperature of the air is to you. Scientifically, there are many reasons why this is so. In simplest terms, bass, like any other living creature, seek out that which is most compatible to them—the most pleasing temperature for feeding, resting, hiding from enemies, and spawning.

Deep lakes (those over twenty-five feet) are stratified by temperature. We have a theoretical cross-section of a deep lake in the summertime to carry in our heads. The relative thicknesses and temperatures of the bands will vary a bit, but starting with the top layer there is merely a three-degree drop in temperature in ten feet of water. The winds force a gradual flow of currents in one direction across the top, with the return flowing across the bottom of this layer, making a large circular flow. In the middle section, called the thermocline, the temperature drops quite steeply. In the lowest layer there is merely a drop of five degrees or so within each twenty-five feet of added depth. In other words, it is possible, by knowing the average change in temperature at different depths, to estimate quite well what the temperature of the water will be at any depth if we start with the surface reading.

As a broad base of comfortable temperatures, bass spawn at around sixty-two degrees, and later in the summer seek a water temperature below the seventy-five-degree mark if a lake has enough depth in it to produce this. They will feed less in water that is hotter than this, except in the shallows. Usually, with the setting of the sun the surface of a lake cools, which is why night fishing is so productive—not merely because it is dark!

Strong prevailing winds blowing for several days across a big lake can push surface water to one side of the lake, forcing the thermocline much lower on the windward side. When the thermocline tilts downward on the windward side on the lake, it tilts up on the lee side. The lee shore shortly becomes devoid of fish, no matter how inviting the shoreline might seem to the angler in terms of fishing prospects as he looks at its surface.

To further case the lake, read and reread the chapters on lake fishing after we fish them together, bearing in mind water layers and temperatures when necessary, and where you'd think the best fishing should happen on your first day out.

As we head the car for the nearest bass water, let's inventory the gear we'll be using for these excursions. Our basic tackle is detailed in the Appendix and often referred to in the text in order to keep the fishing action moving for you, to chew over the failures and do the research after class.

In overall terms, we'll carry a general-purpose eight-foot fly rod of medium to stiff action to be used with double-tapered and weight-forward lines. The single-action reels, large enough to accommodate these lines together with fifty yards of backing, will be labeled in terms of the line they are carrying. The double-tapered line is for short-range, small- and medium-sized bucktails and streamer flies, braces of wet flies, and large dry flies.

Our other fly rod will be powerfully tapered in a nine-and-a-half-foot length with a bass-bug action designed to cast and pick up wind-resistant, fluffy bass bugs or heavy and soggy marabou streamers, weighted flies, and small fly-and-spinner combinations.

For spinning we will again have two rods: a very light one, six or six and a half feet, with a light reel filled with not more than six-pound-test monofilament. This is for short- to medium-length casting using ultralight lures and small live bait. The second stick will be longer, say seven and a half feet, and faster and stronger in the tip, with enough power to use for trolling. It will also cast the conventional medium to heavy spinning lures and weighted live baits. A medium-sized reel with ten-pound-test mono completes the rig.

Our baitcasting gear will consist of a six-foot rod with a level-wind reel. Quite frankly, we'll use it mostly for trolling and drift or bottom fishing, since I believe that casting is more accurate and enjoyable with spinning gear. If and when the need for extra-heavy plugs, spoons, or bait-and-spinner rigs comes up, we'll use this rather than tax the lighter spinning rod. The line test aboard the baitcasting reel should be ten pounds.

We have a stream landing net that, like the trout net, is attached to our wading jackets and carry hip boots and waders in the car for all conditions of river and lake-shore wading. For walking the beach or for fishing from the boat, a longer handled net will be used. We also have a fish stringer, live-bait box, canvas wading creel, insect repellent, an orange in a pocket, some food in a thermal box, and an enormous tackle box with spare parts and tools. (*See* the Appendixes for tackle and gear details.)

My tackle box contains surface popping, surface zigzagging, and surface diving plugs; semisurface popping, zigzagging, and diving plugs; deeper, heavier running plugs that dive, zigzag, and merely run as manipulated, single- and double-blade spinners, and a variety of sizes of spoons, jigs, weighted flies, and hooks. That's it, except for the plastic and rubber worms, eels, and other artificial baits, which are important, as are the artificial pork rinds. Personally,

I prefer real bait to artificial, but there are times when the real is not available and more times when I just don't feel like handling it, preferring the artificial instead.

Of course, because my collection of basic types is small, I carry many backups, since lures are to lose, but prime fishing time is not. Glance at the Appendix for other terminal tackle "musts."

Let's discuss some basic principles of bass fishing. The black bass is a voracious fish, much more so than the trout. He'll strike at almost any kind of lure when he's hungry. Find him in the shallows when he has left the deeper parts of the lake to go there for food. Throw shallow-running, surface-popping, or zigzagging plugs at him and you'll have him. Even if he's stationed permanently in a weedy pocket in the shallows, you'll get the same results, since he's on the alert to guard his lair and to hit anything that moves. If he's stationed in a mid-lake pad patch or grass bed, you'll find him hiding in the holes, waiting for a minnow to swim by or your plug to whip by him.

Fish for him in the deep either by trolling, stillfishing with live bait, or, better still, unweighted baits. Troll for him across the deepest parts of the lake in the hot summer months or over the spring holes where he's waiting out the hot temperatures from above. You'll take him.

Troll the sandy shore, including the points of land where you'll stop trolling to cast the entire point. Troll in and out of the coves, pausing to cast into all the nooks and crannies between the weed patches and snags. Work the mouths of rivers and creeks, for you'll also find him there and catch him.

On the other hand, you may fish all these places and many times come home without so much as a strike, that being the way it goes in bass fishing. I've performed all the tricks I've learned and read about over some thirty years and, more often than not, come home fishless or without a bass worth keeping. At other times it has seemed that any idiot, out for the first time and not knowing the first thing about bass fishing, could take his limit in a half hour. That's bass fishing—the best we can do is to corner the problems and proceed in an orderly way, getting the most out of our tackle, lures, and manner of presentation.

Logic and past performance argue that night fishing pays off for bass and can be the most exciting—and most exasperating— sport ever devised by man. The times I've taken big bass at night (bigger ones than I've ever hooked during the day) have been legion, but I have no record of the nights I've returned fishless. Yet

I've fished for bass much more than most anglers in this country, and I think I know just about all there is to know about what to do. As the saying goes, an expert is a man with whom you go fishing and if nobody catches anything knows all the reasons why!

So start out from where you are. The bass is not a wizard: Like all his brothers of all species of fish, he is only a fish, with no Madison Avenue savvy and very little gray matter. He's not out to fool the fisherman and couldn't care less about his woes but is merely doing what comes naturally. To find the most efficient ways to lure him requires a quick eye, sixth and seventh senses, and a lot of luck, despite all that has been written on surefire methods.

Remember that the good bass *fisherman* is first a bass *hunter*. Trial and error over the years will bring forth opinions as to where to fish and with what. This book contains quite a bit of this "research" plus combinations of ways to hunt for bass.

I do not push coincidence and try to make it seem fact, because this has confounded me too many times. Arm yourself well and by some sort of magical guidance you'll fish with the right lure enough times (unless the lure itself doesn't make as much difference as tackle manufacturers would have us think!). I do believe, however, that the fisherman who knows just how to manipulate a lure so that it becomes a living threat or an enticing bit of food to a bass is the one who consistently catches more bass than most others. He first has to hunt for the bass, which requires know-how and deliberate casing of the lake as well as a routine plan with which to begin the search with the tackle at hand that is best suited to the situation.

This book is constructed around the formula of situations that we fish together so that, first, the situations offer a background for a planned attack and, second, they will recall similar situations you've fished before or ones to look for when you fish again after reading this.

A SHORT HISTORY OF BASS FISHING IN AMERICA

Unlike trout fishing, with its imported dogma and tradition, American bass fishing was spawned in the grassroots experience of pioneer days. At first the bass was considered merely to be a food fish. It was netted, caught on hand lines, or taken on long poles with cord or horsehair lines tied to crude hooks, sinkers, and live bait. Any sport enjoyed while using those methods was purely incidental.

Later, when more men and a few women could afford to fish for the fun of it, bass began to gain the rank of game fish. Anglers were limited to tackle imported from Europe: horsehair lines, long heavy poles, and single-action reels. There were no lures generally available other than big wet salmon flies. What little tackle could be obtained was quite costly.

But sport-loving Americans and those who wanted to catch bass in more efficient ways were quick to develop tackle to fit the nature of this powerhouse of "finned fury."

First, in 1810, George Snyder of Paris, Kentucky, developed a fishing reel with a multiplying gear that permitted four turns of the spool to one of the handle. This principle is still used in the modern baitcasting reel, with some refinements, of course, such as the level-wind and controlled-drag mechanisms that have come from ingenious modern designers. The new reel, originated in England around 1850, enabled an angler not only to cast heavy baits but also made it possible for him to retrieve line faster and offer efficient pressure against the fighting action of this "rough, coarse fish," as trout purists called it. Then came the Meek reel, later popularized by an improved version made by the Kentucky firm of Meek and Milan.

But the reel was not enough. The rods of the day were long—twelve to eighteen feet—and the combination was rather awkward to use. To correct this situation, Dr. James Henshall, the Izaak Walton of young America, designed rods of shorter lengths, in the neighborhood of eight feet, which cast the heavy natural baits and sinkers well in coordination with the multiplying reel. He also wrote the first American bass book, *Bass Fishing*, which has become a much quoted classic.

To refine Dr. Henshall's ideas, Samuel Philippi, a Pennsylvania gunsmith, introduced the use of split sections of bamboo about 1910 and tapered even shorter rods in order to bring the three elements—rod, reel and casting line, and weight—into better harmony.

Hiram Lewis Leonard began in earnest to develop both fly-fishing and baitcasting rods in his shop in Maine, and later moved to Ellenville, New York, near the famed Catskill Mountain streams and lakes. He continued to labor at rod design and subsequently moved back to Maine, settling in Bangor. Old-timers will remember the trade name of Abbey and Imbrie, a firm through which Leonard marketed his rods.

From there came the evolution of the H. L. Leonard Rod Company and the famous tackle store—the first one in New York City—under the sign of William Mills and Sons, across the street from the Woolworth Building near City Hall.

The factory Leonard founded in Maine was moved in the early 1930s to Central Valley, New York, where it is today. For many years it was known and loved for its early American charm, but a fire destroyed it some years ago and a new plant had to be built. The most noted rod makers there were W. Edwards, E. F. Payne, F. E. Thomas, Hiram Hawes, and Frank Oram.

Several graduates of the Leonard rod-building method started rod-building firms of their own and were quite successful, even after the advent of glass rods threatened the trade, as did international embargoes limiting bamboo shipments to the United States, a situation now eliminated by peace in the Far East.

Tapers, handles, and ferrules still undergo steady improvement so that today a customer can just about name his specific choice of rod weight, taper, action, and quality. And despite the invasion of glass, a few custom bamboo rod makers still cater to those who prefer wood.

Up to about 1915, bass fishing was limited strictly to the use of bait held down with a sinker while the rig was raised off the bottom with a bobber. The first artificial bass lure was devised in 1925 by Julio Buel, who cut a spoon from its handle, then attached a line to one end and a hook to the other. He promptly took bass after bass, and soon fishermen were frantically converting discarded teaspoons into bass lures. The new gimmick became a recognized killer, and to this day (with modifications) remains one of the very best (see the Daredevle spoon in Figure 2).

The search for better bass lures continued. Another weapon in the angler's arsenal of deception was invented by James Heddon, a Michigan angler who whittled a length of old broom handle into the shape of a minnow and attached a hook to it. It cast well and when manipulated with the rod tip must have looked to a bass like a wounded minnow. Since then, fortunes have been made in the manufacture of wooden plugs of all sizes, shapes, and actions— floating, diving, and sinking types—and more recently made by the thousands out of plastic.

The early plugs were quite large and heavy, to balance the rather coarse tackle. But through the years, with the development of lighter lines and springier rod tips, plugs have become smaller and lighter, reaching their extreme in the ultralight spinning plugs

Figure 2.   The Daredevle spoon.

so popular for trout, panfish, and bass. Some are even designed for use with a stout fly rod.

In the early 1940s, spinning tackle arrived with great fanfare. I was among the first to try it on trout and bass, having received an outfit complete with the "thread line" or braided line back in the early thirties. Spinning tackle was to add another dramatic chapter to the saga of American bass fishing. The development and further refinement of glass-fiber rods was to continue the revolution in the tackle industry and thus in the entire sport, bringing rods and tackle of excellent quality into the reach of millions of anglers at a fraction of the price of hand-made gear.

During the early days there had been no need for the conservation of bass because they seemed to be everywhere: in lakes, rivers, creeks, ponds, and swamps. Where trout were fast disappearing, bass seemed to thrive, and when introduced into impoverished trout waters bass grew big and full of fight. Today, for example, we have excellent bass fishing in the upper New England lakes and streams, which at one time had no bass. The Grand Lake Stream section of Maine, for example, never saw bass until sportsmen introduced them into those waters in the 1850s.

THE BLACK BASSES

Biologists have had more trouble trying to pin a name on the various species of bass than most anglers have had in catching them. Rather than rehash their troubles, suffice it to say that there are basically only two types of "black" basses, neither of which is truly black—the largemouth and the smallmouth. The variations of the subspecies are so minute as to be interesting only to the ichthyologist. The difference between the largemouth and smallmouth is shown in the accompanying illustration.

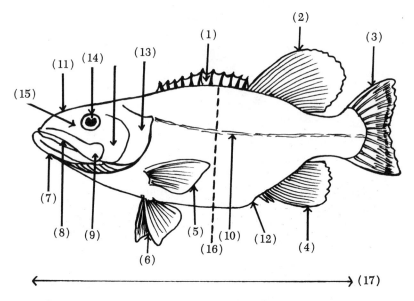

Figure 3.   The smallmouth bass, showing location of parts (which also apply to the largemouth bass). (1) Spinous portion of dorsal fin. (2) Soft portion of dorsal fin. (3) Caudal fin. (4) Anal fin. (5) Pectoral fin. (6) Ventral fin. (7) Mandible, or lower jaw. (8) Premaxilla. (9) Maxilla. (10) Lateral line (sense, sound organ). (11) Snout. (12) Cheek. (13) Opercal, or gill cover. (14) Eye. (15) Head. (16) Depth. (17) Distance from snout to nape.

The spotted bass found in a limited area of the south-central states is a smaller species, rarely going over the fifteen-inch mark. Some say it is more like a smallmouth in its habits and fighting power, but this is a matter of opinion.

As of the moment, the largemouth bass has the Latin name *Micropterus salmoides;* the smallmouth, the label *Micropterus dolomieui;* and the spotted bass, *Micropterus punctulatus.*

Of the three species, the largemouth has always had the widest pattern of distribution, even since the broad introduction of the smallmouth into new and far-flung waters. The largemouth is more adaptable to warmer waters, reaching its greatest size in Florida and near the Gulf Coast. Bass of eleven pounds are relatively common there, where in more northerly waters they seldom grow to more than five or six pounds. Smallmouths are found naturally in more northern waters or at elevations where water temperatures agree with their needs, but they seldom grow to more than five or six pounds. They are long-time residents of the wild southern Canadian lakes and rivers.

There are many similarities between the largemouth and smallmouth. They are both nest builders that fan out a circular nest in the fine sand at the edge of a lake shore or along a shady stretch of a slow-moving river. By fanning and nudging out bits of refuse, the bass protect the nest, which is usually two to three feet in diameter. The male and female take turns standing guard over the eggs. Later, the young fish will fin around in the nest hole until they are large enough to wander into the outside world.

During this time, generally from April to the end of June (depending on the location and the seasonal air and water temperatures), the adults are quite easy to take with almost any lure cast in or near the nest, and many states have declared a closed season during the spawning period for obvious conservation reasons. Where the fish have grown only a little in size but large in numbers from overfeeding and overabundance, the season is usually open during the spawning period, and wondrous sport is to be had. All the angler need do is approach the spawning area either from the shore or from a boat, find a position within easy casting distance of a nest, throw a floating plug over it, and whammo! he's hooked a bass.

Bass are quickest at this time, being on the alert for all attacks from the outside. They will charge into a school of big chubs or even carp that frequent the same shallows in search of their vegetarian diet. I've seen a pair of bass drive off a carp five times their weight, so intent on protecting their nest that they were willing to fight to the finish. Naturally, your lure excites this protective anger, so the strike is usually fast and furious. A plug—any size, shape, or color, plopped down within twenty feet of the nest—will bring on an attack, sometimes from four or five bass all at once.

By the time the little inchlings have grown up, the parents have long since forgotten them, and the little ones, like minnows and other small lake fish, become fair game for the big bass. Both bass species feed on anything that moves, both aquatic and earthborn: minnows, frogs, worms, insects. They have been known to catch young ducks, birds, and mice with much the same voraciousness as the pike and musky. I have seen big bass knock mice off a log and also watched big old bronzebacks try for small birds such as the marsh wren, when it ventures too close to the water surface.

Bass feed most heavily during the early days of the year, but as the waters begin to warm up they seem to eat less and feed with less abandon, limiting their activity to early morning and evening and, in the hottest summer months, to midnight forays, offering excellent night-fishing sport for those bold enough to angle in the dark.

As to the comparative sporting qualities of largemouths and smallmouths, there is much argument. The southerner likes the largemouth because of its size, and strongly considers the heavy weight of the fight more important than the antics of the smallmouth of smaller size. The northerner, working his favorite smallmouth water, glories in the terrific battle put up by such a relatively small fish and, on a pound-for-pound basis, votes the smallmouth tops. Both agree that the trout and, in fact, all other American freshwater fish (other than the heavier pike and musky) are no match for the bass, large- or smallmouth.

Both species are voracious takers of lures when conditions are right and the angler can present the right lure correctly. Both species can, however, confound the best techniques and leave the angler wondering if all the bass have suddenly disappeared from the lake, gone on strike, or become too smart for him. I have taken bass after bass on certain waters on one day, only to fish the same waters on another day and come home fishless, despite the use of various techniques and myriad changes of lures.

When it comes to lure choice and color, note that, throughout, I am concerned with techniques of hunting bass and ways of presenting lures that might appeal to them. The experiences of avid bass fishermen point to approach and presentation as being of far more importance than the choice of lure. This is the opposite, in a way, to trout fly-fishing, in which the same technique, varied by only a slight difference in fly pattern, color, or shape, can spell the difference between success and failure.

All three of the methods I discuss in this book—baitcasting, spinning, and fly-fishing—can be employed for both bass species in lakes and streams, and the lures are quite interchangeable. Basically, the differences in fishing technique are dictated by the situation rather than the species, for where largemouths and smallmouths are found in the same water it is usually possible to catch either with the same lures and presentation techniques, since one never quite knows which fish is present and willing to bite.

The largemouth of southern waters is a terrific fighter. One would think that in the warm water of the south the fish would tend to be logy and soft and to fight with less vigor than their northern cousins. This is simply not so. I've battled medium-sized largemouths in a Florida lake and found them to be just as tough or tougher than the same size fish in a Connecticut lake. A big Florida bass is a real thrill, and under these circumstances many anglers vote for the largemouth as the better fighter. On the other hand, while fishing in some of our larger northern rivers, such as the Delaware or Susquehanna, I've taken smallmouths on light fly-fishing or spinning gear and had far more excitement than I'd bargained for.

There are today many more lakes and rivers that contain bass than there were when America first became settled. Waters have been stocked with both species, and where trout and other game fish have disappeared, under either too much fishing pressure or pollution, bass have hung on valiantly. Modern roads have made prime bass waters open to the public, and extensive conservation practices in the national parks and tree farms have helped develop fine bass populations.

PART ONE

LAKE-FISHING SITUATIONS

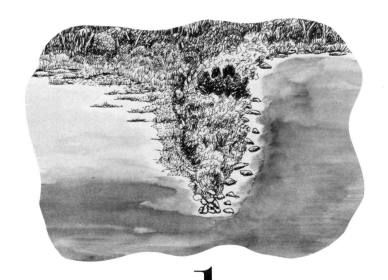

1

SHARP POINT
OF LAND

Whether you're studying a map of the area, scanning the lake from your car, or peering out from the boat dock at the shoreline, the place to look for and one of the most obvious places to start fishing would be a sharp point of land extending into the water from the shoreline. On both sides of such a point, at the very tip, will be good spots to find bass. So it is with the section we are about to fish together, first from a boat and then from the shore, as an exercise in bass hunting and fishing.

Bass *hunting* should constitute about 50 percent of your time on any given lake, no matter how well you know the waters or have fished them before, or how many types of lures you have elected to use. Lake bass fishing is not like stream bass fishing or trout fishing. Fish in a stream are easier to locate, since they are found at certain places doing certain things at certain times. But fish in lakes are spotted only during those times when they are surfacing. Your bass in the lake is hiding; he's seldom seen feeding on fly hatches, chasing minnows, or stirring up any kind of a rise such as those experienced in trout and other types of fishing. The bass is usually quiet, lying in wait for minnows and other fresh food, guarding his lair or just resting and digesting the last prey from his prior feeding spree. This means you have to hunt for him.

So we go searching out the most obvious places, first with our eyes. As we approach our point, you'll see a few boating anglers working this section of the lake. Most of them come from the opposite shore, from the resort that you can hardly see from here. If you were to speed to the sharp point of land over *there*, you'd find that many of those fishermen came all the way from *this* side, which is typical fishing logic.

At the moment, most of the few anglers that are out on the water are stillfishing well off the point. This mile-long lake is a haven for largemouth bass. Its seminorthern location gives it long, cold winters, which breed strong generations of fish. The bottom and shoreline conditions vary from flat and muddy shallows to rocky cliffs, sandbars, sharp drop-offs, and deep spring-holes. The point of land we will fish has two sides, with distinct differences in character. As shown in the picture, the right side is deep and rocky and the left side is flat, gravelly, sandy, muddy, and shallow. As a formula for working the point properly, I like to fish whichever side is in the lee of the wind, since as a general rule bass head for the calmer water when there's a wind that causes waves that rock them about. If the wind is breaking on the rocky, deep side, the shallow side will be in comparative calm, and vice versa. When the wind is coming straight in, you can't win, so if it is too strong you can either skip the location or at best give it a short whirl and then search out another location where neither you nor the bass are at the mercy of the wind and waves. A night when the wind is down is one of the best times to fish "the point," particularly in the summer months, for it is then that the big bass come in near the shoreline to feed. The point offers a wider and usually more abundant source of food than the flat or open shoreline.

The lake in the picture could be in Michigan, Massachusetts, Ohio, or New Jersey. The time of our junket is in July, about a week after the opening-day fishermen have tried and left. Few water skiers are about as yet, but August will see them here in force. Today the lake is calm, and as we look about on the approach the lake shore brings to mind countless ones you may have fished before.

Even the point of land is not an unfamiliar sight. By the time we get through with it, you'll call such locations your very own. Next time you pick such a point to fish, you'll remember our first visit together.

The dry weeks have lowered the level of the lake about a foot from the brush and grassy shoreline. The spawning season is long past; bass are moving about freely in the clear water. Their little ones have become their forage, free-swingers now, not holding down to the nest site.

Our little outboard boat planes the water beautifully, skimming right along on top. We approach the situation illustrated both in the picture at the beginning of this chapter and in the diagram to which we will often refer throughout this "trip" (Figure 4).

The usual angler would likely race in near the area, cut the motor, and cause big waves that would disturb the natural conditions, then wonder why no fish were biting. An equally poor way of approaching is to slow down gradually and come to a stop; the boat loses its plane, sinks down deep to cause big waves, and

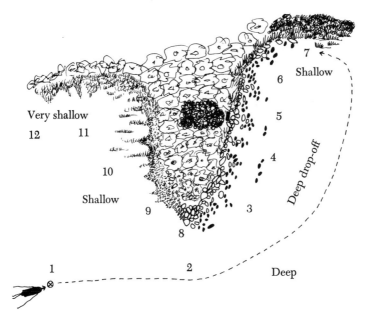

Figure 4. This diagram is typical of those in each chapter of this book. It is the aerial view of the situation we are to fish. This sharp point of land juts out from the basic shoreline of the lake. Note the deep drop-off to the right of the point, the cluster of rocks at the tip of the point, and the gravel that turns to sand and then mud at the left corner. The text follows the number of the fishing positions on the diagram.

plows along at a slow speed. The best approach is to plane in at full speed to within about fifty yards from where you'll start fishing, stop dead, and either paddle in or barely idle the motor so as to slide in with as little wake as possible. I prefer to paddle or scull. (*See* Appendix: Sculling.)

The deep water under the dotted line on the diagram under us shallows up abruptly along the line of the right-hand side of the point and amid the shore and sunken rocks. I prefer to troll this edge for any fish that might be coming in from the deeper water or moving out from feeding along the edges. There is usually quite a bit of movement at this time of the morning, and trolling in this way can bring strikes. Since we are new on the lake we are also *hunting* for our fish, and trolling is a good way to test the environs. Bass seem to like this edge, for the baitfish also hang in here in much the same manner as do the prey of saltwater big-game fish along ocean drop-offs.

A slow troll is called for, for several reasons. For one thing, I prefer slowly trolled lures or bait most of the time simply because I've found that slower pays off better. I've learned the hard way and also by watching others that most bass fishermen troll much too fast. The problem lies in two elements that must balance: lure action and depth. In crystal-clear water, it matters little just how deep a lure is trolled—within obvious limits—since any bass above or below the lure will see it plainly. I try to keep my lure about five feet down, taking in the important consideration of lure wobble or action. Most lures are designed to increase their vibration as their speed increases. I've also discovered that a lure that is wiggling too fast has generally less effect than one acting the way a wounded minnow should act. A wounded minnow doesn't race across the landscape. So try to find the median between these two elements and you'll have at least a sporting chance to connect. You can alter the weight of the lure, and you can pick lures that wobble or zigzag at speeds that match the speed of travel you select in relation to the depth at hand. If you want to use a sinking-type lure, like a saltwater jig gone fresh, attach a cork well ahead of it to keep it up slightly.

After you become sensitive to the action of a lure on your rod tip, you can slow the troll or speed it up. Lures that have no action of their own but require rod-tip action on your part can be activated properly, and the depth of the troll can be adjusted, by the angle of the rod and its height off the water in relation to the amount of line you've got out. This takes a bit of doing, but knowing what you are about is half the game. As a general rule, I fish with no more than seventy-five feet of line out behind me; I find that I can reasonably control what's happening at this distance. When I'm using surface plugs that float I can let out a hundred feet, although it is really not necessary. I've taken many bass (I'll bet you have, too) at even shorter distances. Also, the shorter line length makes boat turning easier.

Now to the actual fishing. Using two spinning rods, I'd rig one with a spoon or spinner-and-bait, such as a nightcrawler. (*See* Appendix: Terminal Tackle.) This makes a good fish-hunting rig. You might even latch onto a pickerel or a rock bass for some action. I'd use the other rod for a semisurface plug that darts and dives as deep as the speed of the troll—in our case, to about three feet under, since the lake bottom here ranges down to about fifteen feet with some huge rocks to break it up. We'll work our way to the point on Figure 4, then turn out and do some casting from positions 3, 4, and 5, then intrude on the shallows into position 7. This will give us thorough coverage of the water with all the means at our command. We could also make another pass or drift so we could cast right into the shore.

Working the point itself is almost too obvious to mention. We'd throw everything at it from all angles: surface plugs, bugs, small spinning lures, and darting-diving plugs, for we are hunting.

Now let's really concentrate on the left side of the point. It might be well, since the slight breeze does not disturb the surface, to try strictly surface plugs, such as the Jitterburg, and cast them right into the shore or, even though you cannot see them, into deep lanes in the gravel and sand, which harbor minnows. A close look will also show that there are channels into the deeper water that the big bass use as highways to their food supply. Remember that a month or so earlier those shallows were being used as spawning beds and that the big bass are quite familiar with the food supply in there. This afternoon, right after lunch, the light will be in position for us to see the true underwater contour of what appears to be a flat beach. In the area of 9 and 10, the shoreline becomes muddy and grassy, and even at this time of summer the underwater weeds have spread a good thick carpet over the bottom. Bass like to hide in there, especially when the sun comes out brightly and the wind kicks up the shallows. So we work the Jitterbug, slowly on the retrieve, so that it just plops along in not too much of a hurry, but with enough surface action to wake the dead. At position 10 we can even break out the fly rod and cast out a couple of bucktails. Perhaps (just for practice) we can try a bass bug, with the idea of exciting whatever bass there might be in the pads and grass. These fly-rod lures would be better at twilight, since the sun will set on the other side of the point and the shadows from the trees will cool the area even before the sunset. Just after twilight is magic time.

I've taken some good fish near where the rocks degenerate into gravel and sand just below 9. I like to fish this area carefully, no matter what time of day and whether or not the wind has disruped the surface. In fact, a little wind here is a blessing, since it allows a closer approach and the line is not as noticeable to the fish. This section is overworked by most anglers, since the majority are too lazy to cast into the shallows, preferring to go for a boat ride along the deep side of the drop-off to make a few casts as they proceed. I've often tried an unweighted crawfish on light spinning gear into the cluster of rocks near the point, let the bait settle a bit, and slowly retrieved it in a "swim." On several occasions bass followed that bait almost to the boat before grabbing it. (*See* Appendix: Bait fishing.)

We have now passed a couple of hours of angling over a relatively small part of one tiny bit of lake. You'll no doubt note, as you look back at your bass fishing career, that you have never given so much time and attention to a specific area as you have today. It shows us that if we're going to catch fish, we must leave our anxieties and eagerness on shore and fish easily, carefully, and quietly, which can be done—without beating the neighborhood to a froth.

We can return here at twilight, fishing first from the boat and later, well after dark, from the shore. There are some big bass lurking in that water.

Let's break for lunch. On our way in we'll drift with the slight breeze right into the rocks at position 7. There's a grove of pine trees about halfway down the point and a spring where we can take a drink of some really cold water. There's also a bench that I put there many years ago. Sitting there, eating our lunch, we can see both sides of the point and its contrasting waters, and watch for any signs of activity.

Look over in the direction of 6. We've just fished through there, but do you see the minnows flashing right along the drop-off? Break out a fly rod and tie on a small bucktail. Wade out for backcast room and catch yourself a bass. Let the fly sink about a foot on the cast and then, very slowly, retrieve, jerking your rod tip to add action to the glinting silver shank and hairs of the fly. Bring the fly to the surface with a modified roll cast forward and slither it along the surface before letting it sing again. (*See* Appendix: Flycasting.) That should do it. If you don't get a strike, continue your retrieve right into the shore. There are a few smallmouths we didn't mention, and they will likely intercept you. They're probably the ones wreaking havoc with those baitfish out there right now. See those water flashes? Be prepared for a hefty strike.

Now let's "walk" leisurely down toward the point to make a few casts, you with the fly rod, using the roll cast, and me with the light spinning rod and surface plug. This walk gives us the opportunity to look over the water we can fish in the dead of night. It is always a good policy to at least scan an area during the day that is to be fished at night, in order to have advance notice of possible trouble spots. My wager is that right now, a cast straight out at the head of the point toward those exposed rocks will draw a rise. Make your cast toward a rock, let the fly sink a bit, and then, without giving it too much motion, "swim" it a bit, then roll cast it up to the surface. Let it sink down again and repeat the process. It nothing happens, get tough: rake that fly over the surface, roll casting it forward, pulling back, and rolling it over the same spot a few times. That ought to raise at least a rock bass.

With a slight afternoon breeze and the sun beating down on the deep side of the point, we can try in between the boulders and along the deep side of the point from 3 to 5. First we'll cast surface wobbling plugs and then try the darter zigzaggers right into the shore, in a conventional way, from as far out as possible, drifting down the shore to the cove. There are deep runs and holes between those boulders and grasses and weeds, ideal conditions for both the bait and the big fish. As the sun begins to fall, the shadowy side of the rocks will be the place to cast in order to provoke a strike. A slight breeze that has allowed us a close approach has now freshened into quite a wind, and wavelets are beginning to form on the lake surface. We'll work out now, and from a position near 4 we'll slow down to a nice easy troll with a deep-running plug on my rod and a spoon on your spinning rod. We'll work our way up to 6, pausing for a few casts to the rocks off the point, and ending our run at 9. That will give us an hour or so of careful fishing.

When we're done we can invade the bait pail. You attach a crawfish—but no weight—to your light spinning line. I'll rig up with a small live perch, also unweighted. We'll drift with the wind and the whims of the waves from 9 to the area of 10 and outside it, almost to 11. I'm using the perch because it will head down, a habit most shiners do not have, they usually require at least a small split shot to put them under. If our weightless baits stir no action, we'll add two split shots and cast the baits into the corner, in the direction of the pads. This live-bait-drifting method can produce, especially on a section that has not been worked over recently, or later in the season, when the water skiers and motorboaters have driven the fish down during the bright light of day. At twilight I like to return to this spot if the wind is not kicking it up too strongly and drift as we are now, casting once in a while in between the rocks and into the shoreline. Quite often a smallmouth will strike here.

Fishing the point itself with a weighted live bait seems almost too obvious to mention. After all our activity of the day it will be pleasant to sit in the shade of those birches and pines, cast our slip sinker and bait combo (*see* Appendix: Terminal Tackle) as far out as possible, and sit there contemplating the cosmos. I can think of no better way to get rid of the need for action and let the psyche eliminate the tensions of modern high-speed living. There is much to be said for what I term stillfishing. The old man I used to fish with down south really knew how to sit on a stump and watch the water above his line. He'd smoke an old corncob and weave slightly from side to side as he sat there almost asleep. In that state one can have strange and wonderful visions, and at just the magic moment some bass may decide to break the spell.

After an early supper and refreshing shower, we're all set for the twilight run on our point of land and the fishing that we'll enjoy well after dark. As you may have noticed earlier, it is possible to wade down the center of the sand and gravel shoreline. As we approach 10, the bottom becomes muddy and unsafe, but you can cast in there close enough for a long cast in almost any direction. The edge of the water is shaded first as the sun falls and light barely filters through the pines. Later the offshore water will be in shadow, and the bass from the deep will work their way first to the edge and after that right into the shallows, finally feeding along the water's edge during the dark of night.

When you are finished with your assignment, I'll pick you up in the boat and we'll troll the edge of the shallows toward the point, using semisurface plugs that wobble our rod tips. We'll also make a few casts to the rocks at the point. By this time the wind is down and the sun also, and the semidarkness makes this a good time to spot cast among the boulders and sunken rocks between the point and 3. For this we'll throw surface plugs of the small variety on our spinning gear. Or perhaps, if one of us chooses, we can break out the bass-bug rod and send a feathered enticer into the boulders, let it sit there for thirty seconds, and pop it slowly back to the boat. We'll also work this point from the shore, since it is good water for dark-of-night fishing. Many bass fishermen who don't own or have access to a boat can enjoy excellent fishing on any lake if they venture forth at night, particularly in the hot, muggy months, when the heat of the day and the action of people on the water have given way to the quiet of a cool night breeze. There is seldom any need to wade in the dark, since bass will be feeding in close and can be reached by casting from the boat. Thanks to its easy casting, the conventional spinning rig will reach out more than enough to cover the water properly with a variety of lures.

After dark, the baitfisherman using a crawfish on an unweighted line or leader can cast it almost anywhere and expect a strike. I consider this bait better than the frog simply because frogs are generally found there, but more likely in the mushier grass-and-pads areas of a lake.

At dawn any bass feeding close into the shallows will work his way out as the light brightens. Sit out there in a boat and cast minnow-sized spinning lures, such as an Indiana spinner (*see* Appendix: Terminal Tackle) and a worm. Put the lure down in the middle of the shallows and retrieve it slowly. A black eel or long nightcrawler, bounced slowly along the bottom, might also do the trick.

On the drive home we can recapitulate the entire day's operation and see how we have considered the direction of the wind, degree and direction of light, amount of water disturbance, and the fish's feeding habits and movements. We've fished in several ways and have tried to present a variety of lures, and have done it virtually from dawn to dawn. Still, we have hardly scratched the surface of the entire lake. But by hunting this way over a spot like the point for an entire season, you'll learn much about nature and its changing moods, its conditions, and how to meet them with your own deductions based on having fun catching fish. We can't do everything the first time out; this first trip was a simple starter, but we'll become more involved as time goes on.

Before we go any further I'd like to put in my two cents for one of the most effective baits or lures-and-baits, and one that can be used on almost all game fish: The pork chunk or pork rind is used either as a pure bait impaled on a hook or in strip form to flutter behind a lure (Figure 5). The monster bass of Bull Shoals, the TVA whoppers, those fat largemouths of the Everglades, and even the smallmouths of Michigan or northern Maine eat high on the hog. You can get pork chunks and rinds in bottles at a tackle store, or you can save some pieces when you carve the family ham (or even sneak a few strips of bacon after breakfast). Fish the bait with no attractor spinners on a weedless hook, or attach a fluttering bit on your wobbling spoons, spinners, jigs, and deep trolling lures

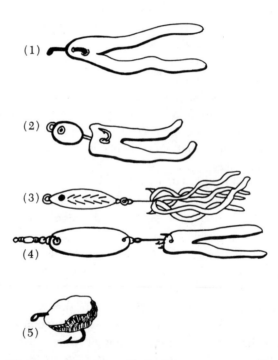

Figure 5.   These are various standardized types of rigs with which pork rind, either real or artificial, can be used. They can be employed for trolling and casting. The single-hook pork rind lure can be cast, trolled, or stillfished. (1) Two-tail pork rind on hook. (2) Pork rind on weighted jig. (3) Thin rubber or pork rind strips on a sinking plug. (4) Strip pork on a spoon. It hampers the action, and the plug must therefore be activated vigorously. (5) Pork chunk on a hook, to be used with a weighted leader or fished unweighted on a dead drift. The latter is most effective, especially in clear water.

—yes, even on your popping plugs if you're surface fishing. When fly-fishing, use a simple, small-size hook (generally a 10 or 12) and stick on a thin strip of pork, not more than two inches long. This works as well as a streamer fly or bucktail. Also, no matter how you fish a pork lure or where, inspect it once in a while to make sure it is not twisting the line or about to tear off.

In the situation we've just concluded, I'd work the point, trolling back and forth with a pork rind as deeply as possible without snagging too many times. This would be the final treatment if the day has been fishless. And if you're offended by handling a pork bait, try using thin strips of yellow, orange, or white rubber or plastic the thickness of a kid's balloon. Cut thin strips of this and use them as you would the real thing. Many commercially made lures have this teaser type of appendage or "skirt."

If you decide to drift fish rather than troll, pick a five- to ten-foot-deep location that is rocky bottomed (smallmouths like this sort of real estate). Attach a strip of pork about four inches long to a jig and bounce it along or fish it very near the bottom. Fish the retrieve in a jittery motion, offering as much action and fluttering as you can make. Bottom bouncing a jig with a pork strip attached is enough to drive the fish crazy.

Remember these illustrations about ways of using pork rind and chunks, for you'll need them later.

2

SHARP COVE

Humid weather, midsummer doldrums, sleepy people, logy bass. We're on the water just before sun-up. It's muggy even after a long, cool night. It's the same lake we fished in Chapter 1, but about a half mile farther along the shore, bound for another of my favorite hot spots and, if you have done any amount of bass fishing one to which you won't be a stranger.

What may be quite unfamiliar will be the way we fish it together. In this book we are attempting to tackle every conceivable and mostly unusual situation, and to tackle them carefully and thoroughly in order to provide you with a kind of systematic approach to your bass hunting. Much of the way we fish will not be strange; some of it will be obvious. Once in a while you'll experience a new technique or, quite possibly, one you've forgotten. We're fishing together so that I can give you my manner of approach, presentation, and enjoyment of angling for bass. The next time you go to a spot similar to the ones covered in this book, it will instantly recall the trips we've taken together.

The "message" of this book is comprehending the proper methods and techniques for bass fishing, for the knowing alternation of methods is far more important than the mere changing of of lures. This is the thread of the book's philosophy.

We'll spend a bit more time here in detailing the presentation of lures and techniques than we did during Chapter 1, simply because there are more "possibles" presented by a sharp cove—more ways to entice the bass that we know are there.

A cove is a harbor for fish, and they generally reside there with more permanence than the fish that come in and out from the shore of an open point.

This is primarily shallow water with the only open water being the ten-foot-deep main "channel." It's about six feet deep in the holes, shallowing in through the grassy fingers or points. At the very bottom of the cove is a spring brook entering from the brushy corner at 7 (Figure 6).

The bottom is muddy. Only once in a while will you see a rock or, if wading, feel a bit of gravel underfoot.

One would think that bass, large- or smallmouth, would spawn in this cove, but they don't, since it is impossible for them to fan away the muck down to the fine sand, a requisite for the proper kind of bass housekeeping. This cove has no pond lilies or arrowbush; instead it is almost entirely grown over with grass, as is indicated in the diagram and also in the illustration at the beginning of this chapter.

We're going to get hung up, there's no question about it. You simply can't fish this type of water without having the lure catch in the grass, old tree branches, and whatnot. But you pay your money and take your chances. In this case it's not half as bad as the lily-pad patches we'll be fishing later.

I've found that the only way to cut down the number of times my surface lures become hung up is to fish them very slowly and kind of ease them along through the grass, rather than merely pull them straight through at a fast pace. This is difficult to describe, but to put it another way, make the cast with a floating, popping, or diving plug and allow the lure to settle on the water. Now, *gently* ease the lure along, almost as if you were "feeling" the grass as the lure passes by. If you pull the lure slowly enough, even the most stubborn grass stems will yield and slip through the bend of the hook or slide by the head of the lure. Given time, they'll usually slide by without gathering. In this instance avoid lures with metal fins at their head, or plugs with fore or aft spinners.

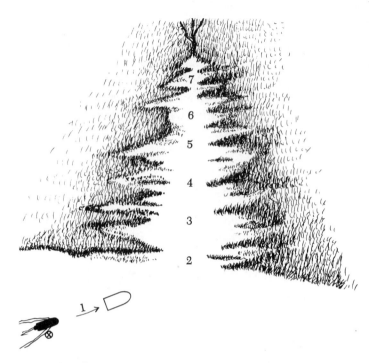

Figure 6. Aerial view of a sharp indentation of the shore as it cuts into the weeds from the main body of a lake. Note the grassy shoreline points and indentations, and the generally straight channel leading from a small spring brook in the weeds. The fishing positions indicated are described in the text.

There are also heavily feathered lures on the market. These have a bunch of feathers tied tight in and around the bend of the hook. I tie my so-called "weedless" bugs or flies by making conventional body, then using two duck-wing feathers tied in so that they bend inwards. Set the feathers so that their tips are angled down toward the barb and lie tight against the lower bend of the hook (Figure 7). Dress the rest of the fly according to pattern and design. It is not the answer to weeds—nothing is—but this rig works well percentage-wise.

As with the surface lure, try and ease the fly through the grass rather than merely pulling it. Stand up. Use as long a rod as you can find for this fishing and keep it high so that much of the line is off the water.

Weeds and grass are put in a bass lake for one purpose only: to strain the patience of the angler! So don't fall for the ruse and

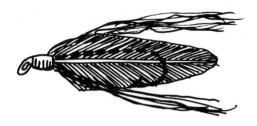

Figure 7. This is one of my attempts at making a weedless bucktail fly. The secondary duck-wing feathers are used because of their stiffness, which helps to protect the barb of the hook as the fly is drawn through weeds.

merely give the water a superficial treatment. Go in there bound for battle. Expect to become snagged, caught up, and sometimes stuck in the grass so firmly that you'll have to wade or boat in to free the lure. It's just part of the game. The rewards are great, however.

The water level at this season is about a foot below the high normal for the lake and the water temperature is in the mid-seventies, and just right for bass. The natural food in the cove consists of crawfish, frogs, and minnows. In this particular section I've never seen perch or sunfish, so our choice of live bait is chosen with this in mind.

Gray dawn now; misty shoreline. As we round the point from our quick boat stop at 1 on the diagram (Figure 6), well offshore, we drift along the trees and make a few casts with floating-diving plugs on our spinning rods, or with whatever lures we left on our rods last night. We're casting now to gain our hand and gauge distances. Our first real tries will be made right into the grass harbors between the finger points of grass inside 2. The reason we're approaching from the left on the diagram at this hour is that we want to fish that side that will remain in the shade a bit longer. We are now going to commence our bass hunting.

Out go our first searching casts, via our same spinning rods and with small-size surface plugs. For variety we snap on a surface popping plug. Neither of us should retrieve too quickly. Most of the casts will involve slow retrieve, the reason being that most anglers, especially when they begin their day, are all pepped up and ready to smash into the fish with gusto. Our way—and I hope to show its logic by our catch count—is to learn to tease bass into striking rather than assume they are just waiting for us to throw something at them. Certainly we're not here to scare the fish into the thick grass. Remembering that the water is shallow and that the cover of the grass is rather slim in contrast to that in the pad beds, we'll let the floating lures sit for a few seconds, give them a twitch at first, and then slowly retrieve. We won't pick up the speed of the retrieve after the lures have technically left the grassy areas. We'll work them to the rod tip, expecting a strike in the shadow of the boat.

We're bound to get hung up at least every third or fourth cast. When we do, we won't forget that we're trying to tease our bass into taking a lure and rush that grassed-up lure into the boat in a hurry. We'll merely reel it in slowly, almost as if we were continuing to fish it. In this way we won't spoil the spot. Usually when a lure becomes caught in this type of grass, it's only a temporary hang-up. A couple of short, quick, snappy jerks will usually dislodge the grass and the plug will float free. Just that much action is enough to entice a bass. He sees the plug erupting during the de-grassing and can (and will) hit it, grass or not, if he has a mind to. So just because you are caught up in a few blades of grass doesn't mean that the cast is a total loss. I've taken bass—and I'm sure you have, too—that have grabbed a plug under those conditions and swallowed it, grass and all!

As we move into 3, we'll be in a position to work both sides of the cove at the same time, although some casts will of necessity be long ones. For this reason, we'll either switch to the heavier plugs, or if you prefer to use the same weights, push our rods a little harder. Try a smallish, jointed, shiny-finish surface plug that will, if you make the cast right, pop nicely on the surface.

Work the near side and throw over toward the grassy inlet. The exercise here is to see just how close to the edges of the grass we can cast without landing the plugs into the thick grass, risking a hang-up. This is close enough for any bass that are lurking in the grass points.

So as not to become tangled up or hook into each other on these casts, let's line ourselves up as shown in the diagram (Figure 8). I always try to avoid getting hooked in the ear or neck even by my best friend.

Now, with several casts, short hits, and no fish, let's proceed farther into the cove, choosing the shadowy side in the direction of 6. Cast into the second point of grass off 2, taking time. The mist

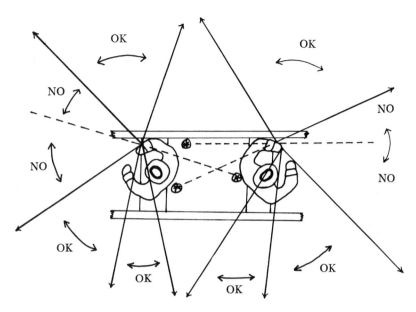

Figure 8. Safety afloat! This diagram shows the proper angles of casting so that backcasts do not come near the anglers in the boat. It is best to stick to these angles and turn the boat for varied positions rather than risk a hangup with your partner.

is lifting now, and I've found that the fish seldom move much before this mist rises, although your experience may differ entirely from mine. There is a kind of dead period between the break of dawn and the lifting of the mist when I've experienced a minimum of action. Perhaps it is because the light changes the quality of the water. A slight breeze is coming directly into the cove now. If you had listened you'd have heard it approaching as it skirted the tops of the trees. It took away the lid of mist and the slight damp-coolness that lurked with it. Time now to shed the light jacket.

Now, with your spinning rod, try a popper plug with weed-less wires on it. I'll angle the boat for you and hold my fire. I took a good bass in there last season, so maybe you'll catch his brother!

Ooops! One thing you're going to have to learn is the perfection of precise casting. Many of the baitcasting clan claim that spinning gear isn't half as accurate as a baitcasting rig. They say this because with spinning gear the user is much more haphazard in his casting, so obsessed is he with the delight of the distance to be had with a spinning rig. Learn to throw that plug not sky high, where the wind will catch it, but straight out over the water so you

Figure 9. This diagram shows both a good and direct flow of the lure with its minimum of slack line (below) and a sloppy, uncontrolled cast into the air, bringing with it too much slack line (above). If a fish were to strike the second cast as the lure hits the water, the slack would offer problems.

can measure the distance and stop and control the fall of the plug to within inches of the proposed target. (*See* Appendix: Spinning.)

When you're doing this kind of casting, you learn to release the line a split second into the downward thrust of the rod, bring the rod tip up sharply to absorb any slack, and then immediately engage the pickup and be ready to crank in and pull back farther on the rod to stop the lure if it is going beyond your intended distance. Practice this against a barn when you are on shore. Try it at varied distances and try to remember those distances when you are out on the water. This familiarity with your cast timing and a specific lure weight will be necessary when you do any serious night fishing. If you don't master the cast and judging the distance, you'll spend more time in the woods than on the water.

Okay, you have snagged into the grass and your line is lying on the water. You don't want to disturb the spot, since I'm sure there is a bass of good proportions in there, probably at the tip of the grassy arrow point, or if not there, then somewhere between the grass and us. Don't just pull on the snagged plug and strain the rod and possibly break the line. Patience.

First, lift the line gently off the water by reeling and raising the rod tip. Now, by working the rod tip up and down in a kind of springing motion, put tension on the line (Figure 10). Use the flexing or vibrating technique; it is not a sure cure, but if you

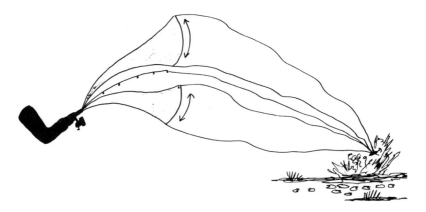

Figure 10. It is usually simple to pull out of a snag if you are patient and don't pull too hard at the lure. Vibrate or "foil" the rod both up and down and from side to side, pulling steadily. This action will gradually wiggle the lure loose from the snag.

vibrate the rod tip up and down quite violently so that the line carries the up-and-down motion to the lure, it will jiggle the hooks up and down, eventually tearing them loose from the grass. As you are doing this, pull back on the rod as the hooks begin to give way. If the up-and-down flexing doesn't work, try whipping the rod tip sideways and combine the two motions, all the time pulling steadily as you feel the grass gradually release the hooks. It works.

There you are, free.

And the plug jumped right into the pocket for an ace. The bass was there just waiting for it. He didn't offer much time for you to recoup. Hit back at him hard, now. Up with that rod tip, keep the line off the water and pressure him out of there by pumping in short hauls rather than exerting a steady pressure.

Now he's out of the woods, let him thrash; ease up a bit, but the second he starts to head for the grass on either side, let him know with a sharp snap of the rod tip that no amateur is on the other end. Your drag is preset so that you won't overdo it.

He's in the open, but don't get overconfident. That largemouth will go three pounds, not earth-shattering, but a nice bit of fun on spinning gear. Had it been taken on the heavier baitcasting stick it would not have offered half the action.

Put him on the stringer and don't forget that he and our other fish are there when you start the motor. You'll drown them if you drag them at any speed other than a very slow troll. The most humane way of stringing a fish so it won't drown is to insert the pin of the clip through the very end of the lower jaw, where the bone is firm and the flesh is tough. If you slip the pin through a fish's open mouth and gill, it can't close its mouth or gills, and so suffocates. Some anglers prefer to insert the pin into the meat just in front of the tail, and leave the head free.

We proceed down to 7. We are poling the boat very quietly so as not to scare bass out from the corner of the cove. (*See* Appendix: Poling.) They see you coming and before you get too far in they elect to get out of there by swimming right by you, headed for the open water. There goes one now that we spooked. With luck, however, there will be others still remaining. You'll take one right in that corner where the bushes part. This end of the cove is the hottest spot; hidden in the brush is the outlet of a tiny spring brooklet where bass and minnows come in for a cooling off.

Uh-oh. There's an angler there. He's sitting under one of the trees. Let's watch him for a moment and see how he's doing. Take a look through the binoculars. See? He's fishing live bait and a bobber. He must have a good brand of mosquito repellent or he'd probably be bitten alive in there. Speaking of being bitten, try some insect repellent right now. Better to be prepared.

Since we don't want to disturb our friend, we can turn around and work our way out of there, perhaps to return later, in the middle

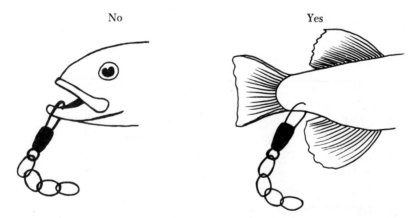

No   Yes

Figure 11.   The fish on the stringer, shown hooked two ways. The most common hooking is through the bottom of the jaw. This, however, inhibits the breathing of the fish. It is better to stick the clip through a section of flesh near the tail, leaving the head free to breathe properly.

of the day. I wanted to have you see this spot and, difficult as it is to fish, to show you the possibilities. You'll get hung up. You may even hook a big one in there that will tangle you up unmercifully. But if you get as much as thirty seconds of a grand fight, the tangle and trip in there will have been worth it.

Now, with a slight breeze coming up, we can work back to position 3 and do a bit of baiting. We could also return here tonight for some great bass-bug fishing.

No, we don't start the motor and whip out of here as if the warden were after us. We pole out and then paddle and *then* start the motor and slowly head for 3. We'll see the channel easily and be able to work it with live bait drifted weightlessly—a tricky procedure but quite effective on the bigmouths that are spooked by baits rigged with bobbers and sinkers. I've missed many bass because of weights. More often than not, the bass will merely mouth a bait that is held almost stationary by a weight and bobber; they seem to know that things are not right with it. On the other hand, a bait that is free to swim around in the water has more appeal. The bass, seeing the bait fin away from him, usually delivers a strike that has some finality to it.

Even though the water is a bit cloudy in here, it is easier to see into it with the sun at our back. It's getting warmer now, and with the breeze behind us coming from 2, we can drift with it down the stretch to the channel. We'll work the channel now with almost anything you choose, since we are again hunting for bass. In the past I've yanked out a decent pickerel from here and sometimes a nice crappie or two. I still like to fish live bait, drifted, so let's put off the casting exercise and rig the bait as shown in Figure 12 with thin monofilament and no weight or bobber. (*See* Appendix: The Merits of Bait Fishing.) I'll use a chub on the soft-tipped spinning rod; you try a shiner on your medium-action, soft-tipped trout fly rod with the mono line on the closed-face reel. I like this rod-and-reel set-up for the kind of fishing we'll be doing; with two anglers fishing from a small boat, with its space restrictions, one fly rod is quite enough. To get the bait out easily without danger of flipping it off, use the sidewinder cost. (*See* Appendix.) We'll both need lots of room. Don't ever try to throw a live bait with a vertical swing cast.

You make the first cast, out into the deep part of the channel. Let the line stay slack and work with extra line coiled in your hand or laid in coils on the bottom of the boat. With the closed-face reel,

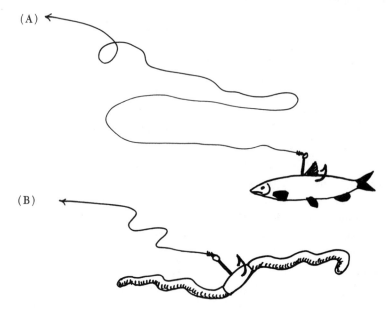

Figure 12. (A) A live minnow hooked through the back. It will live longer when hooked in this way. This is a good rig for stillfishing, but not for casting, since the bait will tend to spin in the air on the cast. (B) Hook a worm through the collar, for this bit of flesh is stronger than the rest of the body.

you can also feed the line directly if it comes off quickly enough for you. In spinning with an open-face reel, the trick is to work with the bail open, but with your index finger placed very lightly on the edge of the reel spool for touch control. I'll keep the boat from drifting and we can let the bait swim around for a little exercise. It will likely head down under, which is good.

Now, with both baits searching for bass, we can settle down for a quiet spell, light a long cigar, and watch that big old osprey circle about in search of wounded fish along the lake shore, or some sucker that's mudding in shallow water. It's nice to be out in such a quiet place. Hard to believe that we're not more than a mile from the highway.

Watch that line. Sure the minnow will swim around a bit, but he won't take the line out that fast. STR-R-R-R-R-I-K-E!

Nice bass. Set him hard now. Sink that barb much harder than you would in a trout or other game fish. The thrashing action and head shaking of a very mad bass can and usually does throw a single hook, and unless the fish has lowed the bait down deep, he'll get away most of the time. Even with two or three sets of hooks, bass can and often do throw the works.

Another subtlety. It is generally wrong to strike the moment you feel light pulls on the line. Unless the bass is absolutely ravenous he will mouth the bait a bit; take it crosswise in his mouth, travel with it, spit it out, pick it up again, place it crosswise in his jaw, spit it out again, circle around it like a cat does with a mouse, slap it with his tail, and bump it with his nose before opening the big gate and sucking it way down into his throat. Only when he really takes off do you haul back.

Working this cove from the shore under the same conditions would be as much of a delight as fishing from a boat, particularly if you enjoy poking in and around the brush and grass and wading along the shoreline of a lake. There is much of interest along the way in the form of discarded bird nests and holes and markings made by muskrats, raccoons, and perhaps mink. There will be some tracks left by herons and bitterns, snipe checks in the mud, a chirping frog that bounds from almost underfoot, a snake perhaps, and a complement of songbirds. The quieter your approach the less the wildlife will be disturbed. You might even see a grouse or a deer. When you emerge from the trees you'll move slowly through the brush, out into the open above the grass. If you're fly fishing, roll your casts and use a large-size bucktail or a marabou. I overdress my bucktail flies for this kind of fishing, and they look much more bulky than those usually found on tackle counters. I also like to cast two very small bucktails and risk even a worse hang-up, since these little flies have always done well for me on both trout and bass.

It's fun to start out from the brush and cast into the gap of one of those open "V's" between the grass points, at first dropping the fly practically at your feet. A surprised bass will make a lunge almost as the fly hits the water. If you don't get a hit, you can count on a strike as you lengthen your cast to go out farther from the shore into the "V."

Since the bottom is muddy you won't be able to wade too far out with any comfort, and as your feet sank in your casting would be restricted by your lower-than-usual height on the water. Conventional fore-and-aft casts can be made up and down the shore where the grass allows. If you're spinfishing, try a popping plug or my variation of the popping-diving plug with hairs, as shown in

Figure 13.   This is a very overdressed bucktail fly for use in lake fishing for bass. The usual trout-stream bucktail is about half this size in proportion to the hook.

Figure 14. This creation works wonders in grass. It's better than the usual plug with the "weedless" wire extensions that sell so well.

When you fish this cove or any cove, sniff the wind first and work the side that is less windy. Work with the sun at your back so you can see into the water. Don't leave without making a few casts as far out as you can reach, for example, in Figure 6 from 1 to 5. The big fish that will come in from the main lake will have to pass the two grass points, and if you are there at the right time, you should connect.

After a thorough working over of the cove by day, you can take part in its treasure by night, working the same way as by day and going over familiar footing. There are great sounds in the night: an owl hooting at you from the brush; a bat whisking by. Best of all, you'll hear both near and far the thrashing of bass on the feed, just waiting for you.

Surely you've fished this kind of water before, and if you remain in the ranks of bass fishermen in the future, you'll fish it again in its varied forms. Try and remember our experiences together and relate them to the problems you'll be facing, snagged lures and all! I'll wager, right here and now, that in the past you've tended to skip over or at best have merely thrown a few casts into such a spot. You became snagged and gave it up. Next time things are going to be different. Go armed with the most weedless lure to fit the problem, the one likeliest to survive the hang-ups, and fish it slowly. Bass in this situation are not choosy about pattern, size, or color. They go only for *action* in the grass. So hit first and ask questions afterwards. And remember that most anglers will skip the best parts of the cove. That's why the fish are big in there!

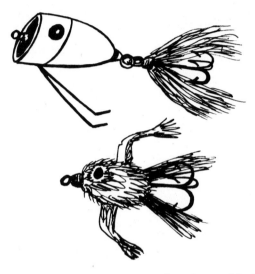

Figure 14. Note that these bugs are tied with a treble hook. This is seldom done, the usual bug having only a single hook. The treble hook seems to nail bass quicker and more securely, but the lure tends to hang up more often when fished in the weeds or grass.

3

ROCKY SHORELINE (DEEP)

A deep, rocky shoreline is a very common type of situation on most northern smallmouth lakes that have a variety of terrain surrounding them. High hills, rock-strewn valleys, cliffs, gravel deposits, and shale drop-offs and clefts all go toward making up the basic strata for the formation of good bass lakes. Somewhere along the lengths and broken shorelines of these lakes are deep stretches of scattered boulders and the broken remnants of rock formations partially disintegrated by time and erosion.

Bass like this type of water and thrive well in it. Many lakes in Maine, for example, that did not naturally contain smallmouths have become loaded with them since the first plantings over a hundred years ago. The shoreline may be as shown in the drawing at the beginning of this chapter, a section near where large shade trees grow almost to the shore of the lake, or it may consist of more

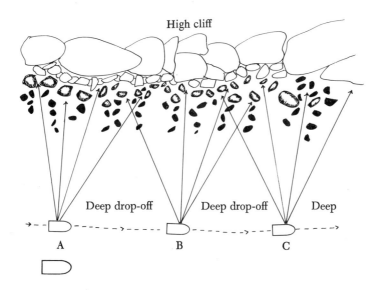

Figure 15. *A typical rocky shoreline that can be approached from either direction. It is best to keep the boat as far out as possible but within comfortable and accurate casting range. During the day it is not always necessary to cast the lure right on shore, but at night and in the evening or morning, try to target in on the actual shoreline and make your lure imitate some form of life coming out from the shore into the water.*

Starting at A we note the sudden drop-off from the high cliff indicated. We cast from a comfortable distance, bouncing our lures right off the rocks. At B, the boulders are close together and we cast as shown, right in between them, bouncing our lures off rock tops as they travel back toward us on the retrieve. When the lures are in the clear, we can pick up for a re-cast. When working a sinking-diving plug, we allow the lures to sink once they are free from shore snags. Move the boat ahead slowly to aid the action of the lures and to cover more territory.

At C is the same problem cast. When you are finished casting in the area, cast back over B and A—you might raise a bass that did not hit on the first tries.

open stretches that once were fields or washed-out areas, now grown over with thin brush. The edge of the lake drops off in gravel, large stones, and small boulders to a depth of about four or five feet and then slopes down, sometimes almost vertically, in a broken, plate-like shelf. Beyond this line is the deep water of the lake. Springs are often found in this kind of set-up, and in the summer fish abound wherever there is a source of cooler water than is found generally in the lake. It is the opposite in the fall, when the fish will tend to go to the warmer water.

On the other shore of the lake is about a mile of water like that shown in the picture. There are deep pockets between the boulders, that can be seen, and even deeper water pockets and holes between the boulders, that cannot be seen. Smallmouth bass abound in here in company with rock bass and good-sized white perch. In areas where there is more gravel, a gentler slope, and sand bars, you'll see evidence of bass spawning beds, and the fishing there during the spawning season (when legal) can be great.

It is common knowledge that if there are too many bass in a given lake, their average size becomes smaller. It is in such lakes and under such conditions that fishing over the spawning beds in the spring should be allowed and also recommended. The season lasts only a few weeks, and unless the lake is over fished, there will be plenty of bass left to survive and prosper. In this instance then, it is not unsporting to fish for bass when they are over their beds. Check the local game laws, however.

In the case of heavily fished bass waters, you will discover that the bass are usually big and cautious. This means that the ratio of bass to their food is in a better balance, and that fishing over their beds might seriously reduce the population. Of course there are many attitudes about this touchy problem. There are some who would rather catch more and smaller bass than fewer and bigger ones.

Debates on these points rage at boat liveries, at rod and gun clubs, and in the laboratories of conservation departments. The lawmakers try to accommodate the most popular concept and to enforce practical laws as best they can. Personally, I find it most difficult and am most reluctant to fish over the spawning beds, in a heavily fished lake, regardless of the points raised above.

Certainly it takes little talent to throw a floating plug almost haphazardly near a spawning bass or its bed. Any fish within fifty feet will come out and grab the lure, since he has been convinced that the thing is there to invade his home and privacy. But perhaps we all have to do it a few times to get the thrill of action out of our bones before we can get down to serious fishing for the hard-to-get bass that are just feeding or guarding their lair when their homemaking duties are over for the season.

The conservation departments of various states regulate the bass harvest. That's why it is important to help them in recording your catches and reporting your luck on a given lake. For many years, while fishing a group of lakes near my home, I would send in reports at the end of the year. The department thanked me and other contributors for doing this, and used these figures as evidence of the relationship between bass and angling-pressure in those lakes.

Meanwhile, back at the lake, this is water to be worked equally from the shore and from the boat. Actually it can be tackled in much the same way as a trout stream if you are fishing from the shore or wading along the edge of a drop-off, being careful to keep out of the holes.

Our first consideration, as always, is the wind. In midsummer select the shore where the wind is not rushing waves onto the shoreline. Also, if you fish in the morning or evening, select the section that is likely to remain longer in shadow or that will receive the cooling shadows first. Given this directive, we can proceed to fish. We have diagrammed two samples of ways to cast to a rocky shoreline when boating (Figure 16) or wading (Figure 17). Let's

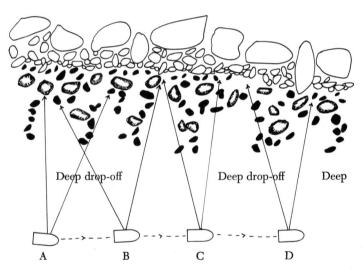

Deep drop-off   Deep drop-off   Deep

A   B   C   D

Figure 16. A variation of the rocky shoreline, with a much more shallow lake edge. The same general rules of position and casting apply for any rocky shoreline, however, although I prefer to use lighter lures, and more especially fly-rod lures and bass bugs, for this kind of water. Note how we proceed from A to D on this water. Remember this routine when you come across a similar stretch of water.

The casts may look obvious to you here, but experience will show you what to look for on the water. Proceed slowly and pick your shots. Return to the area at another time under different conditions and study it before you make your first cast.

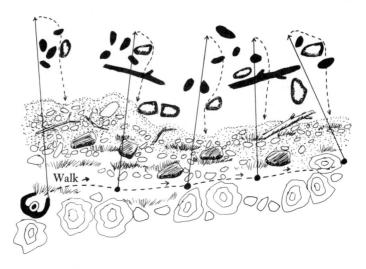

Figure 17.   This is a diagram of the manner of casting and retrieving a bucktail (or a surface bass bug) along the rocks, both visible and underwater. Note that the cast is curved in near the exposed rocks to allow the lure to be fished "around" the rocks, and then retrieved in short jerks back to the rod tip. (See Appendix: Fly Casting; Bass Bugging.)

take a look at the bottom with prying eyes, as if we were swimming along the shore edge in skin-diving togs. The time is midsummer, the water is warm.

The water is clear, for there is no mud to stir along the bottom. A scant few bits of grass and underwater weeds grow in these rocks. Large bright spots and dark shadows are carved out by the shape of the rocks from the direction of the light. Where it is about five feet deep these areas are quite well defined, but after about eight feet the entire area becomes dimmer and the contrast between light and darkness is less noticeable.

Look carefully. There are fish in here: small sunfish in the shallow sections and a few rock bass or a passing school of perch. But look beside those rocks. Once in a while you'll see the eye, the snout, or the tail of a really big bass. He's just sitting there, resting, or perhaps moving about a bit looking for something to feed his insatiable appetite. As he wanders about he is alert for any movement, particularly that of a straying or wounded minnow, or a school of small minnows away from their cover. He knows from experience that it is almost useless to chase minnows unless they are balled up in a tight school or are near the surface, well away from cover.

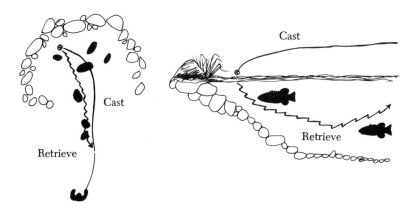

Figure 18. This is the cast and roll-mend technique that can be used instead of the conventional straight retrieve back to the rod tip. Note that the fly lands near the rock, is retrieved a bit, and is then rolled forward and to the left to again be retrieved and fished. It is possible to fish the four positions without the retrieve becoming necessary.

We take our cue from all of this; let's get back on shore and into our fishing garb. We are armed with a fly rod and a spinning rod with which we can throw the small lures that should imitate the bait minnows well. (*See* Appendix: Tackle.)

From the brushy shore we can poke our rod through the leaves and cautiously step into the open. If the area is in shade we can be less mindful of our sudden movements; but on a bright, shiny day any sudden motion might send the nearby inshore bass out into the deep. Quite often during the day these bass will harbor up right next to the shore, especially if the water is in the low 70s, unless and until the wind causes waves that would rock them and make life a bit bouncy. Given quiet water, we are also warned of careful fishing, not unlike careful stream tactics.

Since our bass would feed on minnows here, not generally crawfish or frogs, let's try a bucktail, ordinary trout-style. By roll-casting, if we cast directly out from our position, we can aim for the pockets between the rocks, allow the fly to sink about a foot or two, and then, in very snappy but short jerks and pulls, retrieve the fly to our rod tip. We can cover the area in this way with one pattern.

But since the fish will usually get bored with seeing one particular pattern, we can change patterns after every five or six casts if they have been following our fly but not taking it.

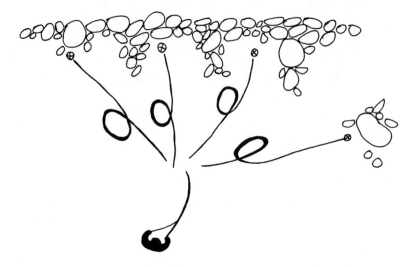

Figure 19. Forward roll casts to a target.

Another technique that the rollcaster can use is the quick, surface-disturbing retrieve. Cast the fly holding the rod high, drag the fly across the surface for a few inches, pick it up with a forward rollcast and conventional back rollcast, and then replace the fly in exactly the same spot (Figure 19.)

This gives the impression of a wounded minnow or a frantic one and will engage the attention of any fish in the area. Even if the bass are not feeding they are suckers for the escaping-form-of-life motion of the fly. A black-and-white marabou is excellent for this, and so is the red-and-white, particularly in the bright light. As always, I prefer black or at least dark brown for early morning and evening fishing, once the shadows are over the water. Try the old rule of a dark fly for a dark day, and a bright one for a bright day. As you work along the shore, do not neglect to cast *ahead*, right next to the "beach." Most of us have a funny tendency: when fishing the shore we cast *out* as far as possible; when casting from the boat we cast as far *in*.

Quite often, in order to work the shoreline ahead, it is desirable to wade out a bit from shore so as to gain back-cast room and a proper angle for fishing the shoreline in between the rocks. If the drop-off to a deeper level is seen, the fly can be worked right along this line, often with good results.

In early morning and at twilight I have taken good smallmouth

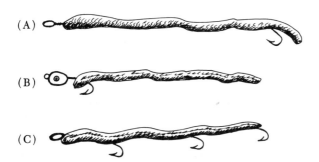

(A)

(B)

(C)

Figure 20. Three ways of using the plastic worm or black eel. The top rig is best for grassy or weedy water since there is only one hook. The lure can be used either with or without weight. The second and third rigs are good for trolling and deep down drift fishing as well as casting. Activate the lure, don't just pull it along, to make it appear like an eel. (A) Eel or plastic worm threaded on a single hook and leader. (B) Weighted jig—single hook. (C) Three single hooks.

bass in this way, fishing trout-stream style with a big Wulff dry fly, skittering it between the rocks. Playing and landing a good bass in that kind of water with such light gear is a pleasure.

A small spinner, notably the Colorado, with a worm or pork rind is an excellent next choice, or even an excellent starter, if the wind is well out from the area. Diving and zigzagging plugs are third choices. But as I have learned from so many years of failing, it is not the choice of lure that is important, it is the way of fishing for bass under certain conditions that really counts. If you can present a lure properly over the bass—almost any lure—there is a good chance they will respond.

Fishing this shore from the boat, we could go through the bucktail, marabou, spinner-and-pork, or spinner-and-worm bit. We might even choose a small spinfishing popper plug or a fly-rod bug.

Now, however, I'll give you the pitch for my most successful lure for such water. I've saved it for last here, just to show how many alternative possibilities there are.

This is the place for the artificial eel or plastic worm (Figure 20) in black or dark brown, or the large-size plastic worm (use a real nightcrawler if you prefer, or even a grass snake!) Remember, we are still in the boat, lying a bit offshore.

You'll get snagged in the rocks, but no matter. Put that rig down and drag it along the bottom, over and between the rocks. Let it pause right on the bottom. Bring it to the surface, run it fast, run it slow; experiment. Chances are that you won't have too much evidence of a specific technique that pays off, but bass like this type of lure, especially on a weed-free, rock-strewn bottom. I'd hate to fish it in the weedbeds!

When you are finished with the inshore area, work the eel or worm down deep, letting it bounce on the bottom. *Fish it slowly.*

If this still doesn't get you a bass you're in trouble. Bait up a live worm, and as a last resort, since the lady is waiting at home for a bass to bake, try a generous piece of pork dead-drifted deep along the drop-off.

If you are still fishless, don't go home that night!

Our second, earlier, set-up of the rocky shoreline (Figure 16) is a bit different. This is much shallower water in the first fifteen feet out from the waterline. There is good shade and cover right overhead, and when this side of the lake is in shadow it is a good area to fish at almost any time of the year. It is easier to wade here, excepting that you must watch the quick drop-off. I've used conventional small wet flies just as I would if I were fishing for trout. In fact, the wet flies pay off in northern lakes where there are brook trout as well as bass along the shores. They must appear like small minnows or big natural flies or nymphs. Rock bass will also take these small flies, with utter abandon, and can provide some fun fishing after a day of casting for the big ones that simply did not materialize.

Big bass do not usually harbor in this water. If you do catch one baking size, he has probably cruised in from the deep to feed or rest. I've seen fish like this in spots similar to the one pictured, flipping the minnows right against the shoreline. This is also good water at night for wading; and just as good fished from a boat if you can work quietly enough and keep the tackle and oars from rattling about. If possible, it is best to fish it from the shore first, to get the layout of the "inside" water, rocks, holes, and flat places where the minnows school up. Later, at twilight or in the darkness of a moonless night, you can lie offshore a bit and make leisurely casts into the rocks, landing the plug or lure just at the lip of the drop-off—not necessarily into the actual shoreline, where you might get hung up.

While fishing from the boat, remember to cast up and down the shore, for quite often a good fish will have come in after you have left a short stretch, or will be lying just offshore ahead of you. Angle your casts so that you retrieve across the shelf edge.

Shallow trolling with light spinners and small spinning-rod-size spoons also can be productive along this kind of shoreline, although it is not too easy to get these lures through it without hanging up in the rocks. But worth it? Yes!

Again, try the pork rind, particularly behind a light spoon. Keep the line short and the rod tip up when trolling. A pork-rind bait can ride just a foot or so under the surface. Gauge your line length for this to happen, and troll slowly. If you're fish hunting, not having seen or felt a fish, use live bait. It is the perfect teaser at almost any time of the day throughout the season. If the wind is ruffling the surface, go down. Slow troll or drift the bait, weightless. If you fish from shore, sit there, cast a slip-sinker bait rig (*See* Appendix: Terminal Tackle), and light up a cigar.

I'll bet you have skipped over this type of water before. You merely trolled past and perhaps gave it a few casts. Maybe you have even picked up a small bass or two, but this book deals with the times you haven't, and I'm trying to offer the most techniques to try over a given spot rather than merely going for a nice boat ride.

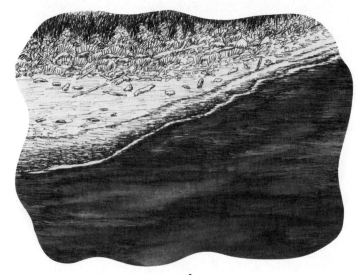

4

SANDY SHORELINE

You'll find patches of this kind of shoreline on the more northern lakes. It will be spliced in between all kinds of rocky drop-offs, muddy sections, and gravel reefs. In some of the midwestern states, the lake will contain much larger proportions of sandy shoreline. Florida shorelines are exclusively sandy unless the lake is lined with old cypress and palms. This is the kind of water you usually troll by once or twice, fishing it while you're on the way to something that seems better. The lakes you are used to fishing are much more interesting, with their coves, inlets, points, deep drop-offs, and grass or pad flats, so your reasoning is to leave this barren-looking water to the bathers. At times you'll be right; at others quite wrong.

You can say that about almost any stretch of water. If you are fishing on the wrong side of any lake, wind-wise, you won't see a bass. If they're all down in the deep sleeping out the hot sun and high temperatures, or are logy on a low barometer, you'll find your choicest shorelines—as well as the beach—devoid of action.

If time allows, of course, fish the entire lake, choosing the best times for each type of water. I've never been the kind of angler to fish a specific spot for a few casts and then dash out and away for a greener pasture across the lake, spending more of the day in transit than in fishing. I prefer to fish rather than travel.

So we have come to this sandy bit of shoreline. It is open and bright; few wavelets are washing the clean sand cleaner. We're offshore about a hundred feet and over about ten feet of water. From here into the shore the beach shallows gradually and it is only inches deep for about ten feet from the dry sand. Not much life here, you think, since there is little place for bait to stay in residence and less opportunity for the big fish to stalk their prey. Actually we are fishing the beach where, years ago, I took the biggest bass of my career. It was a four-pound smallmouth, big enough to thrill any angler. So it is quite worth our time to try a few tricks and see if we can duplicate the experience. If not, we'll try it at night.

Look carefully into the water, whether you are on shore, wading, or in a boat. The water is clear. Under its surface you may see minnows and other baitfish moving in small schools. Since this particular area is exposed to winds and any lake currents that exist, it is not quite spawning territory; still, it does hold small baitfish. In a few minutes that bright sun will be shaded over by billowy clouds and you'll be able to see under the surface. We can assume that there are bass in the neighborhood of those minnows; however, it is most difficult to approach and present a lure here that will not scare the fish away on the first cast. And if you're on shore, there's scant brush cover to offer a backdrop to your approach. If you fish any of the midwestern lakes that have stretches of this type and sandy or pebbly shores, you'll recall having been skunked here. Yet as you will see, there are great possibilities to be realized the next time you encounter such water. Try some of the tricks we are about to suggest in our next hours of fishing together.

Look at Figure 21. Boat fishing offers perhaps the best vantage point for fishing this beach, since the intruder, if he proceeds quietly, will drive any big fish in toward the beach and won't disturb the fish that may be working the shoreline. Casts made from 1 toward A and B, for example, will sink deep and actually touch the sand before being retrieved. This is the spot for small spinning lures, and the ultralight spinning addict with his tiny tackle can put his miniatures to work, unhampered by snags,

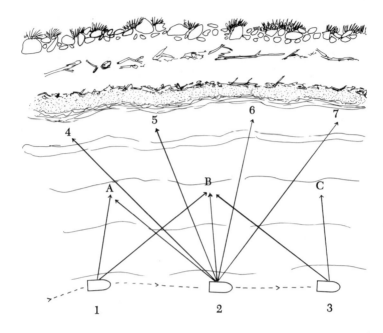

Figure 21. This bland-looking, sandy beach shoreline looks as if no bass would ever be found in it except possibly at night. This isn't so, however. Troll it along the deep edge during a bright day, but work the bugs here in the evening, casting them right up to where the waves meet the dry sand.

grass, and the like. A big bass on that tackle will produce some thrills even if the fish is never landed. I also like the small feather and bucktail saltwater-type jigs that ride with the hook up. Cast ahead of your course. The area is as yet undisturbed. Cast straight along the shore. If you have approached from 1, cast toward 2. If from 3, cast toward 2 and 1. Don't work inshore yet, there may be a bass lurking in the deeper water. Save the shoreline for later. When you cast that jig, let it rest on the bottom for a second or two and then *slowly* drag it along, causing the sand to "mud up" a bit, imitating a small fish nosing the bottom. Now pick it up off the ground, jerk the rod tip, reel in a bit, and let the lure sink to the bottom again. Repeat this process until the lure is almost under the boat. It gets bass.

Say you choose a spoon for the next try. Continue working the open water. Use that spoon in the same way as the jig. If you get no response, then go for a sinking-diving plug (*See* Appendix: Lures) that activates the faster you pull on it as it heads down deep. If you still get no action, you can proceed to fish the inshore section inside positions 4, 5, 6, and 7 on the diagram. You are now fishing from 2, having worked both 1 and 3, with the exception of having used live bait or even a pork chunk.

In this situation, I prefer fly-rod lures, bucktails, small hairless popping plugs, or maybe even a popping bug. Cast these right to the edge of the water. Let the disturbance from the line disappear and then, in very slow, twitching motions, cast that lure over a thirty-degree arc, covering the area without moving the boat. When all else has failed, impale a big nightcrawler, your black eel, or a plastic worm of large size on a plain jig. Cast it right to the dry sand and drag it into the water and over the bottom. Do not pick it up off the bottom, but instead let it crawl back to you. This also works well on sandy bottoms where there are some weeds and a few boulders. You'll use this technique often in your shore fishing.

Quite naturally, this beach and those like it are best fished in the early morning or at twilight, for it is then that the big bass will be coming in for a meal or hanging around after the nighttime foraging. The prime time here is, of course, at night. We'll get to that later.

While we're here, you and I are really going to get to fish together; I want to show you a synchronized method of duet fishing that has paid off for my partner and me for many years.

Unless two men fish together a great deal, their casting seldom fits into a mold of instinctive cooperation. It is usually each man for himself, so to speak, and this can be awkward and dangerous.

Take a look at Figure 22. This is the casting set-up for what I have dubbed "duet fishing," which resembles the skindiver's term "buddy fishing." Two anglers casting in this manner, using two quite different lures, can take fish more often than they can with unorganized casting and certainly more than one angler can.

The boat direction represent the slow troll of your craft, loaded with you and your partner. You have both just retrieved your lines and are into the beach area (not shown) in the foreground of the diagram. First, Angler A casts to the point labeled 1 in the diagram, well ahead of the spot usually cast to by the man in the bow (angler B in the diagram). When angler A's lure has traveled to point X on the diagram, angler B casts to the same spot that angler A had cast to. The fish thus has a good choice of lures. Angler A then

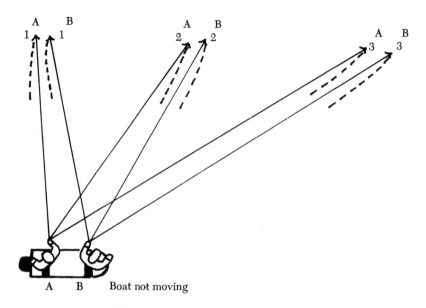

Figure 22. This diagram shows the way in which two anglers can fish their lures closely together in sequence and thus offer the fish a varied fare. Often the number one angler, being in the second position, gets more hits.

slowly retrieves his lure, and when B's lure reaches point Y, A casts ahead again in the same way that he did before but this time toward point 2 in the diagram. Angler B's lure is now brought in so that as soon as A's lure reaches point X, B can cast to point 2 on the diagram. Again, A's lure is being retrieved so that he will be prepared to cast to point 3 as soon as B's lure reaches point Y. Note that the sequence is alternated between the two anglers, offering different lures and angles to the fish, with equal chances for each angler. The casting is not haphazard; there are no tangles and no dangers, and there is much good water coverage.

Look now at Figure 23 for a different method of trying to gain the best coverage and variety of lure presentation, fishing two in a boat while it is moving slowly.

Angler A makes his cast to the target. As soon as his lure travels behind and he begins the retrieve, angler B casts to the same spot but retrieves faster than A so that he can get the first

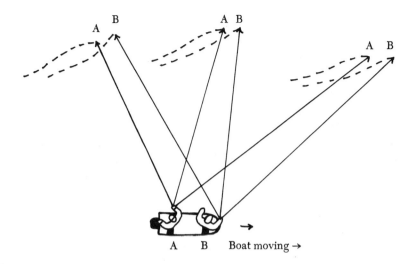

A   B   Boat moving →

Figure 23.   Anglers A and B are targeting in to the same target, and the retrieve also goes in parallel as the boat moves slowly along. This is a great way to entice stubborn bass.

cast at the second target. When B has cast and his lure lags behind from the second target, Angler A makes his cast to that same spot and retrieves more quickly so that he can get first cast at the third target. This system allows the two anglers to take turns making the first cast to the advance, hot-spot target.

Of course you can always fish in the conventional, parallel way, both casts landing at the same time, one ahead of the other. Both lines will then swing together on the retrieve if the boat is motored slowly along.

When fishing the beach, it is quite an advantage to be the man at the motor. Since the water is shallow and all of it is of practically the same quality, the man in the back of the boat can allow his lure to swing very wide and out from the shore behind the boat and can even troll it a bit over the area that has just been fished. I've often done this, reeling in the lure to about twenty feet behind the boat and keeping my eye on it while lighting a cigar. You'd be amazed at the line of fish following the lure that we didn't know were there. When this happens I drop anchor and use live bait, letting it settle right on the bottom.

Bass will frequent this beach particularly in the summertime, in the evening after water skiers and other surface factors, including speed wakes, have kept them in the deep during the day.

They'll come inshore to feed long after the bats have digested their first insects. I also like to wade this beach armed with a fly rod and small bass bugs, or a light spinning rod with a mini-Jitterbug. Sometimes, if I'm really quiet and the bass are really in and feeding, I hold my casts until I see one particular bass and cast directly to him rather than follow the usual "hunting" method.

Imagine another type of beach or a sandy shore—the kind of shore where the heron watches long after the bass have spawned. It can be good even during the bright light of day, since it is protected somewhat by outlying grass and pads that keep down the big waves from speeding wakes. I've reserved this fishing for you. Kill the motor well out from the pads. Pole your way in here. (*See* Appendix: Poling.) Allow the waves and water motion to subside for a minute or two and then, *very slowly*, work your way in and pick your casts with care, limiting them to perhaps one or two throws to each spot. That is probably all you'll need, for it is almost guaranteed that there will be big bass in there just waiting for you. The little ones spawned earlier by the big fish are now fair game, and they know just where to find them. I like to try a very small bucktail lure, but you try whatever you like.

Let's go night fly-rod bugging along this beach; we'll try with the boat first. The usual idea here is to cast into the shore, and we'll do this even if it means more boat handling to move from position to position, followed by squaring the boat off for two casters, with the inside man working the shoreline and the outside caster working about twenty feet out from the shore. In this way many a backcast that feels too low can simply be allowed to drop down on the water so you can work the area behind you. If any bass are heard feeding well out from shore, specific casts can be made to them. As far as lure choice is concerned, anything goes.

The second method of fishing this beach is to move slowly along the shore a convenient distance from the edge of the water, cast the bugs right to the shoreline, and pop them out toward the boat.

The angler fishing from the shore can fan out his casts from a single position or walk slowly along the shoreline, casting ahead and once in a while behind him in order to cover the water well. The tendency in all of this is to cast too much and too often. Remember, it is better to cast less and perfectly than to make a great many casts that are sloppy. Fish can easily be put down here, even at night. Too much casting will also discourage any fish from coming into the shore to feed.

The next day, even if your physical constitution and your usual routine of life make you fight stubbornly against it, get up early and fish the same area, even if you have fished most of the night. Get a cup of coffee. See the sun rise—and catch some fish. There's plenty of time to sleep when you are back on the job!

The early riser hits the payoff. For one thing, the world is still and mostly (except for you) asleep. Only nature is awake. The birds are singing even before the sun actually rises. Ever been out digging worms when the cock crows just before daylight? The sky is beautiful at that time—deep blue and almost black in the west but beginning to glow in the east. And when you reach the lake at that hour and fumble for the bow rope, the water is still. It bounces a star back at you.

Only a few birds twitter. Perhaps the crows are about, putting an owl to rout.

Listen. The bass are feeding up along the shore. Hear that? *Slurp,* he's mouthing something. Another *slurp.* Then a tail swish. *Bang!* That bass up there caught something. Better get up there before the sun rises and puts him to sleep for the day.

The air is cool and fresh. Your collar is up around your neck. A few mosquitoes are after you but will stay ashore when you depart onto the lake. Hurry.

Don't start the motor yet. It will break the silence and shatter the mood. Row for a bit, dragging a couple of lures behind the boat. A Jitterbug, perhaps, a small one on the light spinning rod; a jointed Pikey-minnow plug on the other, heavier rod. Cast a midget popper plug on the ultralight rod. A big bass will smash it to pieces. Are you game?

When you row quietly and spot a bass feeding under the overhanging beech boughs up the shore, you can pause, reel in, and cast to him with the other lures, such as zigzagging or popper plugs.

A deer comes out to feed. She's touchy at first, looking in all directions and sniffing the wind. Then she comes out boldly, hardly expecting to see a human up and about at this hour. As you fish by the sandy shoreline you scatter the first bass near you. Stop the boat. Remain quiet for a spell, then quietly cast ahead of the boat and toward the beach, where the bass have been attacking the minnows that have just become active with the light. You'll throw a big, fluffy marabou bucktail on the heavy fly rod. You'll let it sink and bring it back in short, snappy jerks.

There is a mist on the lake. It shows first as a pink haze, with only the tops of the trees and distant hills appearing against the lightening blue sky. Let's try some light artificials or even small bucktails on this sandy shoreline.

We'll beach the boat and wade along. At the end of the beach is a cluster of rocks. There are bass in there, as we have discovered in past night patrols. Maybe we can get a big one to take home for breakfast. We select the big fly rod—the bass bugger—and tie on two small bucktails, one a solid black with a tinsel body and the other brownish-yellow, perchy looking one, to give the fish their choice.

We make several casts up the beach, and when we have a good false cast going, we let the flies drop down in the water behind us, slightly out from the beach. To give them time to settle a bit, we drag out the cigarettes. It is light enough now so that a match flare won't scare anything.

That, of course, is when the strike usually happens, so we'll let you write this part of the sequence. It never fails, and it's a big fish. So we drop the cigarettes in the water.

The morning star splinters. We use the net, and it comes up heavy.

Lots to do today!

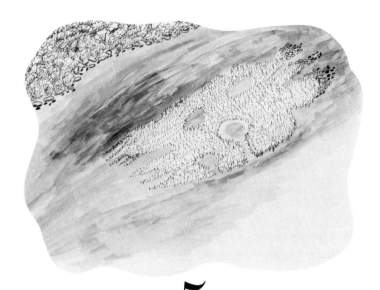

5

MIDLAKE GRASS FLAT

We're in a plane, flying over one of my favorite lakes in New England. To the right is a dark forest of spruce, fir, and pine. Between that shoreline and the light spot in the middle of the lake is the deepest area. Note how the water shallows quickly to the "almost island" that we'll call the grass flat. It is nearly as if an island were forming here, or once formed and is now sinking. Whatever the case, this shallow, midlake shelf is present for some geological reason, with the main part of the lake bottom sloping away from it.

Many bass prefer to stay in the flat unless scared off by too much fishing pressure, speedboat wakes, or a high water temperature. They also tend to hole up in the deeper grooves or potholes of the flat that are shown in the diagram (Figure 24). From our high position these potholes look like pockmarks. We'll catch bass

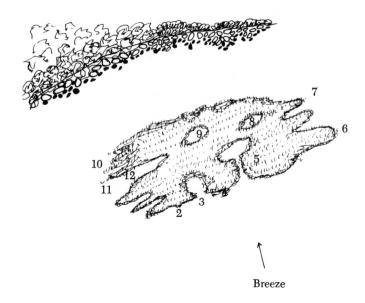

Breeze

Figure 24. This is the view looking down at a typical grass flat that is found offshore in a lake. Note the levels indicated (in a rather orderly and conventional manner) and the three basic holes. There are no two midlake grass flats alike, but we fish this particular one from memory.

in them, or at least bring up some action. Besides the resident bass, the flat is constantly invaded by bass that come to it from the deeps that surround it. These bass generally come in at twilight and depart after sunrise. You'll likely hook into a few finned lunkers.

Viewed from the boat, the features of our "almost island" are not always so obvious. The most prominent flats can be spotted by the tips of the grass, some pads, and an occasional rock or large boulder that protrudes above the water surface. Other grassy flats are located well underwater, as much as ten feet, for example. The grass and pondweed will reach up three feet or more above this, and it is at the level of the grass- and weed-tops that we must troll or work our sinking-diving plugs or cast spoons, jigs, and bait. If you don't get them down to the right level, a lot of action can be missed. The view shown in the chapter-opening illustration is typical of a partially exposed grass flat, since grassy areas that lie under the water cannot be seen.

Most fishermen work the grass flat much too hard, so let's try to fish it properly.

It is eleven o'clock. The sun is almost at the zenith. A slight breeze is developing from the deep, midlake direction. Nice day. No humidity. A joy to be out.

The deeper part of the lake is colored a tan-to-greenish-yellow, and the water is olive where it shallows. Potholes are a bit darker in shade, giving us the tip-off to their location. Later, when the sun is down at an angle, the holes will appear as caverns.

With deep water around our "oasis" it is worth trying a slow troll all the way around, offering us the opportunity to have a good look at the entire area to see what's going on, if anything. Pickerel hold out here, too, as well as sunnies, crappies, and both large- and smallmouths.

We'll troll two spinning rods, since we'll also be using them for casting as we proceed. You can try some long-distance throws right to the edge of the grass as we move along. We might use a floating-diving plug, such as the Pflueger "Pal-O-Mine," so that it will go down quickly with the speed of the troll plus your manipulation of it. You'll have lots of deep water between the grass and the boat. I'll troll a light spoon on one rod and a floating-diving plug on the other. No use in fishing on the top; save that until twilight, or work the surface plugs at dawn. Right now, the fish should be well down out of the light.

We land a pickerel, a nice one, and get several hits from something or other, but nothing to shout about. But we did get a good look at the grass flat, and from here on in the diagram is our fishing layout.

In this fishing exercise we will probably use all of our basic tackle. Since we will troll, a medium baitcasting rod rigged with ten-pound-test line and the usual terminal tackle will be right. Two spinning rods, one lightweight and long, for throwing heavy bugs and light lures, and a medium-weight one for the bigger plugs, spoons, and spinner rigs will be needed. We will each have a nine- or nine-and-a-half-foot fly rod for bucktail casting and bass bugging.

While it may seem a bit confusing to have so much tackle aboard, you will discover that switching rigs is not only a relief but a necessity if you are going to really get the most out of the day's work. So many of us tend to stick to the same rig and fish it for hours rather than switch to something entirely different. Of course, it takes a logical decision to make the switch from, say, bass bugging to throwing light lures or even switching to trolling. Also, as shown in many places in this book, trolling and casting can be done at the same time under certain conditions. Quite often after a stretch of shoreline has been worked, perhaps with plugs, it is quite right to reverse and work over the same area with, say, bass bugs, or, if you are tired of casting, to leave the shoreline and troll for a while or even anchor or drift and fish with bait. So, it is better to take all the gear aboard and learn to use it, getting into the habit of changing rigs often.

In fishing an offshore grass patch you will note that infinite varieties of fishing styles and techniques can be put to good use, and the enjoyment of being able to perform well under all circumstances and with adequate and well-matched equipment adds much to a day on the water, whether a lot of fish are caught or not.

Let's look again at Figure 24, just as if we were actually fishing it and see just how we can plan our moves and decide what tackle and rigs to use. Grass flats such as this one are common fishing grounds in many lakes but are often fished too hard and in ways that tend to put fish down in hiding, or worse still, drive them out of the grass into the deep water. So it is wise to plot our moves first.

From our position 1, as we approach the grass flat, we slow down almost to a stop. In order to get a good look at the possibilities, we will troll all the way around the flat over the shallow side well out from 2, 3, 4, and 7. The water is about ten feet deep some hundred feet out, shallowing up to the grass. The water on the other side facing the shoreline shelves off deeply from the grass flat, and it is deep all the way to the shore.

Let's troll two types of lures. I'll rig up with a deep-running gold spoon that will sink well down. Not knowing the contour of the bottom, I'll likely get hung up if we troll too slowly, but that's part of the game. You can pick a zigzagging diving-type pug to offer some contrast.

Let's go. The boat is pointed off 2 and 3 and we slow troll, noting the two indentations at 2 and 3 that we will be fishing later with surface plugs and even bass bugs when the sun begins to set. Those are fairly deep indentations with their edges sharper than the grass at 10.

Our slow course brings us out from 4, where we see a tempting indentation with its quota of pesky lily pads, but there is at least one good shot in there for later on. Let's troll in a bit closer to that spot. Since it begins to shallow up there, we'll move a bit faster to keep my spoon off the bottom. As we come by the opening, pick up that other rod now and, just for kicks, throw a surface plug in there toward the mouth of the hole.

A strike—but you missed. We'll hit him later.

We see another but deeper entrance into the center of the grass flat at 4, with its channel leading to a nice opening almost caked with pads except right in the middle.

I just had a hefty strike to my spoon. . . . He's on, so I'll kill the motor to play him on a drift. . . . He's off. Goes to show that there are bass along the outside, so trolling can be productive as well as offering a look at our prize bit of lake.

As we round the point, note those three indentations with their rocks and short gravelly bars leading out to the deep water. With the wind picking up a bit, let's rerig to a live bait setup such as the one in Figure 25 and drift well off 7 until we almost reach the lake shoreline; we just might hook a good one. Rig your line with the old-style cork and sinker with a live minnow on the tippet as shown. I'll fish a free-drifting live minnow just for contrast. One of us may connect.

A nice day; it is a relief to just drift quietly without the sound of the motor blocking our ears.

Evidently the gravel and rocks extend quite a way out from the point here at 7. A bottom such as this is usually a good place for

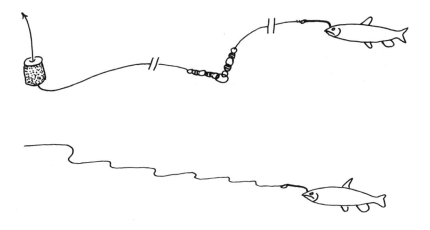

Figure 25. A typical live-bait rig: a cork and sink with a live minnow on a tippet.

live-bait fishing. On trips to this section of the lake, I have often noticed other fishermen anchored where we are now drifting. They fish their live bait right on the bottom, leaving it sitting there for hours.

With all that potentially good fishing with lures and flies, you probably wonder why I suggested this kind of angling first. Why not go in there and fish with plugs and bass bugs—why wait?

Well, for one thing, the sun is high now and bass could easily be spooked in all that glare. Also, the breeze is not exactly a help in the accurate spot casting you'll be called upon to deliver later. Besides, we are actually on an exploratory trip around the flat to spot where we'll hope for action later. We are just getting acquainted with the area now.

Now reel in and we'll troll along the flat toward 10. This time let's use the two rigs shown in Figure 26. I'll use the one with the minnow on the tippet with a sinking plug trailing behind it. You can tie in a spoon on the tippet with a live minnow. Use two weights and then a live minnow at the end. Again, two anglers can present more variety this way.

It's about time we caught something.

Note that this side of the flat is rather stiff and straight in contrast to the other side. This tells us that the water deepens quicker on this side. Note the amount of rocks and gravel here, somewhat like the shoreline.

We can troll in quite close now, hopefully without snagging the bottom. A look at that shoreline tells me that we should troll along it too, one day soon. We'll have quite enough working the flats today. Prepared to stay out here until dark?

You can't say we didn't have action along there—three baits stolen. These bass must be experts.

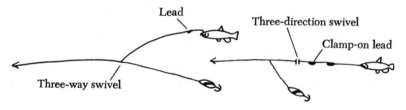

Figure 26.   The two-line set-up using two Indiana Spinners for live bait; the second set-up is weighted to offer a double chance if the exact depth at which to fish is not yet known. Use the second rig when fish are touchy with light hits or few strikes as the test.

With a bit of time behind us, the sun is now at a low angle and the afternoon wind has died down a bit, promising to calm completely in an hour or two. It is time to attack the grass flat with everything in the book.

From 1, we'll first work those two fingers at 2 and 3, the number 2 first. Let's plug it. Use a Jitterbug surface plug and I'll try a fore-and-aft floating plug for variety. We'll alternate casts and I'll square the boat off so that we both have easy casting and plenty of room to work. We are now about seventy-five feet out from the grass points. It looks quite shallow in there. Good pickerel water, so we may connect with one of them, if not a good bass. You go first. Place that plug right in the corner of 2 and let it stay there. Don't move it for a few seconds, then very slowly retrieve it, and then give it a jerk if you get no action. . . . Now retrieve it so that its built-in action begins. Stop it now and let it rest. Bingo—a bass on the first cast.

Now that you have hooked your fish on the stringer, I'll work my plug in the same kind of situation at 3. No response, so I'll retrieve slowly, just in case a bass might be following the plug but not taking. The plug is now only about twenty feet from the boat. Ah ha—see, it pays to fish out each cast, figuring that the bass will follow the plug—except it isn't a bass, it's a nice pickerel.

Next let's try a couple of casts off 4. That is a nice little cove, although it is loaded with lily pads. You will have to throw an accurate one in there and very carefuly ease the plug out through the pads. You can do it. Careful now. That's a hot spot. Good show, now retrieve, easy. No action? Well, let me try. *That* one was a bit too far to the right and I caught my first pad of the day. A few snaps on the line and it will be free. A strike!

For variety, now, let's try a nice long cast with the bass bugs into 5. The slight breeze is coming from behind us, and we can slip one right down the center of the path that leads to the cove. Should be a whopper in there. This situation is very similar to many we have fished or will fish in this book: mucky shorelines, pad flats, and even rock clusters. With the kind of accuracy I've seen you display with your pet fly rod, you should have no trouble here.

Around the tip of the point at 7 is a mixture of grass and gravel, a perfect spot for bass that come in from the deep to feed on crayfish and other aquatic goodies. How about working this water with two small bucktails. I'll guide the boat for you this time.

You can make quite a few casts in there without disturbing the water. No luck . . . well, it was a good exercise to remember. I strongly believe in bucktails in bass fishing, even though many other experts will disagree, which is what makes it such a controversial sport.

If you remember from our original circular tour of the flat, there are two holes deep in the center. Believe me, these should produce some instant action. You won't have time to retrieve the plug or bug or fly, since the bass, if he's there, will grab it the instant it hits the water. Nor will you have space to do any popping or retrieving before getting hung up in the pads or grass. Now, you will make one cast right over the grass so that the lure will plop down right in the center. If you get no response, don't try to drag the lure back to you. Rollcast it forward with mucho power, then make a strong double-haul backcast to get it up and out of there for a recast. That's the trick. You performed well, even though nobody was home.

One more chance at 9. Do it again, like an expert. I'll angle the boat square on for you. There's a bit of breeze heading into you, so use a bit more power on the forward throw. That's it. Strike . . . missed. Give it a few moments and try again.

While waiting for a second throw, why not cast to the right and left, skirting the shoreline grass in both directions. Retrieve slowly along there. A nice twilight, isn't it?

Notice how we are fishing thoroughly but not overworking the flat. An angler could be following right behind us and fishing over potential water. While we have not beat it to death, we have not overlooked any good spots either.

As we approach 10, cast a few times right along the edge. Ah—strike. A big sunfish, of all things. Try again now.

Our grass at 10 is thinner, with more openings, so it might be well to pick up the spinning rod and cast that Jitterbug plug in there to see what is around that is hungry.

This is once around the flat, and you've had action aplenty. Don't forget to fish 11 and 12.

Now let me try a bucktail fly in there. Mind if I stand for the casting?

Now, to fish that fly back to the boat, I flip forward almost as much as I retrieve, so as to raise the sinking fly up and skip it over the surface.

There's a hit! Missed. Again. They'll do that to you quite often. It's hours later—almost twilight—and we're back at the flat.

Our fishing grounds are shaded now, but a slight breeze is fanning wavelets along the entire length of the flat as they come from down the lake. So I'll troll a Colorado-spinner and nightcrawler bait. You can work with a live minnow of you prefer, behind a couple of Indiana spinners. We'll go it slow a couple of times around until the sun sets behind the trees and the breeze subsides.

We've just gotten started and there's a school of white perch surfacing, chasing minnows. I'll grab my ultralight spinning rod, snap on my smallest silver Colorado, unbaited, and try to catch a couple. There. Go ahead, take the rod and savor a pesky little game fish.

With the water almost calm between the shore and the flat, it is worth a troll or two, but instead of a fast one or even a conventional one, we'll drift at the whim of the lessening breeze, hook on two nightcrawlers to each of our weighted hooks, and drift the works as we go along. (*See* Appendix: Terminal Tackle.) We do a good deal of drift fishing throughout the book, but we might as well detail this sample here.

We take advantage of the wind and drift with it, letting our lines trail behind the boat. The lines are paid out slowly until about twenty feet of line are trailing behind. This slight drift will let our baits cover this good bit of water in a natural way. Our reel drags are set light or, if you prefer, you can hold your spinning rod (the one with the open-face reel) in one hand with your thumb on the reel bail and the bail open. Pay out line when the boat moves faster and reel in slightly when you get too much slack from slow boat movement.

This is the technique for "anytime" fishing on any lake while you're waiting for the magic moments when more sporty methods are in order. But I must confess that I enjoy this dead-drift method of fishing, especially after hours of paddling or casting. Somehow, worms and a good big, long smelly cigar go together. I get sleepy, too, performing this ritual, which is another profound reason that I suggested it today at this hour. It will rest us for what's to come just before dark and, provided you haven't worn out, for some great night fishing.

It's darker now and time for some bass bugging. The sun is down, partly behind the trees. We can see right into the water with our backs to the sun. Looks like our private aquarium. And we know there are good bass in there.

The bug is a lure about which you can't be label-conscious. For some reason, there are so many bass bugs tied by local anglers and sold in the stores that it is practically impossible to classify them, much less hang a name on them. Which bass bug? A cork popper, a deer-hair swimming-popper, a wooden one with spread hackles? You name it. Just make sure the hook is sharp. Since the wind is down, you don't have to pick one that is less resistant. Some bugs are veritable abominations to cast, especially if there is any wind at all. The whistle through the air like a jet and most of them take a good bit of power to direct with any accuracy. Color? Shape? Size? Action? In bass fishing I've come to believe that it is what *you* do to the lure when it's on the water, not what the designer picked as the ingredients, that makes the difference. Bass just aren't as selective as trout. They'll hit anything that moves.

The big trick is to remember not to flail the water to a froth. Pick a spot. Cast to it. Let the bug lie there if it isn't taken immediately and then gently, very gently, move it an inch or so. Let it stop. Now pop it violently. Then, inch by inch, move it across the water without any fuss. Now pop it violently again and let it sit there. That's for hesitant bass. But are they so hesitant? Yes. I've had times when I've cast a popper right to the edge of the pads or grass, or to a rock where I knew there was at least one bass, and when the water was glassy and the shallows fairly open I've seen a bass fifty feet away flip its dorsal at the sight of the landing lure. After a twitch, that bass has moved out maybe ten feet toward the lure and then stopped. And after another twitch of the lure the bass has advanced again. Usually on the third or fourth advance the bass is in position for a rush. With this much warning I become nervous and ready for him—both at the same time. At the explosion, I usually strike at the same time he does.

The most nerve-racking times are those when the cast goes out, the bug just touches the water, and is grabbed by a bass before it even makes its splash. When this happens it is best to remember to make the cast good and powerful, shooting the bug well high of the target area, stopping it in mid-air, dropping it down as you raise your rod tip, and pulling back on the line, leaving absolutely no slack. That does it.

Back now at the camp porch during one of those dog days in August. It is just too hot to breathe, so we might as well fish as sit around doing nothing but sweating it out and swatting mosquitoes, or worse, talking theory.

We think about the spots on the lake where we could expect to find a bass that isn't affected by human considerations of the weather. The midlake grass flat comes to mind. Why not try some

deep trolling around the underwater mound, a nice easy slow troll
with the motor barely turning over. We'll rig up two lines, one with
two Indiana spinners and a perch, the other with two minnows,
one on the triangle swivel as shown in Figure 26. (*See also*
Appendix: Terminal Tackle.) The tail minnow will be preceded by
a very small spinner.

Our two lures should offer variety and taste to any bass that is
awake. We'll start at one end and go completely around, about
twenty-five yards out from the edge of the grass. Then, for variety,
we'll reverse our direction, working in about fifteen yards closer to
the snags. This makes the scenery more interesting, and we might
even confuse a bass or two.

If nothing happens in a little while, we'll anchor off some
points that fit our fancies, drop over a weighted worm or minnow,
and sit it out. What's wrong with sitting for a change?

Besides, we may learn something from sitting and watching.
We just might spot some action on the flat and then investigate it.

For example, a bass might surface just outside the ring and
we'd see the shiny, telltale splinterings of little minnows being
driven toward the sky. This calls for instant action, like shoving
some of our smallest trout bucktails into the area, letting them sink
down deep, and retrieving them in short, minnowlike jerks. We did
this in Chapter 1. Remember?

I'll venture to say that not one in a thousand bass anglers ever
use these small bucktails, but because of my trouting experience
and the fact that river and stream bass sometimes hit them with
utter abandon, I include them in the tackle. It may be because of
the early identification of bass fishing with big plugs, spoons, and
spinners that bass anglers still think that the large lures are the
only bass killers. Yet how many times have you cleaned a bass and
found small minnows or baitfish in them?

Moreover, the light fly rod, usually used for normal, easy,
medium casts on the trout stream, is the ideal tool for such work.
Stand up in the boat and sail those flies well into the grass or
between the pads. A strike from even a three-pound largemouth
will have twice the force of a strike from a like-size trout, and the
battle will really be something to remember. Throw the hook?
Sure they will. They're like small tarpon. Land one in five and
you're ahead. Funny, though, you won't lose any more fish on these
little single hooks than you will with a plug armed with three sets
of trebles. Why? The answer is that usually the bass will open his
maw wide for the fly but will merely bang into the plug. Sure

they'll twist with body-roll action to throw any hooks, but that little bucktail, well down in the throat, usually holds them.

Say, it's about time now. Ten o'clock at night. We sniff the air on the camp porch. Nope. Not yet. It isn't cool enough.

Wait for that night breeze. The lake is as quiet as a ghost. After the night airs move, we'll get out there.

We listen carefully from the porch for any feeding sounds out there in the blackness. Not a murmur. So we go inside for another few hands of poker.

The flame of the lamp flickers. Ah, that's the magic signal.

We take the canoe, not the boat and motor. A short paddle and we're between the flat and the shoreline. Pausing often, we listen. No use casting unless we hear a bass feeding.

Careful of that flashlight. Don't shine it on the water. One of the surest ways to scare night bass is to shine a light over them. I've fished with anglers who always use a light to scan the shoreline for snags and to mark their casting distances. They wipe out the bass as they swing that beam. Then they wonder why the fish don't react the way they expect. True night fishing is done in the dark, all the time. When you light a cigarette, cover the flame and bend down to do it. Fish in the dark of the moon.

Now let's fish those bugs.

I've got my pet rod with me for distance work. It is a split bamboo nine-and-a-half footer, with an almost even action in the upper third and a heavy butt. The tip action is far from soft, but it's not "poley" like some of the so-called bass-bug rods on the market. It requires a long cast to make it perform. Short casts are more difficult to make with it than long ones. However, its action is slow; no quick casts of false casts with this stick. The line is a GAF with some of the thin end removed and replaced with a twelve-foot, level leader of ten-pound nylon or a heavy double-taped line. It will cast the fluffy bass bugs well in a wind, and tonight, with little or no breeze, I can use the fluffs or the cork bugs with no dressing. Again, it really matters not what the lure is in terms of shape or makeup, it is the action imparted to it that counts.

We paddle to about seventy-five feet from the edge of the flat. You sit and watch for a bit. Two anglers can't fish from a canoe, both standing, at night or any other time. Your eyes will gradually get to "see" out here and watch the proceedings.

First I cast the bug about twenty feet out in the general direction in which I'll be fishing. Then I strip off about twenty more feet of line and coil it at my feet. I've removed any and all tackle and gear that would snag the coils of line. All set. I pick up the cast in a double haul and the backcast whistles out over my head, high and straight back. You get to know just how high that is from your daytime practice and your nighttime feel. Then I shoot it out to the full forty feet and my cast strains the reel for more line. I retrieve and strip out more line for the "reacher" cast. Ah, that feels good. At just the point where the lure is about to drop down I pull back slightly on the rod and just as quickly shoot it forward in a powerful whip, releasing five more feet of line. This straightens out the leader for a more direct fall. I've seen few anglers perform this part of the cast. It can get another ten feet of distance when the timing is right. It is also at just the point when the lure is about to drop to the water that you can still pull back and stop it from going too far. When the bug hits the water I strip the slack in. I also try to begin this stripping just as the lure begins to fall, so that it lands on a relatively tight line. Bass quite often hit a bug the second it touches the water, and if there is no strike the instant it hits the water I can quickly rollcast another five feet of line, which will lift the bug and send it still farther on. Now we let the bug rest for a second while we catch a breath.

While this technique (or rather two techniques) is not mentioned in the Appendix, it is best to review the casting instructions there if you are fairly new at bugging, especially at night. It is important to really know your tackle, be able to judge your range, and get to feel the rod and line during the cast. In this way you'll discover lots of tricks that will let you lay that line out without any fluffs, directly to the target. You'll also avoid tanges and wasted time.

The retrieve is the conventional pause-and-pop technique, right to the boat, making sure that your line coils are in order for the next cast.

What a time to be on the water, and what a method of bass fishing! There's nothing better. It takes skill and patience and a bit of strength. But when that bass hits that floater out there—always when least expected—and the rod vibrates from the weight of the impact, followed by a thrash of spray that can be dimly seen, you're on!

Yes, fish the flats at night. Take your time. There is lots of water and hours to work out there. Pause between casts. Listen for feeding bass. Keep your attention up and remember to always keep that backcast high.

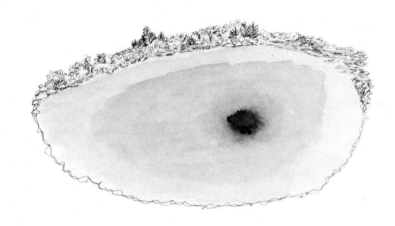

6

MIDLAKE
DEEP HOLE

The most mystifying section of a lake is the part that can't be seen, superficially analyzed, or understood. Today we look out over the vast expanse of water before us, knowing not what lies beneath the surface. Is it shallow? Is it deep? Where are the hot-spots where fish would be found *right now?* Where are they at various times of the year under different temperature conditions, different wind directions, and varied barometer readings? Where are the spring holes where they should be congregating during the warm weather? How do we fish the deep spots? What lures, bait, terminal tackle, and techniques should we use, and more questions.

Given 10 percent knowledge and 90 percent luck, the average angler connects if he fishes a lake enough. But can that percentage be beaten?

We go forth facing these questions, pushing our oars into the

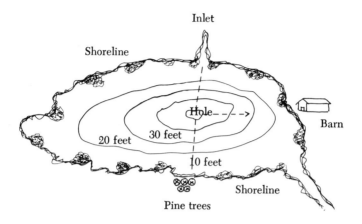

Figure 27. Sketch of topographical nature of a lake, showing the deep hole and the way of finding the "hot-spot" by land markers.

sand, shoving off, and giving the motor one twist. It purrs, sets up some bubbles behind us, and we're off over the surface, bound for some mythical spot, a tantalizing "needle in a haystack."

On first glance this seems like a vague way to start out after bass that may be deep down in a "somewhere" on the bottom. Before we have embarked, however, we've done a bit of research. Long ago, during the winter months, we sent away to the state conservation department for a map of the lake, one of those maps that shows the contours and depth measurements, inlets, outlets, and other characteristics of the lake. Or perhaps we have a U. S. Geodetic Survey map of the region, which also supplies depth markings on the lake portion. Our map in Figure 27 is a simplified composite of such maps, and is of the lake we are fishing.

We have also inquired about the weather and temperature for the past month, and have found that it has been hot and humid. We brought a thermometer along, an almost indispensable piece of equipment for deep-water fishing. It shows the surface lake water to be in the high 70s; almost too warm for bass to surface much, at least during the bright light of day. The wind has recently been blowing from the west, which means that if we are to fish the shore at all, the western shore is it, not the eastern, which would have been stirred up by waves. Out in the deep, the wind direction doesn't matter, so today we can disregard it except for its momentary direction if we decide to do a little drift fishing. But back to that temperature. Since bass like it in the high 60s and low 70s, we can see (and can prove it by lowering a thermometer) that the deepest part of the lake would be their logical hold at this season. So here we are, sometime in mid-August.

Casting, except at night or in the early morning, has been largely unproductive, and we know from past experience that if we are to get a stringer with weight on it, we'd better head for the deeps and lower succulent morsels to the bass right where they are. Now bass don't generally feed down there; they rest out the day. So our techniques must really work well.

That's not all we know. We've also asked many questions at the corner drugstore, where a mounted bass signifies that the proprietor is a good angler, and we are assured that that mounted bass recently came from this lake. We have talked with him and also paid a visit to the local tackle store, where we have overheard conversations about the proper way to fish the lake under the prevailing conditions. Having caught such sentences as "There are lots of deep areas on the bottom of the lake, but only a few where the bass really hang out in numbers," we get a line on one or two of these locations in the conversations that follow. "When you near the center of the lake," someone says, "line your boat up with those hemlocks abeam of you, and the red barn on the hillside should be right dead ahead of the bow of your boat. That's where I took a lunker last week."

So we learn that there are many ways of infiltrating the lake and its secrets. We have also watched with binoculars all week long just where those informed locals were anchoring, and have marked the time of the day and how long they stayed there.

In plain English, though, even when armed with good information, a guide is necessary. With the best knowledge available, he can cut short the wasted effort of trolling an entire lake, casting here and there, and generally fishing on a hit-and-miss basis. Two hours spent in finding a guide, or at least a local man interested in taking the day off for a little pay, will cut down the time spent in experimenting. He may not be an expert, but if he's fished the lake enough or lived in the area long enough, he's got an automatic elimination system in his angling head that will point to a better use of your time.

As far as available methods are concerned, we can try what we've done several times in past chapters and will do again before this book is finished: We can troll deep, drift deep, and stillfish from an anchored position. If we have a good day we'll mark the spot for future reference, a trick described later.

It is nine o'clock in the morning. The sky is clear and a slight breeze ruffles the water surface. Let's troll first, working as nearly as we can the various depth contours around the island end of the lake. Looking at the map, we'll follow the twenty-foot contour, cross ahead of the island, try along the thirty-foot contour, and so on until we get down to the deepest part, which checks out to about forty feet. Somewhere within these ranges will be found a deep spot, and with luck the bass will tell us about it. Bass are primarily school fish and will be found in numbers in the open sections of a lake. We'll work two lines. I'll rig up the baitcasting rod with a spoon on the dropper, weighted ahead of the lure as shown in the Appendix: Terminal Tackle; Trolling.

And since we have found out by inquiry that much of the bass food in the lake consists of cisco herring, I'll tie on a Green Ghost tandem-hook streamer (Figure 28), which imitates this bait fish. It's a killer on landlocked salmon in Maine.

We'll detail this fishing in a moment. On your dropper you'll try a red-and-white spoon for contrast, preceded by a quarter-ounce weight to keep it well below the end spoon on your terminal rig. On the terminal rig you'll snap a smaller silver spoon, and on its hook a thin strip of artificial pork rind. Use the spinning rod, since you're more used to it, but adjust the drag to about a third of the labeled pound test of your line. We'll troll slowly and it will be your duty to discover when your lures are bumping along the bottom.

When you feel the touches of weed or a rock, let me know; I'll pick up the speed a bit and you can also reel in a bit of line. As

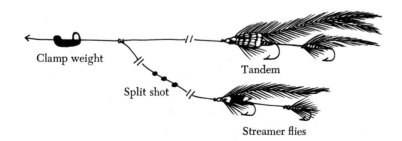

Figure 28. Typical two-hook tandem rig with the weight on the bottom. This is standard for stillfishing with cut or live bait.

we proceed, the motor throbs gently and the lines go out and down behind the boat and into the wake. We keep the map of the lake in front of us as we guide our course as best we can by marking our distance from the shoreline. We can also pause once in a while to check the depth by lowering a weight. It is interesting to note the structure of the hills, cliffs, lawnlike expanses, and gently sloping fields, which can help us determine the depths and character of the underwater terrain. While it isn't always an accurate indication, the contour of the land surrounding a lake can aid greatly in the search for deep spots when a map or local information is lacking. Certainly this kind of observation can give us at least a starting point toward finding the deepest parts of the lake as we go bass hunting.

To fish the tandem-hooked streamer fly, we follow the prescribed methods used by landlocked-salmon fishermen. The fly or brace of flies is trolled from a fly rod or light-tipped (soft action) spinning rod and kept fairly near the surface, usually between the top and five to six feet down. Since the fly has no built-in action of its own, a fluttering is required to make it lifelike. This is done by rod manipulation and line pulling. Also, when two lines are out, one is generally a bit longer, and the flies are weighted to sink them at different levels for better fish finding. From seventy-five to ninety feet of line is sufficient, but fifty feet of line are often enough. In the more northern lakes known to contain both smallmouths and landlocks, one can never know which will take, making angling there a distinct pleasure.

While I've never been one to really love the technique of trolling, even for sailfish and marlin, I've come to enjoy it as a change of pace from constant casting and squinting at shoreline snags in a search for the proper places to cast. I find that if I have done enough research and am not trolling entirely blind, the sport is just that much more interesting. I also tend to become restless. I take the rod and wave it back and forth, or flip the tip as if that would move the lure and give it some action. Most of this rod manipulation, particularly with long, deep lines, is mainly for the benefit of the nervous angler; the motion isn't transferred to the lure, since a slight pullback hardly registers on the end of the line. (*See* Appendix: Trolling.)

Usually, a fish hits when we abandon the rod momentarily to reach for a drink of water or a cigarette or to fumble in a pocket for a match.

No action yet, not even the bump of a bottom rock, so we switch to a spoon and go down below. I'll slow-troll just a bit and see if you make contact.

There, your rod tip bounced a bit. Did that feel like weeds? There are a lot of weeds on the lake bottom at this level. Felt like a rock, eh? Okay, then, no need to reel in to clear your hooks of grass. Also, you know that you're fishing right near the bottom. I'll lower the flies on my rig just a bit by releasing about ten feet of line all at once. We're about ready for the turn now, so we'll gently troll out across the map ahead of the island. It shallows quite a bit on that island reef jutting off the upside point. I'll speed us up a bit until we pass the reef. We should hit a fish on either side of it. This is a very good spot for deep-lying bass, since they come into shore from here in the evening to feed in the nearby pad and grass flats. A few seasons ago, when the lake was extremely low, I can remember seeing the reef partly exposed. There are deep gullies on both sides that make good living for bass and their minnow food. We are right on top of the first approach now, so hold on to your rod and watch that tip.

I pick up my rod and leave the boat headed in the desired direction, guiding the motor with my elbow. Beautiful clouds today, nice full bright ones etched sharply against the cold blue of the sky. An osprey glides high into the whitest cloud and circles for us. Quite a sight. No other boats on the lake; we have it all to ourselves.

There's a hit, and a good one. He's on! Reel in your line fast. I'll kill the motor and we can play this one on the drift.

Let's do a retake on that one. First I'll rig you up with two tandem streamers and weights, as was shown in Figure 28. If we can connect again, we have probably found a hot spot as well as the right lure and presentation. Since the sun is well up now, both sides of the reef are in bright sunlight, so one side is about as good as the other.

There you go. A solid hit. Set him hard! The record in this lake is seven pounds; you're a bit short—some two pounds—but he's a good stewing fish. Before this lake became popular with fishermen, all the bass were small, stunted because of too many fish and not enough fishermen. Then, when fishermen began to harvest the crop, the balance between the bass numbers and available food became better, and six- and seven-pounders were not uncommon. Today, under high pressure from anglers, any bass from this lake is a good one so long as it's legal. I've often wondered why the

conservation agencies, recognizing the need for balance, do not
restrict fishing on such lakes at various times to equalize the relationship of fish, food, and angling needs. It would make fishing
better for sure.

While we are here, let's try for another. I'll let my rig stand
as it is and you work the two streamers again. The map says it is
shallower on the other side of the reef, so we'll cross it and follow
its contour into the deepest part of the lake, do a turnaround, and
then work up the line of the reef again, a bit deeper down.

It was fun taking those bass from that reef, and we haven't
even begun to do what we set out to do, fish the holes. They all
took tandem-hooked streamers, too—lures seldom if ever used on
bass. None of the spoons got takers, yet most of the anglers who
troll this lake swear by deeply trolled spoons. We keep quiet about
our results. Never have I seen landlocked salmon flies in a bass
fisherman's tackle box except in landlock territory. It is also surprising how many salmon- and bass fishermen who do own these
flies ever use them when the bass season rolls around. I discovered
their potency quite by accident: I caught a bass on one while slow-
trolling for landlocks.

We're back at the dock, and some other anglers have just
landed ahead of us. On their stringer are five bass, but they are
considerably larger than ours. I was watching their boat circling
out in the middle of the lake all during the time we were fishing.
They also knew, either by reading a map or by long-time experience,
where the deepest spot is at that end of the lake. They used a slow
troll with a terminal rig of weighted live baits (see Figure 29).

Just for the fun of it, let's try their technique in their spot and
see what happens. Out we go to the deepest part of the lake. We
check the location by shore orientation points. For this type of
fishing I strongly suggest the baitcasting rods, since they are shorter
and react quicker to the strike. I like a very stiff tip for deep
trolling, since instant action must be transferred right to the hooks.
The longer spinning rods just don't have it for this kind of work,
nor are they supposed to. Sure there are special spinning-trolling
rods for both below-the-rod open-face reels and conventional level-
wind or closed-face spinning reels that ride "up." I like to fish
traditionally, with the old-fashioned baitcasting rod and reel, even
if it is only for sentimental reasons. That outfit has taken a lifetime
of fish in both fresh and salt water.

We're armed with ten-pound braided black nylon, and we rig

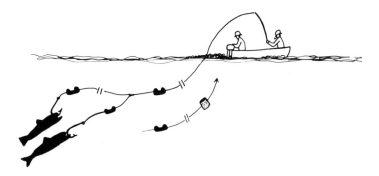

Figure 29. A terminal rig with weighted live baits (cork, below, is optional, to keep the rig from going too deep). Very thin nylon mono is used from the weight to the main line so that the rig can be fished deep. If snagged, the sinker can be sacrificed, and meanwhile the baits will remain at the proper level.

up with a two-ounce sinker, above which we have tied in two, two-foot tippets of nylon for hooks (Figure 30). (*See* Appendix: Terminal Tackle.) Many anglers use plastic-covered braided-wire leaders for this purpose. It is a matter of choice. The metal is safer with the covering, but is a bit more obvious to skittish fish. The line from the sinker to our main line is of lighter-pound-test mono. In case the sinker snags the bottom, this lets us save the rig by snapping off the sinker, leaving the baits to hang free.

We approach the spot as if we were going directly to the corner store for a bottle of milk. We drop our lines until they touch the bottom and quickly draw them up about two feet, hoping that the bottom will be flat enough to keep the sinkers from snagging. Now we drift with the wind across the deep spot and then return under slight motor power, criss-crossing the area. We get some touches and bumps. There are fish down there and they feel heavy enough to be bass, but we cannot be certain. So we try again.

Let's mentally go down there on the bottom and see what goes on when our baits are all set, hanging there in the water. The bottom is rocky. It is not too bright. We can see only for a few yards. Yes, the bass are there. Here comes one up toward the bait. Another bass turns in the same direction, but the first bass shoos him off and sniffs right up to the bait, swims around it, flaps it with his tail, and makes a pass at it, bumping it. Now he circles again, comes in slowly to the bait, and gently closes his hoodlike mouth over it. All we can see is the tail of the minnow. He swims with it a few inches, puts on the brakes, and actually swims backward.

Figure 30. A two-ounce sinker on ten-pound braided nylon.

Now he spits out the bait, picks it up again, and savors it. The other bass comes in close, but the first bass drops the bait and chases him, returning quickly to his "prize." Again he takes it in his mouth sideways, spits it out, picks it up, spits it out, bumps it, flashes around, and slaps it with his tail. But this time when he sees the other fish coming in he grabs that bait sideways with the speed of light, adjusts it head down, chomps greedily on it, and takes off like a shot. All of a sudden he's jerked upward by the angler up above and the hooks find their flesh. He's had it.

That, with infinite variations, is the general picture of what happens down at the bottom. The bass are not there to feed, but to rest. They are not generally hungry, but if you have studied bass habits for any number of years you'll find that they are a voracious lot, hardly about to restrain the urge to pounce on anything good to eat. Saltwater bluefish are like this. I've seen them upchuck a couple of handfuls of crunched mullet that was well down in their stomach only to feed again on a fresh school of bait. Bass have this same deadliness in their blood. They just can't resist at least playing with a bit of bait. This is why you have to get to know the "feel" of a bass when he is fooling around down there. Once you can master that kind of communication you'll know a lot better when and how hard to strike. Generally, if you do strike when he's just fooling around, he'll merely open his mouth and let the bait out. It will be by accident that you'll barb him this way, and unless you're very lucky your hooks will only scratch him. So risk his stealing the bait or at least mashing it up. Wait until he takes off in a good run. Then set the hook.

To be sure, this sort of angling isn't the greatest of sport, but I find that by knowing a little of the game that has to be played, live-bait fishing and even stillfishing in such a spot is a special kind of fun. Certainly the bass that are lying down there wouldn't even give a passing look at a spoon well over their heads and not give more than a passing look at a trolled minnow. The bass on the reef were something else again.

But deep fishing pays off despite all that can be said for active casting, and anyhow, it seems foolish to stand up all day in a boat under the hot sun casting a plug to bass that aren't there or are asleep under a pad or an old fallen tree. You might as well do this in an air-conditioned gymnasium.

But we haven't finished. Drift fishing has its different aspects. It's now another day, like the one on which we had our luck, but we've been fishing the same spot and have each lost four baits. Good hits, yes, but somehow the bass didn't really want to play ball. Either that or they have become smart and able to shred the bait from our hooks and gobble it up while the hooks hang empty.

However, there are two cures for that.

One is the additional smaller hook that we attach to the leader and insert into the tail of the bait. With this, the bass usually won't be able to cut the baitfish away from both hooks without getting nabbed by one. The other trick is to avoid striking when the bass mouths the bait. This calls for releasing the weight when the bait is down deep. To do this, we attach the sinker on a very fine thread, or even by a piece of paper that will disintegrate, dropping it shortly after submergence of the rig. This will allow the bait to swim freely at the desired location, permitting a much more natural action. We fish this either in a very slow drift on a windless lake or when moving with switching winds while hanging on a very long anchor line. To be sure of getting free of the weight at the moment of setting our distance off the bottom, we give the rig a sharp tug; we can then feel the bait itself, free of the sinker. Now we are in more "personal" contact with the bass when he appears. Again, only when the bass starts off for places unknown do we tighten and give a mighty heave-ho. Actually, a bass is more likely to take a bait if it is not held in one static position by a weighted line.

There is nothing that always works, but this system works most of the time. One of the hardest impulses to overcome when in contact with playful summer bass that aren't actively feeding is the itch of wanting to get up and leave for greener pastures, or striking them too soon, or not waiting them out. Remembering that they are not really hungry but do enjoy worrying a bait like a cat worries a mouse, we learn to be patient and strike at the right time.

Another technique I like to use on deep-lying summer bass is

the same general technique that cod fishermen use on their winter
offshore grounds. They jig with a baited metal jig. You do the same,
whether you're anchored or drifting slowly. Use any of the feather-
less jigs, attach an artificial black eel, plastic worm, pork rind, or
real worm—it makes little difference which, send it down there
close to the bottom, and keep it activated. (See Figure 20, page 51.)

THE MIDLAKE SPRING HOLE

While fishing this spot is somewhat similar to what we experienced and practiced in the midlake deep hole, there are some
differences. Actually the two situations and their techniques do
overlap. For instance, when the midlake deep hole is discovered to
also contain a spring, a combination of the techniques used in the
two situations can reap rewards if done correctly. To find the
spring, look at the map for the possible "hole," then lower your
thermometer.

Spring holes, however, are not necessarily located in the deepest
parts of a lake's contours. They are quite often found near rocky
drop-offs or cliffs, between sand bars or gravel edges, or in very
deep crevasses. They are usually found by accident, since maps do
not indicate their existence. Only in extremely low water are they
ever actually seen.

The spring hole is best worked during the hottest time of the
year and during low water. Since the bass, unlike the trout, is not
a cold-water fish that likes low temperatures all season long, the
bass fisherman need not expect to find him in a spring hole unless
the rest of the lake is extremely warm. Walleyed pike are also taken
in spring holes.

Save the spring hole for midday fishing when you are all done
working the shoreline. Now let's get to work. Here we are on the
map and the wind is coming from our back, directly toward the
hole. Instead of whisking right over the hole, dropping the anchor,
and starting to fish, we'll first approach to within about two
hundred feet of the edge of the hole. There is our marker, a bit of
brush supposedly drifting on the surface. Actually, it is stationary,
since it is anchored to the bottom on a nylon mono line and sinker.
Other anglers would pass it by. Now before we drift over the area,
we drop our anchor, and as the boat drifts down on the edge of the
hole, we pay out the anchor rope and the bow of the boat swings
into the wind. As we feed out the rope, we drift to within about
twenty feet of the center of our target.

The bass below are unaware of what is about to happen.

Using our baitcasting rods, we fish still-style with two hooks and live bait, this time live shiners. (*See* Appendix: Stillfishing; Terminal Tackle.) But while we hook rock bass, seldom found in such deep water, as well as suckers, catfish, and white perch, we get no bass.

We pull up and proceed to another spring hole, but this time, since it is in such shallow water—not over fifteen feet deep—we decide to make a few passes with the trolled streamers. This works. Two bass come to the net.

Next we try the stillfishing act, and two more good bass mount up the score.

Just for fun we open them to see what they have been eating and find them empty in the upper stomach, signifying that they have just come there to cool off. They would probably have fed in the shallows at evening time or during the late hours of the night.

Actually, under these conditions it is a wonder that we even had strikes, much less landed fish, since their appetites were not stimulated at that time of the day. It seems reasonable, that the bass would stay in these holes even at night, and feeding on the minnows and other fish that would likewise find the lower temperatures attractive. But such has not been the case in my experience. The spring hole turns out to be a good spot for a summer slumber rather than a short-order restaurant.

There are spring holes that do serve a double purpose, however. These are generally found in a gently falling shoreline that is indented by cuts and almost gullies on the shore. Evidently, the spring freshets carve out these avenues for the water, and much of it evidently seeps into the ground. Following the general contour, the cooler water then slips down under the level of the lake to come out in tiny but numerous openings. In times of heavy rains or freshets the area above ground serves as a trough to bring runoffs, worms, grubs, and the like into the water. These attract the baitfish, and the bass come in for the kill.

Quite often such locations can be spotted by lines of grass or pads, with the channels of deeper water being clear of both. Work over these areas by drifting live bait, casting semisurface lures, and, at times, fishing bucktails weighted by splitshot or clamp-on leads. Evening and early morning are good times to fish here, especially if the area is sheltered from the wind.

Have you ever been caught in a thunderstorm or squall out in the middle of a lake? If you haven't, you're lucky, but you're luckier still if you have and have survived. Being caught in a sudden wind can be highly dangerous, for lakes have a bad habit of whipping up killing waves in as short a time as five minutes.

Uh-oh, a big blow is heading our way right now. See those thunderheads approaching? We had better keep an eye on them. If that gray area below them becomes darker, we had better head for shore. At the moment, there is a pleasant and steady breeze blowing, but if it stops suddenly, our minutes out here are numbered. That is, if we care for our skins.

We'll troll for a while, headed in the direction of the barn. I don't mind getting a bit wet for misjudging the timing of a downpour, but I don't want to have to do battle against the wind even with a good motor. I remember the time that I had to literally limp home through a rough blow. I couldn't run at high or even half speed without shipping water over the bow. The wave chops were so stiff and close that I had to keep down to an almost holding speed. I finally ran out of gas and had to drift with the wind back in the direction from which I had come. When I had rowed the boat home that night after the storm had subsided, I was a mighty tired guy to say the least.

Those clouds don't look too good to me. The wind is slackening. Feel that heaviness in the air? I think that cloud has spotted us and is about to give us the works. Let's head for the island on the way back, just in case we misjudge how soon the storm will hit. We can always hide it out in the comfort of those spruces.

Wow. Now it is as still as a ghost lake. Not a ripple. The sky is darker now, so I expect the worst in a few minutes. Glad that island is dead ahead.

We made it. Now to take cover. Here comes the wind. Nice, isn't it? Relief after the low pressure and mugginess. But you just wait. It'll blow your brains out any minute now. Glad you came ashore?

Don't mess around with approaching squalls. Respect those clouds and don't try for bravery awards; the price is too high.

7

SHORE-ROCK CLIFF HOLE

Here's one of the prettiest backdrops for a day's outing and one of the most productive if fished right. Okay, I know, you can get skunked here too, but it's in a nice environment; a good place for a picnic and a fast swim. As a matter of fact, one of my favorite short-rock cliff holes is well populated by swimmers during the vacation months. One day, a couple of skindivers were working underwater when I arrived to fish the cliff hole shown here. They surfaced just long enough to tell me that there were any number of big bass right under my boat.

Not every lake has such a spot. Most contain but a few really big boulders or rock clusters of any size. Lakes that do have at least one big rock cluster have usually been formed at the bottoms of deep slopes from the nearby high hills. Because of this type of formation, the lake bottom is jagged because of rock formations that contain wide, deep cavities and high spots. These are made all the more obvious by the rock formations that extend above the water. Cool springs issue forth from such rocks, both on the land and under the water's surface, and lakes that have rock clusters as their dominant characteristic are usually full of good big fish, although strangely enough, they are not always easy to catch. Clear cold water, rock instead of weed cover, and boulders instead of muck, ooze, and tangles make the fish fast strikers but extremely wary. They move about a good deal more than the bass that find a nice soft bed of weeds and food to lodge in the year 'round.

This is perfect smallmouth water. As a matter of fact, when I sat down to draw this, several scenes came to mind and I had quite a bit of difficulty settling on any specific kind of setting. I've seen this picture in Ontario, Maine, northern New York, Pennsylvania, and the Ozarks, although the rock formations there are quite varied geologically. Certainly, there are lakes in my memory in Washington and Oregon, and a few in the midwest, that harbor such succulent fishing scenes.

And enticing as it may be, I have fished (even overfished) such areas, knowing darn well that big bass were around despite the fact that nothing—and I mean nothing—could produce action. I can remember working a stretch like this one for a whole day without a bass showing no matter what I threw at them. I'd kept asking the air whether it was because the bass just weren't in there or because they were in there but bored with my whole procedure. I also remembered the skindivers who had spoken of a good supply of bass beneath the boat. On another day in that same week I'd returned to the same location and gone through the same routine, trolling up and down deep, medium, and shallow, anchoring offshore and throwing surface plugs, deep runners, weighted bucktails, and weighted baits, and hooking bass on several of these techniques. I'd checked with other anglers and none had agreed that any set pattern of events or lures was "sure-fire." As far as I'm concerned, then, this type of water has to be struck on a day that luck—pure luck—is with you.

Quite often, as you've probably also experienced, the bottom of a hole like this is most difficult to troll, in that it varies sharply from shallow to deep, and hang-ups are inevitable. Troll deep and you get hung up; troll near the surface and the bass hardly pay any attention. Casting, then, seems to be the best medicine, other than stillfishing with live bait, a guaranteed method of reducing the supply of terminal rigs in your tackle box.

Certainly you can troll outside a cluster like the one that is pictured. As you go by, well offshore, it is a good idea to look into the water as you proceed and see if on the next pass you can work in closer and just as deep. If so, the second pass will afford an even closer look at what's showing that will interrupt your next run. In some cases it is possible to troll right in under the cliffs. If not, you'll simply have to spot cast and be alert to bumps on the line that signify rocks. Often you'll have to put the boat in and spoil the spot to retrieve your lure or come in close enough to allow the lure to fall away from the snag on which it is hooked.

One day, more years ago than I care to remember, light fell on a technique that sounded as if it might work for cliff holes. I was reading my favorite magazine and the author was promoting the use of saltwater jigs for bassing. He sparked something in me. The next day I drove a hundred miles to a tackle store near the coast where I could invest in some striped bass and weakfish jigs, and even bought some plain jigs that had no feathers or other decorations on them. I planned to put these on later if the experiment proved successful. Since then I've taken some mighty fine stringers of bass with jigs, and not a small number of magnificent trout (Figure 31).

I experimented with all kinds of tackle. I threw the jigs first with the conventional soft-tipped spinning rod and found that the tip bent too dangerously and the casts were inaccurate. Then I

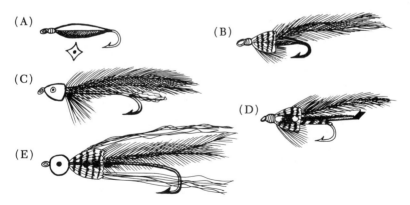

Figure 31. (A) Common weakfish jig. (B) Jig dressed as a typical streamer fly. (C) Standard bare saltwater jig tied as a streamer. (D) Weighted streamer with Mylar added. (E) Saltwater jig extra-weighted and tied as a streamer-bucktail.

switched to heavier, stronger and stiffer tips and found that I snapped them off too readily on the cast. This called for a heavier line and a little loss of distance for the same rod pressure. I also experimented with the lure action. I had learned of its value in saltwater angling, but until I read that article could somehow or other never relate the same thing to its use on freshwater bass. Tackle-wise, I found that the stiffer and heavier the line the better I was able to handle the jig, since a limp line would not communicate to the lure what I wanted it to say to the bass.

The jig is a dead thing when merely retrieved. As far as snagging is concerned, its main attraction is that the properly made ones ride with the hook up, which is a godsend in freshwater angling. You can work them in sand, gravel, rocky benches, and even around boulders and seldom become snagged. I have tied up a few with stiff duckwing feathers turned or cupped to the hook, which makes them practically impervious to snagging. Note the jig shown in Figure 31D. The conventional jigs are also pictured. All of the jigs shown have the necessary capacity to flash, as well as quick maneuverability and a quick response to even the slightest manipulation when you are armed with tackle that can transmit the proper action to them. Best of all, I've found that the bass like them with an enthusiasm equal to mine. Incidentally, I've found that I can handle the jigs very well with a medium-sized baitcasting rod, and they have been responsible for my return to casting with the old equipment, giving the spinning gear a rest. They also cast very well in a stiff wind, and their lack of any wind resistance makes them perfect for spotcasting to a dime-sized target between the rocks.

Note the examples of jigs shown in Figure 31. The weakfish jig (A) is diamond-shaped if viewed cross-sectionally. It is heavy enough for very light spinning gear and can be weighted with a Colorado spinner or even an Indiana if desired attached on a short tippet three feet ahead of the jig. It can be fished "as is" in the silver finish, without any dressing, since it looks for all the world like a small shiner, or it can be painted black for night fishing or dressed in any of the popular streamer-bucktail combinations. You can also attach a pearl flipper to the hook, and don't forget the artificial pork rind flutterers. Long white polar-bear hairs and a flash of golden pheasant on the cheek of the fly work well too.

Bonefish jigs of various styles, one of which is shown in Figure 31B, are also very good. Used for bouncing along the sandy flats of the Bahamas, these lures can be fished in the deep crevasses of our rock pile. Bounce them off rocks, either submerged ones or those with the tops showing. Let the lure fall off enticingly, with either a quick retrieve or a jerk retrieve, and you'll offer the bass something they are not pestered with by the usual angler.

The trolling feather jig, as shown in Figure 31C, is another weighted variety that, if given the right action on the retrieve and fished deep enough, will produce.

To get the best results with a jig, you must put all of the action into it; merely dragging it through the water is seldom enough unless the bass are almost starved to death. But there is a catch here. First, your casts must not be long ones. The shorter the better, since on long casts the action you must put into the rod in order to make the lure dance its needed "jig" simply won't carry through the long line. Axiom: The shorter the line, the more activity is felt by the lure; that is, unless you want to stand up in the boat and wave your whole rod up and down and from left to right until you're exhausted. Just to learn all this, make a short cast into the water where you can watch the lure. Now manipulate the rod tip in jerks, and even pull on the line to help the action a bit. If the jig is bouncing up and down, dancing in the water, its action should be sufficient. When you then figure that twice the amount of line you have cuts down your lure's activity for the same amount of rod tip action, you can see why a short cast is the best.

Figure 32 shows how I suggest you retrieve a jig, given several underwater situations. It is sometimes possible to see the layout if the light is behind you and the water unruffled. If you cannot see, you'll have to do your fishing blind and work deeper and deeper down.

Part A of the figure shows the retrieve for a sudden and straight-down drop of rocks. Part B is for a sawtooth bottom. Part C is for a boulder-strewn bottom beside the cliff above.

Fishing the jig properly in any circumstances is not as easy as it looks. You may feel that you are activating the jig properly by rod manipulation, tip snapping, and line jigging, but make sure that the action you are supplying is felt beyond the springy rod tip. A jig fifty feet or more out or down will not be activated as directly as one fished at twenty-five feet, since the line absorbs most of the applied action. Experiment in a large swimming pool or clear water section of a lake where your partner can see just how you are moving the jig at given distances. Another way to do this is on the lawn. Cast the jig and let your partner pick it up and hold it against your rod action. Or, for a more realistic test, have him submerge the lure and line in the water and hold the jig as you apply the twitching action. Then change hands and you'll know just how well you are doing.

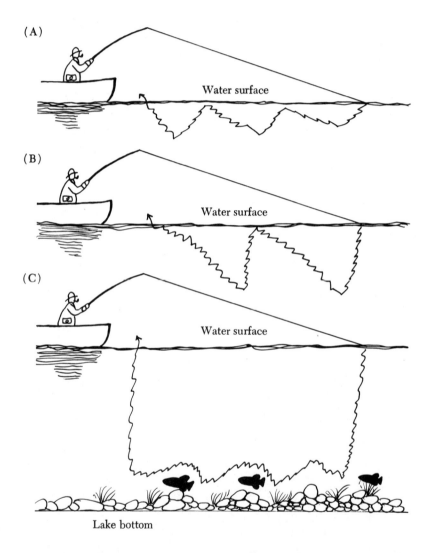

Figure 32. Three ways to retrieve a jig in a rock-cliff situation. (A) The near-surface retrieve with jerky movements, followed by periodic drop-downs. (B) An erratic course, preferably a faster kind of retrieve as a sort of fish-finder. (C) Here the jig goes really deep in a well-spaced retrieve and drop-down pattern.

It is worth recalling here that the jig is one lure that has absolutely no built-in action. Remember also that if you are using a rod with a fairly soft tip you must really overwork it on the jigging action if you want to get results.

Use the two man, "duet" system if you have a partner. It works particularly well in this case. However, since neither of you can accurately tell where your lures are when they're underway, you can signal the time for the second lure to be cast to the same target area by dropping your rod tip (or merely saying "okay" or grunting) when your lure has traveled far enough from the point of impact. In other words, you make your cast and begin the retrieve; when you signify that your partner should cast to same target his cast will go out and not tangle yours on the retrieve. Obviously, it is better to use lures that are quite at variance with each other, to test out the preferences of the fish.

Since the lure is always on the go, a strike will be felt with a bang. Even if the lure is at the top of a "jig" and for a split second on the slack, the hit will come as a shock. No bass can simply mouth a jiggling jig; he'll have to grab it with firmness and finality. About the only additional hooking to be done will be a slight setting of the hook, just to make sure he's on. This, however, can be dangerous, since just that amount of sudden pressure might be enough to tear the jig loose. You can usually tell just how securely a fish is hooked by the "feel" of the way it fights. But since you can only be right some of the time, don't be too concerned here.

With jigs, I've hooked bass in the throat, much deeper than with plugs and the porcupine clusters of hooks that generally grab them on the outside. I've also foul-hooked many bass on jigs, sometimes in the tail!

Mind a brief lecture on treble hooks? Naturally, being a conservationist at heart, I thoroughly approve of the single hook, even on plugs and spoons. I've also found, strangely enough, that single hooks take just as many bass as do trebles. In fact, three hooks are sometimes a hindrance to a really deep barbing of the fish's jaw. I never knew this until I used jigs, and particularly streamer flies and dry flies for bass. Certainly, when you wish to return a bass to fight again, treble hooks, especially if there are three sets of them all hooked into the fish, offer a serious problem. There are also times when nothing will hold a fish, and this goes for salmon, trout, or any game fish worth mentioning, as well as bass. But I suggest that you try singles; you'll have more fun with them.

Another teaser rig in concert with a jig is a tandem bucktail fly attached to a foot-long piece of nylon behind the jig. It is an abominable thing to cast unless you attach the teaser with nylon that is heavier than the main line. This will help it to swing on the cast and not flip or double back on the jig and become tangled. Your jigging action on the rod then makes the tandem irresistible to any bass in sight.

The tricks I've learned and am passing on to you here work exceptionally well for the kind of water we're talking about here, but don't consider them limited to this kind of situation; use them also where you can fish in the grass or pads with the possibility of few snagged lures. Obviously, don't try them where the situation is impossible.

Nighttime angling along ledge drop-offs near a cliff hole is best done from the boat at a good, comfortable casting distance out. Cast surface popping plugs right into the rocks. Bounce them off the rocks. If they're not taken on impact with the water, let them sit for a few seconds as I always advise with any surface popping lure.

Later, on several of our bass-hunting trips, we'll use jigs again under varied conditions.

As a postcript, I might add that you have probably snapped off a great many plugs and spoons during your bass-fishing years. If the tip of the rod is too limber, this has probably happened because a power cast tends to snap the thin monofilament that anglers like to use under the illusion of wanting to "fish light." Of course, you can also use a too-heavy line that would render the whole rig useless or at least make it hard to work accurately and effortlessly. But if you suddenly want to throw a heavy spoon quite a distance, you have to be careful on the cast not to let the rod tip flip too fast, or your line will snap. The trick is to balance your line, lure, and rod weights to your particular temperament, remembering that it is better to either change reel spools and use a heavier line or to switch to a rod with a more evenly graded tip action for casting a heavy lure.

Many fishermen, especially spinfishermen, try to make one rod do all the tricks to fit all circumstances. Like the fly rod (and more so than the baitcasting rod), the spinning rod must be chosen first and then the line and lure balanced to it. Or, if you prefer the other system, start with the lure weight and usual distance you'll be casting it, and then fit the line and rod to the combination. If you don't achieve a proper tackle balance, your casting will be inaccurate and bothersome.

One of the main reasons that you'll hear the old-time baitcasting-tackle gentry pooh-pooh spinning gear as inaccurate is that some guy with a spinning outfit bought unrelated elements, or worse, tried to use well-related elements in the wrong manner. The wrong baitcasting outfit can also be an abomination.

It is true that very light spinning rods can perform unbelievable feats in casting the light trout stuff. But don't expect that same outfit to handle the big terminal lures used for bass. As in bass-bug fly-rod fishing, you need a rod that is not only powerful enough to cast heavy plugs and spoons, but one that is also strong and firm of action, with enough spare power to set the hook fast in a rough-mouthed fish and even drag it through the weeds if necessary (and this goes for the line too). (*See* Appendix: Baitcasting; Spincasting.)

As for that rock cluster and bit of cliff-dwelling scenery, don't be discouraged if the first time you work it you don't get a break. By the same token, don't become overconfident if you score the limit your first time around. Of all the situations you can dream up, this one is a real dilly.

8

STREAM INLET
AND OUTLET

STREAM INLET

Let's fish a wilderness smallmouth lake in New Brunswick, Canada. The lake lies just beyond the Maine border. The province is separated from Maine by the St. Croix River system, which drains from lakes in both Maine and New Brunswick. These lakes and the streams that belong to the system harbor landlocked salmon, big brook trout, and some monstrous smallmouth bass. Even a week after the ice has left the lake, when the landlocked fishing is excellent, I've been tempted to switch to bass tackle and try for one even though it must be released. The fish are not too fighty at this season because of the water temperature, nor do they tend to strike as hard, but it is fun to catch one or two, especially if trolling for salmon has not been productive. I hanker for action, especially after warming the hard bench of my rowboat for hours waiting for a salmon to strike.

The inlet we are about to fish is where a good-sized trout stream enters the lake. It does not just simply fall out of the woods onto the shore but curves a bit as the water gently slows down to a deep, meandering current that follows a timber-lined shore. I've seen many a deer and quite a few moose here in the early mornings, and most of the time ospreys circle overhead, since there are several nests in the old dead trees that stick up from the greener, second-growth spruce and the alder-fringed edge of the lake.

The ice has been out for about three weeks and we are fishing a cold day in early May. We've swept the lake several times for salmon with no results and have decided to come in out of the wind to try for bass and, upstream, a trout or two for lunch. There are bass in the slow water all along the lake shore itself and for quite a way up the inlet. Laying down the trolling gear, we switch to spinning rods and light spoons. Yours is a gold and mine a silver, so that we can give the bass a selection. Following our system of duet fishing in parallel or in rotation, we proceed up the shore preparatory to entering the inlet. Some large rocks break up the grassy shoreline and some old timbers have fallen into the water along the deeper stretches of the shore. In places, the shallow gravel and grass extend for quite some distance from the shore. Large underwater rocks are a constant that we will cast near and around while trying to dodge the highest ones with the propeller.

These are good casting spots, and later in the season, when the water is lower and warmer and the lily pads are present, I can guarantee that anyone casting for bass for the first time in his life will take fish here. It requires no talent whatsoever, except to try and keep from snagging one's lure on the rocks. I've broken many hooks off on these jagged rocks after hitting their tops or dragging lures over them.

So we begin our casting. For some distance up the shore we do not get any action, although we have been varying our retrieves from deep to surface and from fast to slow. Oh, I forgot. There is a chance to hook a good brook trout on these spoons, and once in a while you can get a smashing rise from a salmon, so you can expect anything on this run, particularly when we reach the inlet. That's why it has been a ritual for me to drive eight hundred miles from New York City for many seasons just to fish this lake and the neighboring inlets and outlets, chains, streams, and rivers of the

St. Croix system. It is the same territory I visit late in the fall for grouse and woodcock and, a month later in the fall—if I can—for really big whitetails.

There's a hit. Salmon? Trout? Bass! A good bass, too. Fights heavy, doesn't he? A bit sluggish, but he's bending your rod quite a bit. Keep that rod tip pointed up and don't let him gain any slack or he'll file your line.

Uh-oh. That's just what he did.

Now I've got one on. He's not as big. Look at him jump! Not bad for a half-frozen smallmouth. It's hard to believe that they'll even bite at all. Remember when we arrived here two weeks ago? We couldn't have gotten the boat up in here for the slushy ice.

I suggest we switch to the fly rod and streamers as we approach the inlet, since we'll have a better chance at all three species with single- or tandem-hook streamers, especially in this clear water. The game fish feed on smelt at this season, and since smelt ascend the brooks, the fish will be lying almost anywhere in the mouth of the inlet. As shown in Figure 33, there are three main inlet channels that are deeper than the sandy bars that form as a result of silt coming down from the stream above. We want to fish all three of these in several ways. As shown, we'll first troll across the outer fringe of the inlet in our bass hunting and then work the deep runs by taking the boat over the bars and casting into the channels with a variety of lures, starting first with the streamers.

There's the first shallow bar. See the deeper water between it and the next one? Then there's the second deep, another bar, the third deep, and the last bar. Later on we can fish the shallows, since excellent bass-fishing areas lie along the shore for almost half a mile, until we come to the outlet of a little creek where (if we catch no trout) we'll try for some pan-sizers.

Okay, you're on, trolling a tandem streamer about a hundred feet behind the boat. I'll sink mine for variety and work it a bit closer than yours. There's just enough wind to hide our motion and wake. We may be lucky enough to hook a salmon. Now we're almost over the first deep. Watch out.

Zing. You had a strike. That was a salmon, no question about it.

I've got something heavy on mine; a bass. I've always said that I would rather get one good big bass on light gear than all the trout in creation. Even in this cold water he feels strong. But just wait until we fish this same spot in July. You've got kicks coming and you had better have a good strong heart.

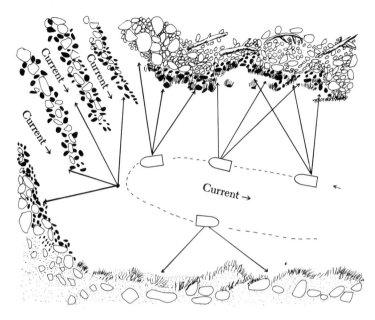

Figure 33. Fishing the approach and into the inlet. Note the advancing path from the far right side as trolling and casting is done into the shore amid the sunken and visible rocks. (The main current or body of water has been trolled previously, so it is now time to get down to work.)

The path rounds out at the foot of the inlet and crosses the shallow bars. (Casting can be done up and down the deep grooves if you can hold the boat steady.) Then a swing over the bars farther up is made, and finally the return to the spot where you began.

The bottom side of the pool is generally unproductive, as it is too barren and offers little attraction to the fish. Later in the season it is bone dry.

Now let's try trolling over the second finger of the inlet. How about switching to a plug, a zigzagging River-Runt (just to name one) while I stick to the weighted streamer. You may have a better chance with the plug.

No luck with either, so we'll proceed to the last channel. Let's try some wet flies and see if we can pick up a trout. It will be lunchtime soon.

All set? Here we go. Make your cast right into the stream, hold the rod high and skitter the flies across with a flipping rod action and strong pulling on the line to make them jump. That's it. We've got two fish on, both trout. This is nice country, isn't it? And since few people have discovered it, the fishing is great.

Some months have passed and we're back again. It is now July.

Our heavy lumber jackets, scarves, warm trousers, and knee-length boots are packed away, and we're working the shoreline dressed in light wool shirts, open at the collar.

What will Mr. Bass take at this time of year? We finger the tackle trays for an inspiration. Let's try a surface zigzagging plug. We have a number of them. You try the peach-colored one. I'll snap on my old trusty, the fore-and-aft frog-colored spinner plug that sinks a bit. We'll run the same shore that we did back in May and see how differently the bass are acting now.

Notice that the water's down quite a bit; about three feet. Those rocks that we cast to earlier in the year are virtually on the bank, which is now grown up with grass and weeds. Most of the rocks we glided over with the outboard are exposed now, and we can target in between the ones directly on shore that are shown in Figure 34. Follow the diagram and see just how thoroughly we can fish this together, casting in rotation, putting our lures right next to the dry land, and, as the water deepens, picking up our retrieve speed to send them down and on their mission.

Just as you begin your retrieve, I cast a bit upside of your lure, let mine sink a bit, and hope I don't become snagged. There are some old boughs and windfalls in that water. You can see a few of them, so it's a gamble either on the surface or underwater. The odds are against me, but it's worth the risk. There are bass in there and it is up to us to prove it.

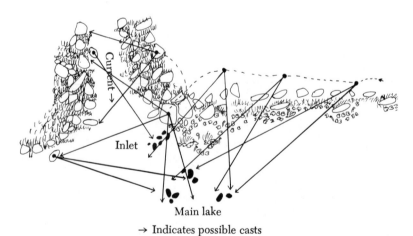

Current →

Inlet

Main lake

→ Indicates possible casts

Figure 34. A typical bend of an outlet stream or connecting bit of slow water between lakes. Note the variety of possibilities as indicated here for all techniques.

There's your first one. Look at him thrash. I'll bet you never had a smallmouth from more southern waters fight like this one. Keep your rod up now to avoid those snags.

Now cast between those rocks. Put your plug right between them, next to that old burned stumphead. There, another hit. And we haven't even reached the inlet.

With that fish in the boat, let's get up there and work the curves of the slow stream that flows down from the brook. We'll spin-troll one line, keeping it on the surface and fishing a streamer, and you can cast a spinning lure. Just pick any one, it makes no difference which. Trout or bass now, so watch it.

There! Right on the splashdown. Do you still think that fish are lure-label conscious?

We'll release that one, since it will go only about four pounds. But I'll bet you wouldn't have let him go if you had taken him from your favorite Connecticut lake.

As we work up and around the bends, nothing happens, but I have a valuable tip for catching those bass, and that is the use of big, gaudy wet flies (Figure 35). I'll be the guide, poling the boat downstream while you tie on three big flashy ones on a stout leader. You can stand up for the fly casting. I'll angle the boat so you don't catch me on the backcasts. Keeping those fluttery, wind-resistant things up is quite a chore. Go ahead. Put your cast right into the bushes; let the flies sink by mending the line ahead of the current drag, and then flutter them out toward the center of the stream for your recast. Glad you have a long "pole" instead of that overrated "light tackle"? You need a good rod here for the purpose of delivery. Sure it's heavy enough for a salmon, but the point in se-

Figure 35. Four gaudy wet flies. These are typical of the flies tied fifty or more years ago. They are not used too much today, but that doesn't mean that they cannot be effective. If trout are about, they like these flies too.

Flutter these in your presentation, three at a time, right on the surface. When trolling, cast them out from the side of the boat and allow them to swing into the boat's wake, dropping them back about twenty-five feet more than the original cast.

lecting the rod is the proper delivery of the fly, not its light qualities in battle.

That's it. There's your first one. By golly, it's a trout. Try again.
Good. A nice bass this time, but keep that tension on and get him
out from under those alders. He made such a commotion that he
put up two woodcock. Let's remember that location come fall.

At sundown we drift across the lake, casting into some rings
made by big fish. I can't tell what's making them, but the wet flies
can. You'd expect trout out here, since there are insects hatching
on the water. Nope. Those are bass. Throw the flies to them.
There's one. Wrist tired? Let's see, you've released twenty-eight
bass today. I think it's time we head in.

For contrast, let's go to a Massachusetts lake. We have no boat
here so we'll have to fish the stream inlet on foot. It's still July, but
the weather is much hotter down here, and clammy. The bass don't
know this, though.

Our inlet (Figure 34) is a large, slow one. In fact, it is hard to
make out the difference between the shore of the lake and the edge
of the inlet except by the right-angle turn of the water. Right at
the corner are some large boulders, a lot of high lake grass, and a
few pads. That should be a good spot for casting, and just beyond
the rocks is a better spot for live-baiting. We have about two hours
of fishing time before sundown and that should give us enough for
a taste. There are both large- and smallmouths in this lake, so we
have a choice. There are also walleyes and crappie.

Study Figure 34 to see how we'll cast to this spot with spoons
and plugs from the shore. If we were to work this from the shore at
night, we'd use surface plugs, since the water is shallow. Bass come
in here at night to feed, and it is almost a guarantee that you'll get
a fish well after dark.

For live-baiting, we select a slip-sinker rig and some shiners.
It has been a hard day, so we'll wade out to one of the rocks on
the outer fringe of the corner of the inlet and let nature take its
course. It's nice to relax for a while. Live-bait fishing may not be
active and glamorous, but it offers a tired angler the chance to let
the fish do all the work. Besides, it's a nice day and the clouds are
fun to watch as they shift around up there in the blue. Here comes
a couple of fishermen up the lake in their boat. I wonder if they'll
fish near us? Yep. They see us on the point and select the same
spot, although quite a distance out. We can talk back and forth,
and they seem friendly.

"Any luck?"

"Not too good. You guys get anything?"

"We took a couple casting along here with surface plugs, but we haven't had our baits in for long enough to know what's going on, if anything."

"We'll try out here in the channel. Minnows."

"Okay, we'll see who has the winning tickets."

I think I'll have a cigar. Hey, look at your line! It's peeling off your spinning spool like water off a duck's back. Okay, now. Raise the rod tip with a quick snap, and as a good second motion lower it, reel in quickly, and snap it up again. You must have a good one on there. Not enough to mount, but plenty to bake.

Not much happens for some time. After about a half-hour of baiting without a strike, our friends take off for the other side of the inlet, a good stretch of water about the same as ours. We watch them for quite some time as they fight four fish. Now what I want to know is why the fish bit there instead of here. I fished that shore last week and caught nothing, which was why I wanted to try this shore with you today. Well, that's bass fishing, and I thank God that there is no expert, much less one who can write, who knows all the answers.

I'm feeling restless. While you're sleeping alongside your rod, I'm going to try a saltwater jig just to see if I can stir up something. This trick often works. I know darn well that there are bass along here. They couldn't all have moved out or been caught since my last try.

First I'll cast straight out and let the jig sink for about three feet. It's about ten feet deep out there, as I remember from my baitfishing experience. Now to retrieve. I'm having trouble with this light rod and flimsy tip. I should have known better. Well, I'll try again, casting out from the center in both directions, alternating from side to side. There's a bump. No connection. Another cast. Another bump. What could that be? It wasn't a rock, for sure.

Here, you try casting this jig and I'll rig up another rod. Try out there, just where your bait is.

That's it. Strike! Come back on him, *hard!* He's off. That's one fault I find with most lightweight spinning rods; when you really want to set the hook into a bass, they just don't have what it takes. That's why I prefer a baitcasting rig or at least a very stout spinning tip for most heavy-lure bass fishing, as I've mentioned before. That light wand of a rod is okay for trout, but when the chips are down and you want to set the hooks into a big bass, especially one that has hit light, it takes quite a "pole" to do it. If we spent more time in selecting our gear than in getting all hung up on plug labels and brand names, our lives would be a lot simpler and more productive.

We have one more type of inlet to work, the small stream. We pick a hot day in August, on a Connecticut lake. The water is as warm as stale soup. The birds have quit singing. The weather is muggy and we should be in the shade of the local tavern instead of out here in the sun. With no luck for a two-mile stretch of casting, we'll head for the inlet, which is near us now, and if we don't connect there, we'll call it quits for the day. I want to save some strength for fishing another inlet at night.

It's a nice little brook. Not much of a trick to know what to do here; we merely make passes well away from its outlet, working in gradually, trolling and casting. If we were working from the shore we could really get up in there, but I don't think it's necessary to go ashore now. Let's try trolling some streamers across the mouth. Although streamers are lures seldom found in most bass anglers' boxes, I'm partial to them merely because they work.

This time, however, our tactics don't produce. Still, those bass must be down deep somewhere. We spot an angler coming along the shore headed for the stream. He's carrying a fly rod. Let's see what he does. He's casting what looks like a wet fly but not flipping it in the air with the usual abandon. It must be some kind of bait.

"What are you using?", we call.

"Hellgrammites."

Hmm. We watch to see the results. We don't wait long. He's into a bass before we can reach into the live-bait box. Two casts by each of us, even in our offshore position, net two bass and we call it quits. We should have known that big underwater bugs such as hellgrammites or even crawfish would be called for here. We'll know better next time.

The big thing to know is just how to fish the bait. First of all, learn to hook the hellgrammite properly. Through the collar, yes, but be careful not to kill the beast in the process. Then, using a very light nylon leader, attach a very light bit of sinker, either a short piece of wraparound lead or a small splitshot or two. Clamp on the first splitshot six inches above the hook and the second about two feet up. This spacing will allow the cast leader to "bend" rather than double back on itself and tangle up. If you're using spinning gear (and fishing in shallow water), you can attach a plastic bubble to the line end to keep the bait up off the bottom. I usually attach it to the very end, but some anglers like to let the bait flow free on the end with the bubble about three feet up. This is awkward to cast, but it works when it gets in the water. Once the bait is in the water, leave it alone, letting it sink and drift for a while, and then very slowly retrieving it with little jerks right to the rod tip.

For our final go at inlet fishing, let's try a lake under extremely low water conditions in late summer. It is useless to fish this during the day, since the water is shallow all around and there are few rocks in the inlet for fish to congregate near. The area is as open as New York's Fifth Avenue on a Sunday morning. Instead of using the boat, we work it on foot. It is black as pitch out here, and cool. As our eyes become acclimated to the dark, we can see the bare outlines of the water's edge. We listen. No fish are feeding, but I know they're in here from past experience fishing here at night. Surface plugs are in, and we work two Jitterbugs. You work one side of the inlet and I'll take the other, and we can cast in rotation, toward each other's shoreline. Now take it easy with that Jitterbug. Retrieving it that fast kills all the real action. You might just as well be using a hunk of wood. Let that lure move with the action that has been carefully built into it. Slow down. That's better. Don't be in such a hurry.

On these excursions we have used a variety of lures, as we have in the other situations in this book. Sure you might have come up with just as good choices, and perhaps even have made out a good deal better. But at least we have tried to follow what I consider the most direct ways of casing the lake, scanning the problems at each spot and adapting our lures and tackle to each situation with enough flexibility to make quick changes as well as unorthodox moves in the bass chess game. Just how we came upon the routine ways in which we choose our lures and use them is often quite by personal preference; almost all of us have our little ways of personally attacking the situation that confronts us. Usually, the personal rules over the logical, although they can many times be identical.

Generally speaking, if two people are fishing together, I like to start with two distinct weapons, even though the circumstances may argue for one particular type of lure. Certainly night fishing from the shore or from a boat over shallow water would argue for a floater or popper of some sort, but most other situations call for variety, if for no other reason than to hasten results so that both anglers can switch to the hottest technique or lure choice. I've seen times when even the same type of lure is called for—say a spoon— yet a red-and-white will gain hits over a green-and-white or a black-and-white. Had both anglers been using only a single color combination, such as the black-and-white, no fish would have been taken and nothing at all would have been learned from the experience. Even when fishing alone, I try to troll two lines with varied terminal attractions. When casting, I usually load up with three and sometimes four rods equipped with varied lures and terminals, even though it is much quicker and easier to snap the lures on and off when I'm using only one set of tackle.

And remember, it is always best to have rods and reels of different weights available for the different methods that require them. This attention is far more important than being "picky" about lure labels and variations of a basic lure action.

Thus far we have been dealing strictly with stream inlets, that is, the inlets of streams that have their headwaters in springs and creeks, not the inlets of rivers that are passageways between lakes. Fishing the inlet of such a chain river is quite a thrill when the fish are in, since the chain allows the fish free passage up and down, from one lake to another. Trout and salmon, and certainly pike and muskies, use these waterways frequently. Bass do not use them to the same degree, although they will be found spawning in the spring some ways up these rivers.

The fish's main attraction to the inlet of a chain river is that there are always a good many bait fish riding down the currents. Also, the water temperature is cooler—a blessing in summer. Therefore, all the fish have to do is wait there and be fed. When there has been a prolonged dry spell and the chain river is low, the action is naturally at a minimum. But comes a good rain and the river rises, the fish from the main lake will respond and head for the inlet. If you can strike it at that time you'll strike it rich.

Some of the finest chain-river-and-lake fishing is to be found in the upper New England states, particularly Maine, and into New Brunswick. Ontario is also cluttered with endless chain lakes. The St. Johns River in Florida is another great example of a strong river punctuated by broad expansive lakes all along its northward run before it enters the sea at Jacksonville. These lake inlets are always good, particularly for live-bait fishing right where the silt drops off and the real floor of the lake begins.

The lake outlet is as popular with fish as with fishermen, for the same reasons the inlet is. The techniques of fishing the two are also somewhat the same, but the timing of the good fishing periods is something else.

Fishing a lake outlet that is not part of a chain—that is, a stream leaving the lake to go downstream for good—seldom provides any bass that would be coming up the stream and into the lake. True, there might be resident bass in the stream that trade it for the lake once in a while, but the numbers of fish that make this trade would be minimal. The fish that come down to the outlet to feed do so merely to follow the baitfish that will be spilling down into the river below, and this happens only when excessively high water brings them down. The only regular attraction to the baitfish, and thus to the bass, is the amount of cooler water moving toward the outlet, a point that the fish appreciate only in the hottest time of the year. Bass seldom if ever go downstream to spawn or even to chase after bait.

I have included in Figure 36 a kind of routine to follow in fishing an outlet. Again, we are bass hunting, and, since the conditions in and around inlets and outlets can be so tricky, I think that if we were going to fish one together right now, I'd do it in the manner shown in the diagram.

Figures 37A and B show the manner of fishing two types of backwaters along the course of a main river. If, however, the outlet is one into a chain river, the times to hit it are when the lake above

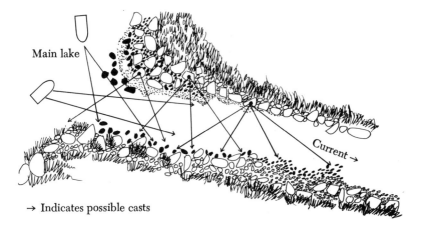

Main lake

Current →

→ Indicates possible casts

Figure 36.   A suggested sequence for fishing a lake outlet.

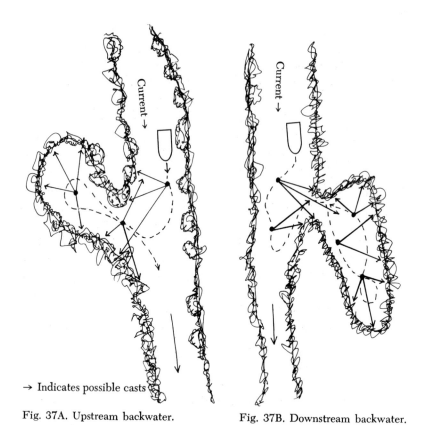

Current →

Current →

→ Indicates possible casts

Fig. 37A. Upstream backwater.　　　Fig. 37B. Downstream backwater.

Figures 37A, 37B.　Suggested sequences for fishing river's-edge back-waters.

the outlet is rising or has risen from high water coming in from its feeder streams. The bass in the river below will then come up to feed in the outlet. Some fish from the next lake below will also work their way up, and certainly the bass in the main body of the lake will favor the shoreline near the outlet for their feeding sprees when they come out of the deep at sundown for their evening forage.

Fishing these backwaters is really a tricky business. The casual fisherman will have to take the breaks as they come. If you are on a short vacation and don't have the time to watch the seasonal changes on an inlet or outlet, merely give it a pass-over by trolling and casting. If you can hit it right, you'll connect far better than in most other parts of the lake. But when it is zero time, no matter how expert you are, you'll be wasting your time.

9

GRASSY SHALLOWS

We fished some grassy shallows a few chapters back when we invaded a midlake grass flat, but the grassy shallows we'll be talking about here are vastly different from those and therefore merit a separate trip. Even here we will be fishing several kinds of flats under different conditions, calling for a variety of tackle and techniques.

My first real experience in grass-flat fishing was in Florida. I had been given the opportunity to catch some of those really big bigmouths and I can remember standing at the dock hefting that first ten-pounder, raising it up and down several times to let the significance of such a fish sink in.

It was on the next day that my host took me out on the grass flats of a big lake, but not before letting me cast my arms off throwing lures into the big cypress roots and some of the most inviting holes in the swampy ring of the lake. I didn't get a rise but was amazed at the accuracy with which I could spot those casts. My host used patience and finally said that if I wanted to combine talent with results, we could now fish the flats where the bass were and catch some.

Having been brought up to believe that bass hung out in the kind of place that I'd just been casting to, I was a mite less than stunned. I've had these comeuppances several times, such as the time in Maine when a guide let me cast for brook trout for hours over the most delicious flats and runs of the broad Allagash. Boy, my flies looked good, but all I caught were chubs. Then he took over and put me onto some of the finest brook trout fishing I'd ever had. The Catskill brown trout technique was of absolutely no use there.

Some of us have to learn the hard way.

Having boarded our Florida craft, we zoomed over the water and headed for the shoreline ahead. The lake was broad, and when we left the cypress forests ringing the edges and were well offshore, I saw the pale green tips of grass bending in the wind. In the middle of the lake there were small waves. The object in this kind of fishing is to find a grass flat where the waves are not kicking up too strongly for the fish underneath and also for the comfort of the angler. It is a tough enough business casting across that steady wind.

Finally we found a spot where the waves were down and stopped the boat. The grass was not thick but there was quite enough of it to snag lures, and I wondered just how I'd manage. I'll take you with me now and we'll fish it together. You are armed with a spinning rod—not a flimsy-tipped one but one with a fast or stiffer tip than generally prescribed. Your line is eight-pound mono on an open-face reel. Lures? There are plenty in your box, but don't bother to open it. I've got the medicine right here: a plastic worm on a jig head. You can cast it almost anywhere. You are also in for a snag no matter where you go with it, but don't get alarmed; that's part of the game. We'll just drift with the wind and you can catch yourself some grass.

Now the way to try and avoid getting snagged up is to watch that retrieve. Take it slowly; ease the jig along and zigzag it constantly—a process that might seem to be one to catch grass but that actually shakes the jig free of grass. That's right. Try it. Okay, you came through that bunch with flying colors. When you feel the lure tugging at the grass, stop for an instant, and give the lure a slight jerk; then, as the grass begins to let go, gently pressure the line with the rod tip, and with the jig free for the moment, take advantage of the opportunity to manipulate it. Follow the steps in

Figures 38A–C. It is surprising how much of the retrieve of the lure will be in the relative clear; most of that grass out there presents more of a mental problem than a real one.

Now make another cast. There is no point in trying to find a clear spot. Just cast.

Raise the rod tip and begin your retrieve. Feel the hang-up? Okay, relax the jig. Now ease it out and retrieve again. Okay, it's caught again a little, so jiggle the rod tip until it is free. Now retrieve once again. Repeat the process. Hey! You're not hung-up, that's a bass! Well, you've discovered that catching a bass isn't half as difficult as learning to worm that jig through the grass.

You could cast a plain jig and do almost as well. Try it. Here's one of my Upperman bucktails, on which I have taken almost every game-fish species in both fresh- and saltwater. It's a wonderful largemouth lure down here. Let it sink down; there are few if any snags out here, just grass and sand. Now jig it along the bottom. Hooked on a clump of grass? Pull on it, but take it easy. Use a steady pressure. Now jig it a bit. There, you're free again. Now retrieve it, using the same routine you used with the plastic worm. Don't let that grass bother you. There's another hit. The lake out here is full of bass.

It's now the next day and we are both a bit hot, so how about combining a swim with our bass-fishing. We can wade it. Hop overboard, but bring your bass-bug rod too, and I'll show you some

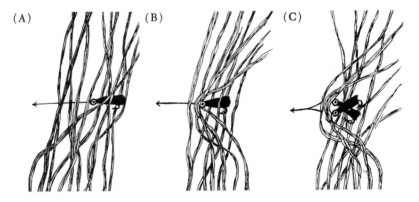

Figure 38 A–C. Moving from right to left in this picture, we see (A) the jig approaching trouble and getting snagged. Only a slight easing and pulling (B), with perhaps a bit of a jerk motion, will keep the jig moving through the grass. Do not pause at all, for the jig will then sink too far down (C) and become badly snagged.

tricks in this grass. Tie on a black-and-white marabou. Now, with that wind to your side, make a few casts into that fairly clear area and see what happens. Boom! That didn't take long. Remember that marabou the next time you're down here. In fact, you have approximately fifty acres of bass-fishing ground here, none of it over your head. So fish to your heart's content, and by the law of averages at this time of the year, you're bound to connect with a ten-pounder. You may not land him, being used to those little northerners, but you can try.

With your fear of grass behind you, and the technique of fishing through it beginning to develop, you'll make it well in the waters we'll fish later.

Let me have that marabou back. I think you missed the special dressing of that fly and the reason why it is so weedless. Figure 39 shows the construction of the marabou with the fuzz removed so that you can see what protects the hook.

Certainly you would get hung up if you cast a red-and-white spoon in there or a plug loaded with a porcupine set of trebles. You don't fish the grass flats with such tackle, at least not here. Where the grass is intermittent or not thick, you can get away with almost anything, but it pays to use a little sense about what you throw into the flat itself. Sure you'll get hung up once in a while and have to reel in a handful of spinach, but so what? You'll also draw meat once in a while too! Remember that pickerel fly that we used way back? It would work well here and on any grass bed.

On our trip back from the lake, let's go fish a grassy shallow in

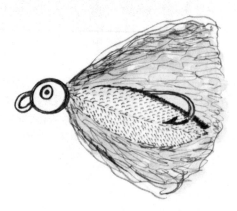

Figure 39. My weighted jig-marabou with a built-in, hard-feathered, weedless hook. Stiff, clipped duck-quill feathers are used.

the bend of the St. Johns River in Florida. We could wade it, for it is all level sand until you come to the actual river. There, the bottom drops straight down to twenty and sometimes thirty feet, so I'll put you in quite a distance from the edge. We can pole or drag a light anchor, since the current swings into this flat from the river proper. The breeze combined with the current moves us along slowly, over water that averages only about two feet deep. We'll fish the famed black eel, for it was on such a stretch that I first learned the killing qualities of this lure, a rubberized version of a small black snake or oversized black worm, take your choice. Anyhow, when the lure first came out in the early days of the rubber (and later plastic) imitations, its fame grew so fast that it was hard to come by one in the tackle store.

Just why such a thing as this lure represents would be traveling out in the open grass flat of a lake is quite beyond me, but perhaps the bass figure that it is something good to eat and go for it. Whatever the case, take a thousand anglers, each throwing it around, and a lot of bass come to net and a lot of talk begins. The results are the same with almost any successful lure. I can recall when John Alden Knight wrote an article in *Field & Stream* about the killing qualities of the ancient red-and-yellow bucktail and called it the "Mickey Finn." From then on, tackle dealers had to order it by the gross.

Anyhow, the chap who introduced me to the black eel said nothing when he handed it to me. In a typical close-mouthed southern drawl, he merely indicated that I snap it on and make a few casts. He was not impressed when I landed an eleven pounder a few minutes later.

Using the black eel that afternoon, fishing it just like a jig, really set me afire. Old blackie is also a great lure in the shoreline rock cluster, as well as in the midlake rock cluster that we'll be fishing later. In fact, it is a good lure any time you have confidence in it and sufficient know-how about when to use it. This, I have come to believe, is the crux of the business of lure selection, for if either of these two elements is missing, it doesn't really matter what you use.

Now let's tackle a really tricky bit of grass on my favorite lake in the Midwest. The deeper stretches are comparatively clear, while the shallows are thick with grass, reeds, and other growth. The grass grows in rows because of the contour of the bottom. Since lily pads are found in abundance, we can bypass them for the time being, even though good bass are often found lying under them. We can

Figure 40. A typical surface darting plug rigged with a single hook and duck-quill "packing" to avoid the weeds.

try the black eel, or a plastic worm on a jig, or a marabou the way I tie it. But here's another trick. Look at this surface plug (Figure 40). It is a wobbler, not a diver. The treble hooks have been removed; only a single hook is attached to the back end, and that one is feathered over tightly. Just the rig for grass. You can fish this on the surface almost with abandon. I'll bet you never saw one before.

Cast it along the open stretches between the thick grass. It works well. Now try it across the thickest grass, easing it along on your retrieve. Sure it will snag once in a while and you'll get a handful; nothing perfect has been invented yet. But about the only other lure that is as snag-free as this one is the heavily dressed bass bug or a dry fly that can be dropped in, rolled forward on the pickup, and dropped down again.

It is also important to note that only under certain conditions will good fishing be had on a grass flat. Take, for instance, the case when the flat is under constant pounding of a wind. The waves cut through, and any bass in such shallow water will depart soon after the baitfish that were in the flat have left for the while. Instead, pick a grass flat on the lee side of the lake and fish that. If you have just arrived at the lake and have no idea of what has been happening, inquire about the wind direction and force for the past few days. It will save you a lot of time, not only in grass-flat fishing but in all your fishing with the exception of deep-down baiting.

And if you still are scared of the grass, stay away from spinning lures and stick to the fly rod and bass bugs. Try these areas at twilight when the wind is down; grass flats in the early morning or late twilight are magical. Pop that bug through the grass. Climb it over the stems. Roll-cast it forward on the pickup and let in fall right into a fresh set of rings. Walk it around in a semicircle by mending your forward roll cast to the right or left. That'll drive 'em crazy.

10

PAD FLATS

That alarm clock has an awful sound this early in the morning; nobody but an idiot or a bass fisherman would be awake at this time. Ah, but I must thank the Great Creator for creating the bass and endowing them with so much activity at dawn. And I must confess that one of the best and most delightful times to be on the lake is during that magic period at sunrise. The slight damp chill can be refreshing, since in summertime the bulk of the day is usually overwarm and, in portions of the country, such as lower New England, apt to be muggy. And if there are high hills between you and the sun, the cool dawn lasts much longer; the dim shadowless light lingers before the first piercing rays of the actual sun slant out across the landscape. It is just those few seconds upon awakening that try to change my mind, roll me over, and make me go back to sleep.

In that early hour, it is advisable to find a fishing spot under one of the hills between you and the sun, for this will remain in

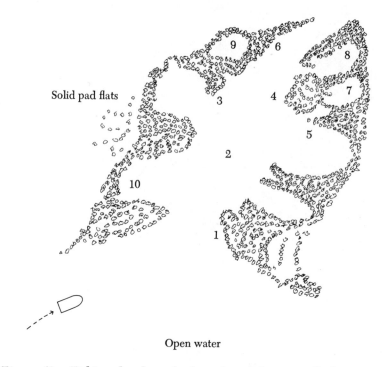

Solid pad flats

Open water

Figure 41. Fishing the channels through pad flats, a really hot-spot of weed bed off the main lake. Fish this one properly when the wind is up "outside" and the lake is being boated and skied to death.

comparative darkness for a longer period. Fishing on the other side of the lake would expose you to the direct light and glare of the sunrise.

In midsummer there is generally a dense fog over the water, or, failing that, often a dainty kind of mist that rises off the water with the coming heat of day. All you can see, generally, is the outline of the trees or distant hills beyond the lake. As you approach in the outboard, there is a big white gap between the upper hills and the immediate foreground: the mysterious line of the lake in which we can expect to find bass on the feed.

Moving along over the water as if gliding over glass, we cut the motor long before reaching the lily-pad section of the lake where we will be fishing. It takes a few minutes for our wake to fade in the pads of the nearby shore. Probably the waves travel to the distant and fog-shrouded shore to wash the gravel, sway the grass, or lace the faces of the boulders, making them glisten to a loon as he swims by looking for his breakfast. We can hear him from way over here, for his shrill, eerie call pierces the fog.

Other birds are awake and have been singing ever since the beginning of the dawn. Now, in summer, their songs and calls are of a more sedate nature than they were in the mating and creative time of spring when they were courting, building nests, and caring for their offspring.

We look ahead to the pad flats and begin to make out the dim lines of the shore. A big, stiff-necked heron suddenly becomes like a rubber band, and great gray wings lift the body and long, dangling legs into the air and away. This ancient species of bird, so angular and stiff when still, is a poem of grace silently gliding into the mist. Our approach is discovered: a small group of mallards pops into the air in an almost vertical explosion, their gilded blue wing-patches glinting in the sun. The light moves up a notch and the fog begins to burn off, revealing the pads. Our minds begin to focus on the prospect ahead.

Why did we choose the pad flats on this morning?

We could have stayed in bed or trolled the lake shore from one end to the other, or we might have concentrated on live-bait fishing off the deep cliffs near the bottom end of the lake. When it comes to early-morning fishing, the possibilities are endless. And just as we might have caught bass in any one of these and other situations or might have caught nothing, we may or may not be successful fishing the pads. The choice is arbitrary, and this is the case most of the time in bass fishing. It is up to the angler to choose the kind of water he wants to fish and what his tackle and approach will be. It is what *he* does with his time, equipment, and talent that counts. The pad flats *could* be a potent spot to connect with some good fish; the pad areas are quiet and will remain so well after the main lake becomes speckled and later waved up by the breeze. The first magic moments in the protected areas where the pads are located call for surface popping bugs or surface plugs.

Since the wind is nonexistent, the bass-bug rod is our choice, and we will use it until the pesky breezes make bugging more of a chore than a delight.

Theoretically, our bass are lying at the edge of the pads, or a few feet in from the open water. They might be working their way out after feeding there during the night. They might also be residents who have taken up their positions along the edge of the pads to find their food in the stems, or lying in wait for schools of pass-

ing minnows and other baitfish that dart in and out among the
stems. From past experience, regardless of the reasoning, I have
found that fishing such places at dawn pays off.

On another morning such as this, we can try something dra-
matically different if you like, so with no wind to bother us, we'll
pole up to the edge of the first line of pads shown in the illustration
at the opening of this chapter. We can position the boat parallel to
the "shore" and both cast our bugs, although it might be easier on
both of us if we alternate casts. Just for variety we can use two
different popping bass bugs. You tie on a hair-body bug with
feathered wings and I'll use a plastic-bodied bug with little dressing. Chances are that we'll either both connect or both draw a zero.
I've seldom found the bass at all selective with these lures. It is
mainly a matter of presentation and the enticing motion of the lure
that gets them.

The rod action feels good as we unlimber and stretch its fibers
into a powerful fore-and-aft rhythm. Coiled line is ready in our line
hand. Now, away the first offering goes to the very edge of the
pads. There. Right on target. One pop, just to set the bug and bring
in the spare line, and we're ready for the strike. Whoops! A good
solid swirl right under the bug. We strike back out of surprised
reflex. It is most difficult at the beginning of a fishing day to instantly recognize that that swirl is not a take. Usually we strike
back furiously by trained reaction and remove the bug from the
scene rather than allowing it to stay where it is. In this case we
let the bug stay where it is for a second or two and, if no action
comes, we rollcast and flip the bug right back to the pad edge for
another try.

There we let it rest, for perhaps the bass will return, or possibly
there is another big one in there. I hand us cigars and we light up.
Your next cast goes out to the pad edge. Get that slack line in,
slowly, without disturbing the bug. Fine. Now you are ready. But
remember, you should try and take in that slack even before the
bug hits the water, for more often than not the bass will hit quickly,
even as the bug hits the water, and if there is any slack line out,
he'll often reject the bug before you can "get to him" on a tight line.
Your cast hasn't gotten a response, so pop the bug gently and let
it rest. I'll pop mine too. Now, slowly swim your bug toward you a
few feet and I'll do the same. With the lure about ten feet from
the pads, we can lift our rods, rollcast forward, and replace the
bugs at the pad-line about five feet to the left of their original spot.
Now let's repeat the line-control process with a few pops.

Still no action.

We pole the boat along about twenty feet, leaving the lures on the water while working them toward the boat for a recast. We work the shoreline in this manner, casting into the inlets between the pads. We take our time, for the sun is still behind the hill, the air cool and still, and the waterline glassy calm.

I notice that you hold your rod high, pointed to the sky most of the time. It is better to have it more parallel to the water. The reason for this is that you'll have much more of an arch for your fast strike if you start from the flat position. True, the line is then more direct to the fish and it is theoretically more possible for him to break it if he strikes hard enough. But to offset this, you keep constant control of the line by holding a coil or two of spare line for the strike. If you steadily hold your rod in the vertical position you have to pull back much too hard for the strike. Try it my way on your next cast. When the bug is out there, lower the rod tip to the water, gathering the slack in as you do this. Make this habit a part of your routine and you'll find yourself in a better position for action. There. Good cast. Bring the tip down and gather in the slack. He hit! Now strike back and up, *hard.* See? You've got him and in this position you have enough spring in the rod to hold him out of the weeds. Nice fish.

Here's a match. Your cigar went out. You forgot to puff on it when you were tangled with that largemouth!

Before we move on, we'll pop just one more cast in that "V" between the pads, if we can do it without getting hung up. Boy, that spot looks inviting. Any bass around? You know, in this type of fishing, you have to talk to them as well as cast to them. Don't expect that they'll just be there waiting for you. Talk to your bass. Wake him up. Tell him that you've made your offering. Nobody can prove that it helps, but by the same token nobody can prove that it doesn't.

The pads are now beginning to take on a shape and form and color. A little fog has risen, revealing more of the shoreline and, since this is a favored location, we unconsciously look for identification signs along the shore that will tell us of good spots to fish. We move, ever so quietly, from spot to spot. A few strikes, a swirl or two beneath our bugs, but not a fish in the net yet.

This has been a good practice session, the main point being to learn the subtle trick of landing that bug right at the pads without getting hung-up, for we will be working in much more difficult water later.

I can recall casting to the pad edges in the hyacinths that line the edges of the St. Johns River in Florida. The boat glides downstream, directed by the guide. The best spots are along the deep and sudden drop-offs that edge the main river current sweeping by the shoreline of pad plants. The bass live in close to the drop-offs, and when your bug lands with a plop well ahead of the boat, you have but a short time to work it. Where the plants are growing in shallower water, away from the drop-offs, you'll get few hits. But since you can't tell just where the drop-off line runs, you fish the whole border as if you could expect a strike at that moment.

Those Florida bass are quick, make no mistake about it. The average northerner thinks that because the state of Florida is semi-tropical and the water warm, the bass will be logy. This is far from the truth. I've had strikes from those trim Florida largemouths that would rival the punch of a Maine smallmouth. The same goes for the river bass encountered on an Ozark float trip, and the identical technique of bugging can be used there on the downstream drift. The big point is to master the spotcast and quick manipulation of the line, taking into consideration the downstream drift of the boat. It is almost like dry-fly fishing upstream; there is little time to waste. You make the cast, quickly adjust the slack, and get set for the strike (if the bass gives you that much time).

There's a bass swirling to your plug. Leave it. Let it rest. He'll come back. Now, gently turn the bug around as you gather in the slack. Ah, that did it. Up with that rod tip. *Strike!*

He's on, but keep that rod back now. Glad that you didn't start that spring from the vertical? If you had, you'd be breaking your back right now before being able to gather in line while lowering the rod tip and still maintaining the pressure on that fish. He threw it, but our point has been well made; that's the whole idea of such a practice session. There are more bass ahead in the lake.

The sun is higher and it is beginning to feel warm. The air is soft; a slight breeze wrinkles the water. Another cast. This time up the shore a bit, since the boat has drifted to a new position. Still no action, even with the perfect handling. Watch it. That sloppy cast put your bug into the pads and you got hooked as you drew back. Now hold on. Don't louse it up. I think you can pull free and at the same time make that bug irresistible. First let everything settle; gather in your slack. Raise the rod high now, tensing the line slightly against the hooked bug. See? You can lift the bug and the pad to inspect your situation. It may pull out right now.

Jiggle it a bit while the bug and pad are up off the water surface. *Splat!* Well, it didn't matter to the bass. He knew something was going on there so he grabbed at the works, pad and all, and you've got him. Boy, what an explosion! He's up in the air, having done you the favor of unsnagging you, but look out, he's heading back for the pads. Strike him hard out of there. That's better.

Here comes the breeze straight at us. We've had it unless you want to fight that breeze. Let's go ashore for some breakfast and we'll return to another pad flat farther down the lake for a different set of circumstances.

The pad flats have produced as I knew they would. I like going in the morning, before the sun or anything except the birds and some nice bass are stirring.

Casting in a pad flat is a bit easier when there are channels through the pads. It is then possible to paddle a canoe, row a boat, or even slow-troll a small boat through the more open stretches. If the wind is right, it is advisable to avoid using anything other than a pole to make your way along, since any disturbance of the water should be avoided. Sure, bass are bold fish and will stand for a lot of abuse and disturbance, but all the same, I prefer to fish for my bass with the helpful element of surprise on my side.

If we were to hover over the area shown in our diagram (Figure 41, page 118) we'd see the flats. Note that there are four distinct open legs, a channel, and several "holes" in the pads. In the springtime this is fairly open water, with some grass showing. If the water is low, the ground itself can be seen before the summer weed growth has started. By July, the whole area is overgrown except for these holes and channels. Why are they still open? Believe it or not, there is usually a slight current draining from the nearby shoreline, a spring or series of springs coming up near the shore. Many years earlier, there may have been a drainage area and the bed of a brook coming right in at the shore. In such situations, you'll find a mucky bottom in the pads in most cases, while in the channels themselves you'll find little growth, some gravel, a few rocks, and sometimes great expanses of sand.

So much for the background. How about the food supply? Lots of it in the pads. The area is literally crawling, and if you were to look carefully you would find lots of little underwater "trails" through the pads that the big fish use as paths. I've seen pickerel trace their way through these avenues, carefully twisting and turning, bumping into a stem once in a while, with the motion of the overlying grass or pad a telltale sign that something other than a minnow is present. Hook a big one in the weeds and he'll use one of these paths as his escape route. Still, you're hardly likely to recognize it as such, since you'll become snagged instantly in the stems of the pads.

The aim in fishing this type of set-up is to lure the fish out to the edge of the pads by any means at your disposal. Let's fish this problem together and you'll see what I mean. We'll try and avoid having to pole the boat in to unsnag a lure, but by the same token we won't sacrifice the fishing potential because of any fears.

If there is a wind, I use a stiff spinning rod and heavy line with lures that balance. If there is no wind, I like to use the fly rod, even though handling the line over the snags is quite a bit more difficult. The least wind-resistant bug and one that is as weed-free as possible is required. Ultralight spinning gear is out except for casts into the open water, and even here you're kidding yourself to use it, for this light gear just won't be able to control a bass that heads for the snags. In any event, long casts are out, since overshooting, casting under a tree branch or snag, or a slight error to left or right can be fatal.

Regardless of tackle, the first rule is to keep that rod up as high as possible, just the opposite of what you do when fishing from clear water to the edge of the pads, as we did earlier in this chapter. It is best to stand in the boat and much of the time hold the rod up at almost a straight arm's length while retrieving and playing the fish.

Don't be afraid to wade this water. Most bass fishermen are lazy, and you'll seldom find them wading such stretches unless they're troutfishing-oriented. It took me many years to discover the pleasures of wading rather than sitting and casting from the hard bench seat of a boat. Wading offers a change of pace, and you don't tend to stiffen up as much as you would if you sat in a boat from dawn to dusk.

Speaking of dusk, that's one of the best times to fish this well-padded inlet, and twilight is as good or better because once the wind is down you can usually see or hear the bass in the weeds and can call your shots over a specific fish. For nighttime sport, learn the technique by day and then, after the sun has set and your evening meal and brandy are well settled, come in here with the boat. Kill the motor well out from position 1 in Figure 41 and as soon as the water becomes shallow enough for poling, work into the stretch and fish it as you would during the day. It won't be as necessary to land the lures immediately next to a pad or weed as it is during the daytime. At night, it is best to err on the side of caution and place the lure near enough to the pads so they will see it.

Right now, the summer sun is beating down on us as we make our first trial run on the diagram. Entering the pad bed from the main lake at the lower left, we're out of the passing breeze, and it suddenly becomes hot. The summer is upon us. Even the temperature of the water is higher. All is seemingly still, yet once we are in and moving along quietly, many birds pop out of the pads and flit along the shoreline. Insects of all descriptions fly from pad to pad, especially dragonflies, and there are quite a few frogs well in toward the shallower sections.

Following our ritual of fishing the nearest water first and not moving until we have thoroughly covered it, we make a cast to the side of the channel, to the left of 1 as it is seen in the diagram. If we stick to the open water we can use a floating-diving plug or even a shallow lightweight spoon. Without moving, we cover the water down to 2 and along the right bank of weeds, using everything in the book to try and find out what, if anything, will arouse action. This, as I have said on all of our trips, is bass hunting. Usually there are good fish at the outside of a pad area like this one, so we concentrate a bit more here than we will in the interior of this location. We move the boat cautiously. This is also a good spot for live-bait fishing later, before we leave for the open lake.

We remember that if we proceed slowly, we won't frighten fish away from the pad and channel area for the main lake as we approach. No sense in scaring the fish into the main lake and then working over the territory they have just vacated. Have you ever noticed fish swimming by you as you entered an inlet? They know you are coming and want to get out of the way for you.

In working this pad flat in the past, I've tethered the boat and waded the little cut-in that empties out of 3. A bass-bug rod is real fun here, and the wading on hard ground is pleasant and the water not too deep. All you have to remember is to keep your back cast high, preferably using a roll cast most of the time and not using a heavy or wind-resistant bug. A stiff leader is needed, since you want absolute and accurate direction for the lure. If it becomes hung up, you also want enough pound test in the leader to avoid having to wade in and unhook it. The little hole to the left of the small channel produced a fine bass for me last year, and I want you to try this spot. The bass hit my bug and quickly sought refuge in the stems before I could gather in my slack line, and even before the rings had settled from the landing of the bug on the water. Fortunately, I was able to raise the rod high and pressure the fish for a surface battle. It was a great show, and never once did that bass gain enough footage to reach the cover of the tangles. As I remember, it was a bright day, one that would not have been expected to produce a fish.

As I first approached the main channel, I cast to its smooth mouth from the inside, and a big fish hit but missed. He never rose again and must have gone into the "big" water to take up residence elsewhere. As I waded back to the boat, I worked the channel, throwing a long, wild cast toward 5. I hooked a nice little bass in the center of that arm of the channel, but he quickly threw the hook. The stretch from 2 to 10 is another good alley where it is better to wade than to drag the boat.

As for wading, it is sometimes a hairy problem to get in and out of a boat when you're decked out in waders. If your boat is of the small, low-sided, car-top variety, you can slip out of it more easily without strangling. I usually move to the side of the boat, having my partner balance the craft, and then stretch one leg straight out over the gunwale or top edge and move the other leg almost parallel to it. I next move my outside leg over the side and bend my knee. If I can't touch the bottom, I lean over the gunwale and roll out, touching the bottom first with one foot and then the other. Another technique is to submerge your waders overboard, step into them, and pull them up. It's a matter of water depth and boat height. Take your time doing this, so that you won't split the seams of your waders.

Back in the boat again, we can fish either toward 6. Since the sun is overhead and there are no noticeable shadows, it makes little difference which one we choose. The wind direction will not affect our casting either on our way in or on the way out. These considerations should be kept in mind, however, when we look to our next moves. A slow drift of the boat along one shore or the other is in order. It is foolish to proceed down the middle of the channel because you tend to scare more fish with the boat in the open for all to see. This is an important point to remember. Think back: how many times have you boated your way through the dead center of a fishing spot or seen other anglers doing this?

Remember these situations the next time you are in this type of water and you'll recall fishing with me.

When you reach 6, say, after some thorough fishing, you can rest the area a bit and wade through the pads to the holes at 7, 8, or 9 for some bugging, and then, by the time you return, can begin casting back toward 5, working the centers of the channels, since your presence may by now have moved the bass to the open water there.

Back at 1, as you proceed looking in the direction in which you are going, do not forget to make a few casts directly behind you. Quite often you can pick up a bass this way.

Out on the open water you find the passing breeze refreshing. You can pull your stringer alongside, count your fish, and put them in the well to keep them alive rather than dragging them in the water. Now start up the motor and whisk away to the next spot.

A pad area like this is usually considered a maze for angling mice and is easily passed up or at most superficially covered in good safe casts and with little or not action. If you really learn to penetrate such water, you'll find it can be easily covered, turn by turn, move by move.

11

ROCK CLUSTERS ONSHORE AND OFFSHORE

It is a strange bit of illogic that makes a fisherman work a great many areas of a lake, casting to almost all of the spots that he likes—often with no results—and saving one of the very best as a "last resort." Most of us are prone to do this; perhaps it is the gambling instinct. We work the pad flats hard. Sure, there are great possibilities there. Then we take in the midlake grass flat, and certainly this is no area to pass up. Next we'll troll the entire length of a lake, hoping to pick up a bass the easy way. But we'll save an ace up our sleeve. I've seen guides do this many times. I've been their victim: they fish me all over the lake and give me a workout with every conceivable lure and technique in the book. Then, after either mediocre luck or no luck at all, they finally take me to where the bass are. Now the obvious question is: Why didn't we go there in the first place?

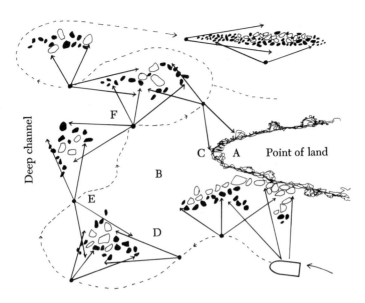

Figure 42. Some excellent bass water if you fish it properly. Look at those rock clusters and spaces in between for the baitfish to school and play and the bass to feed in. The anchoring spot is G.

The rock clusters, either on- or offshore, are wonderful aces in the hole. Where the rocks cluster, so do the bass—all season long, with the exception of the spawning period. One of the best kinds of rock cluster occurs where the shoreline changes abruptly from gravel, mud, or sand into groupings of larger stones and big boulders, spaced just far enough apart for a good growth of grasses and weeds. The minnows hide here, a key to our choice of lures and bait.

The next time you case a lake in advance of your actual fishing, look for such an area. Save it as a last resort if you like, or fish it first if you are greedy for initial success. Fish it the way we'll work today and it is my bet that you will not be disappointed. It is also a good spot to take a friend, particularly one who has not been too successful at bass fishing, since it is not very difficult to fish for anyone who can cast half decently.

Let's go. There is just such a bit of shoreline off that point of land up ahead. The season is early July, and in this northland lake are both large- and smallmouth bass with a smattering of walleyes and pickerel. Years ago the lake also contained landlocked salmon and brook trout, but with the warming of the water due to timber

cutting and flooding, the trout have vanished. In their place, however, bass thrive to draw outdoorsmen from faraway cities who
come here each summer to boat, water-ski, and fish.

The water level is down from a month ago about two feet.
Just a few of the rocks in the clusters can be seen as we approach.
On a windy day you can see the foam flecks from waves that sweep
up the shoreline. A month from now, when the water is still lower,
perhaps even two feet farther down, many of the rocks will be
exposed almost to their bases. But farther out from the center of the
clusters are still more of them, well spaced, that harbor good-sized
fish.

Today we are fortunate in having a slight breeze coming away
from that shore, which means the water surface near the rocks is a
virtual mirror. I've found that fishing this shoreline (and ones
similar to it) is best when the wind and waves are not pounding it.
When the water is rough, the fish seem to either hold down tight
or move off into the deeper water. So if you can, pick a rock cluster
that is in the "calm."

As we have done before in our bass hunting, we slow down the
boat well away from our objective so that little or no wake tele-
graphs our approach. Bass are easily spooked by the noise of the
motor or the wake of the waves, so it is good policy to approach
quietly. Since we will be fishing the edge of the rock clusters, section by section, we can drop our anchor a bit to the side of the
rocks B and allow the boat to drift a little at a time, so that we
can be in the best position to cast to the rocks to try a variety of
lures and methods. Our working of the area will resemble the
approach we used on the midlake grass flats (page 63) and the
routine we followed on the deep side of the sharp point of land
(page 19), which, if you remember, had rock clusters a bit offshore from the actual point. Take a look at the diagram in Figure 42.

As we approach our anchor spot, we can try a few casts right
into the shallows off the point C. These first casts are good as start-
ers, just to get the range and the feel of the tackle.

Let's try a dozen casts with zigzagging plugs that float when
the line is relaxed. Why this type of plug? First of all, the only
food that would be found here would be minnows, sunfish, perch,
or other baitfish; no frogs, mice, or other small goodies. Second, a
deep-running plug would tend to snag readily, especially if retrieved
slowly.

Now we could have a good argument here. You might want to

try bass bugs. Why not? Well, I can't say that you wouldn't connect with a good fish, but I think that the bugs would be better here at twilight or even well after dark. Let's try the most obvious way first. After you take three good bass, can I say, "I told you so"?

Live bait? Now you are really on target. This kind of water is just perfect for live-bait fishing, but we won't stillfish it. Instead, we'll cast our minnows unweighted, with light spinning gear, retrieving very slowly. We'll also use yellow perch. If this doesn't work and more action is required, we'll use our black eel and the spoon decked with a trailing strip of pork rind. If we get no response from these, there just aren't any fish in this lake!

We are now resting over about ten or fifteen feet of water. The water shallows a bit between us and the center of the rock cluster B. Careful scrutiny of the rocks nearest us shows many big boulders underwater. We should work these first rather than cast beyond them to the exposed rocks and so disturb the area unnecessarily. Would you have done it this way, or would your eagerness have demanded that you cast to the rocks that are showing out of water?

Okay, we're rigged up. Your medium-weight spinning rod with the six-pound line has a hook tied to the end. Since we'll be casting short distances, you can impale the minnow by hooking it just ahead of the dorsal fin. Usually, for longer casts, we would hook the minnow through the lips to keep it from spinning. We can hook it as shown in Figure 43, since it will remain alive longer when hooked in this manner. When using a small perch, I quite often hook it through the base of the tail. This allows it to swim freely in between the rocks. Remember, no weights.

None of our casting will be for long distances; it isn't necessary if we can fish quietly and resist rattling the tackle, boxes, and oars in the boat.

Incidentally, few anglers do it, but have you ever used the

Figure 43. A minnow hooked through the back; used mainly for still-fishing or drifting.

bass-bug fly rod for this kind of bait fishing? I'll bet you haven't. Funny how stylized we become. Try it, just for kicks. We can each use two rods for this type of fishing anyway. Cast with your spinning rod, and after the bait settles down, set your drag and rig up your bass-bug leader with a single hook. No, you won't false-cast that live bait. You'll stand up in the boat, lead out about ten feet of line from the rod tip, and coil about twenty feet of line on the bottom of the boat or hold it in your hand if you like. Swing the rod gently and out she goes. Now you have two chances to connect. Both of your baits can remain in the spot where they land. The bait will wallow around enticingly. For variety, I'll pick out a dead shiner and hook it with two hooks and a BB-shot sinker ahead of it for casting and retrieving. I won't let my bait get the chance to settle into the bottom weeds. We'll see just what the bass prefer at this moment.

Nice day. Good to be out here away from the din of civilization. Hey. Look at your spinning rod! That tip is dancing, and no minnow can do that with it. No! Leave it alone. That bass is playing games with that minnow. There, he's taking it out. Strike him!

I'll reel in your fly rod. Glad I had my rig in the boat, out of the way at the moment.

He sure took that one down deep.

Now let's work something else. Sure, we could probably take more bass stillfishing, but just for the exercise let's rig up with two of the most deadly baitlike lures on the market and give this picture all we've got. You cast the black eel with your spinning rig and I'll try a spoon with a fluttery bit of imitation pork rind. If there are some big bass in here we can lug one home and throw back all the others.

Before we cast, let me work the boat a bit farther in for you. Cast that eel between the rock clusters D, E, F, let it drop down about two feet, and then raise the rod tip up and begin your retrieve in short jerks. If you feel the lure roughing along the bottom, speed up your retrieve a little. Remember, there is a legal limit for bass in this state, so keep only the ones that weigh over five pounds.

The accompanying diagram shows what the path of the eel should be throughout its course.

Now to let this area rest a bit, let's pay out about forty feet of anchor line and let the slight breeze sway us back and forth near the outer lip of the rock cluster. It's deeper here, and we can see some underwater grass below the boat, so we've got to keep our lures clear of it. Let's go artificial now, just to see what may happen by comparison. How about your using a jointed Pikey-Minnow perch imitation while I put on a sinking fore-and-aft spinner-plug.

Well, we've cast out a few times with no results. But I have found that if there is going to be any action at all from artificials under these conditions, casting the same lures time after time does not produce. From my saltwater experience I can recall that the fish will take or follow a specific lure for the first two or three casts and from then on become bored. You have to change lures constantly. Granted that we could continue to take bass here on live bait, either cast or stillfished, but we're not trying other methods for the fun of it—tempting luck, if you will. It is a good exercise for a bit of learning. So we change lures—colors, shapes, and actions—after the second cast. If we still get no response, we know that live bait is the only answer at this moment in this particular spot.

Before I leave an area like this, I fall back on one of my favorite lures and methods: the twin bucktails with the big fly rod that we used in fishing the sharp cove (page 30). I guess it comes from being a trout fisherman, but I like to fish this combination on bass too, and it seldom if ever fails me. There is just something about those two flies that will bring a big old bass up from his dreaming. It's a long cast to the farthest rocks I can reach, so I'll try three casts, and if I get no response we can call it quits for now and come back tonight, perhaps just as the sun is setting, and work with bass bugs. There, my first cast goes out. The flies landed with a slight plop. Strike! Almost immediately. Rock bass. Well, it's a fish, anyway!

When fishing a lake that contains both large- and smallmouth bass, your percentage of smallmouths will be bigger in the type of situation we're fishing now, since smallmouths tend to feed and

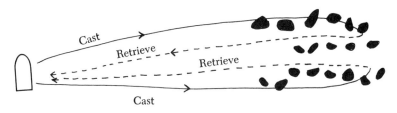

Figure 44. Two casts made with the black eel or plastic worm. The upper course is through the rocks, risking hang-ups. The lower retrieve is made right alongside the rocks. It is all worth the gamble.

live away from the muck and padded shoreline, preferring gravel and rocks. Although this reads like a very general statement, you'll find that it is quite measurable by experience. So, go loaded for some real action.

While this sort of bass ground is fishable at all hours of the day, on this lake I like to work it late at night, particularly in the mid- or late-summer season, since the activity from water skiers, boaters, and other people on the water becomes pretty intense during most of the daylight hours. Wakes, howling motors, swimmers, and boats using the rock clusters as centers of activity keep the bass down, or at least restrict the fishing for anything, even perch.

Still, this point has an advantage in that it limits the feeding activities of the bass to late night. After you get to know an area such as the one illustrated here (Figure 45), you'll find that many of the fish to be taken come from the deep channel just outside the clusters. It seems also that the bass come from the protected nearby shallows that are crowded with pads. In a similar lake where the bass are all largemouths, you will experience the switch of the bass from the pads to the cluster. While you'll get action in the pads during the day, for example, you'll get little action there at night, when switching to the rock cluster will give you a better response. Again, this is generalizing, but a point that can at least serve as a theoretical basis for the choice of water to be fished.

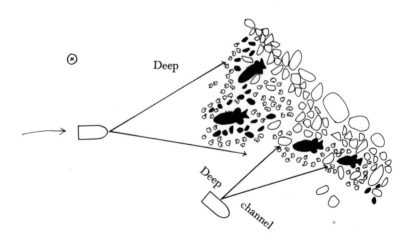

Figure 45. I'll leave it to you to plot a course here. That hunk of water between the marker and the shore should fill the fish-well if you fish right.

Since the bottom depth varies here, we cannot rule out the use of conventional top-surface lures, but basically, live bait, naturally presented, will really produce the big ones. They are out here for a big meal, and the cover of darkness makes them take well-fished baits, sometimes with abandon.

The preferred baits here are the hellgrammite, the crawfish, perch, and many species of minnow. There is sufficient grass and lakeweed underwater to provide havens for small fish and insect life, with plenty of caves and holes for the big fish to hide in and wait.

We can work out a variety of tackle tonight, and we've brought all of it for this trip. But we haven't loaded the boat with all the gear piled up in a bunch; we've spent the time at camp rigging up specific rods for specific uses in the dark, so that time we spend with tackle on board will be kept to a minimum. I have always believed that the time onshore is expendable but that those precious hours on the water are to be used only for fishing, not figuring or fussing. Our two fly rods are all set for bass bugs, or even large bucktails. The light spinning rods will handle small plugs and spoons, and these lures are in the top trays of our tackle boxes, ready for action. For the heavy live bait and bigger plugs and spoons we can use the baitcasting tackle, which is also available for trolling. All of our terminal items are placed in an orderly way, easily accessible in the dark so that we don't have to do any hunting.

Now, at the risk of becoming repetitious, we accent the careful and quiet approach, something that has become an obsession with me over the years, since I have found that such behavior is not only necessary for catching fish, but also more enjoyable. Approaching quietly is also nicer because it lets us "feel" our natural environment and soak up the scene in our being, and so become a part of nature. When I lived for many years in the big city, I'd drive on the broad highways at a nerve-wracking pace, but as the route to some favorite lake took me over smaller and smaller roads I'd have begun to calm down. By the time I got to the lake I'd have left all the nerves behind and begun to really enjoy just "being," for many hours not caring whether I took a fish or not.

As we approach, let's rig our tackle and have all the gear at hand, for a minimum of flashlight glare will be required if we are to take any decent bass.

Can you tie on a swivel in the dark, in case you need one as a replacement? Can't find the hole through which to push the nylon line? Simple. Place the swivel or snap on your tongue and then, by feel, stick the nylon where it belongs, in the hole. It's as simple as that. Actually, you'll be surprised (if you keep resisting the flashlight) how well you can see and feel in the dark. Even under a starless sky there is light, without any glow from a nearby town.

For our approach, we steam our way down the main channel of the lake. The rock cluster we spotted during the day (and fished a bit to explore it in advance of night fishing) is almost in the center of this arm of the lake. There is a pole with a flag on it to warn boaters of the treacherous shallows around the cluster. In high water, the rocks are not exposed. As of now, in mid-August, a few of the larger boulders break the water surface, and later in the season quite a number of them will be well exposed. For a diameter of about fifty yards from the pole, the cluster fans out gradually as the water becomes deeper, especially on the channel side (see Figure 45). The shallower side stays shallow for quite a distance until it reaches the shore of the lake, where it blends into a sandy beach at one end and muddy flats at the other. Since the pad flats can offer some fun, we'll approach the cluster from them, gradually working out to the rocks.

Technique? Lures? Always the big questions in bass hunting, and as I've stated many times, the choice is almost a blind one, based on past habits and personal choice. We could debate the technique and lures for an hour and not really come up with anything surefire. However, it will soon become evident that much more will be learned from an hour of trial, for what we discover will be exclusively for this specific time of this special night. A week from now, or last week, something else might be required.

So we begin with a slow-troll and casting combination. With this we should pick up a few fish or at least get some good action before we reach a hot-spot. You snap on a Jitterbug and I'll put on a plain floating-diving plug. Both can be slow-trolled as well as cast.

The motor is out now. We'll drift and I'll guide with the paddle, allowing my lure to move with the speed of the boat.

Quiet out here, isn't it? Let's listen while we fish and try and find out whether any bass are actively on the feed yet. They should be active by this time.

Try a few casts in there, toward the shallows and pads about seventy feet away. Let your plug sit for a few seconds and then begin the retrieve. I'll cast another plug behind you and do likewise, and we'll have three lures working.

No action, so let's move along. I'll cast my plug way behind the boat and you send yours out toward the shallows on an angle slightly ahead of the boat. As we move, they will move enticingly. Still no action, but the best is yet to come. We have practiced a combination of trolling and casting and have done it with ease out here in the dark, and that's important since it leads to teamwork. If you do this when you are fishing alone, you can cast two rods armed with floating plugs, one well ahead and the other well behind, so as to let one rest and "follow" slowly as you proceed on course, casting as you go with a variety of lures.

Hear that? Slurps. Bass on the feed.

The sounds seem to be coming from the inner edge of the cluster. Just to go against logic, make a cast on the other side of the boat, out in the deep, and see what happens. Ouch! How about that? That old boy is making a hoop out of your rod, but the most important part of the experience is that once you find feeding bass here, it means that others are out there in the deep, with their noses near the surface, cruising along toward the cluster. Set him good and hard just in case he's hooked lightly.

Okay, now let's proceed to working the cluster.

Two bass are active over there. One sounds big. Try for him with your Jitterbug after retrieving the trolled lure. I'll pick mine up too, for we'll be better off just casting from now on, without

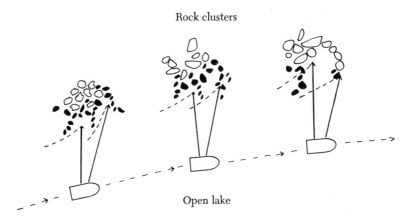

Figure 46. This diagram shows a pattern for a boat with two fishermen working along the shore. It is possible for them to both troll and cast at the same time. The broken lines show the cast lure trolled as the boat moves. A surface plug or bug is used for this purpose. The gentle motions of the boat will activate the lure when it is cast away from the shore, arousing any bass outside while the anglers concentrate on casting to the rocks on the shore.

any complications. I'll work the outside water and see if I can pick up another fish. We'll move along the cluster slowly.

We don't seem to be connecting, yet those bass are on the feed, albeit lightly. Perhaps they'll take something smaller than plugs. We'll switch to the fly rods and move in a bit closer. With no breeze, casting will be a cinch. Just remember that you can't see what you're doing, so get the feel of the cast in the air. I'll square the boat for you so you don't tend to angle your casts near me. Note how the line feels on the backcast, and try and keep it higher than usual so it won't come sailing by at a low angle and smack you (or me) in the pants or shoulder. Now that you're working well, I'll join you with some of the same medicine, and between us we should get some action.

Remember how this spot looked in daylight. Big boulders, deep holes, and paths through the grass. Don't get flustered, there are bass in here.

A slight breeze. That might help fish-wise, although it can offer casting problems. I'll move us about ten feet. There, now.

Something brushed my fly. I pricked him, but he switched to you. He caught you off guard with too much slack, but he hooked himself anyway. I'll pick up and ready the net.

Now that he's in the boat let me ask you, in all openness, whether you would have ever thought to bring bucktails and the fly rod for night fishing? In many years of bass angling I've never found anyone who went in for this sort of fishing, especially at night. Everyone seems to think that the surface plugs and bugs are all that is needed. For this instance on this night we discovered differently.

Now that we're in on the cluster, where the water is shallow, how about parking the boat and wading it? We can work through the cluster for about fifty yards before the water begins to deepen. Better to wade than invade with the boat.

After that, just before we quit for the night, we can rig up the baitcasting gear and deep-troll two chubs.

Well, we're approaching the dock and nothing much is happening. The lines are beginning to sink with the slackening speed, but wait—both lines are tightening. We're fast to two good fish! Imagine. All that activity around the rock cluster and rock ledges and there were two good ones just waiting for us at the dock. We don't dare make a cast for fear of further embarrassment. But you must admit, we've had a good night of it.

ONSHORE GRAVEL REEFS

Gravel beds, gravelly shores, and shallow and deep gravel beaches are found in most bass lakes; few lakes are purely boulder-strewn or, with the exception of Florida and some sections of the country, have nothing but pure sand bottoms.

Much fertile soil is found in the shoreline gravel, land grasses, and weeds that blend into the underwater growth that rings these lakes. In high water, the natural lake growth is covered, and the fish, both bait and game, slither in and out of the thicker shoreside growth for their food. When the water levels fall, the insects and the fish harbor in the slime and underwater growth. In extremely low water, below the usual depth at which there is any extensive growth, only a brownish slime is found.

The fishing in such lakes can be good at all levels, and except where the gravel is absolutely bare of some weed life, bass will be found in and around it most of the year, and especially at night.

The approach to a grass-and-gravel stretch of lake shore like this should be made with as much care as we have taken in the other situations we have been in. A variety of lures and casting angles such as those mentioned before are used to suit the conditions of the moment. The main point is to first fish the deeper parts of the shoreline, just outside the gravel bar or reef, and then slowly work your way into the shallows where the minnows play. Working along such a reef should be done by poling or paddling, never with the use of the motor. If possible, let yourself be drifted with the wind, lessening the work of guiding and keeping the boat moving and angled properly for casting.

A gravel reef that juts offshore is also a blessing to the shore-bound angler. He can fish it from many angles that are difficult or impossible for the boater. Since we have fished from a boat at our offshore rock clusters, let's work the gravel bar in the diagram (Figure 47) from the shore and see just how well we can cover all the possibilities from dawn to late at night, using all the tackle at our command.

Since our course leads to a boat landing site at point 1 on Figure 47, near the shelter of a grove of high hemlocks, we are immediately confronted by a deep, dropping beach of stones and gravel. As we can see from our high vantage point on the bank, the water becomes deep rather quickly, following the contour of the beach. However, as we look out toward the point of the gravel

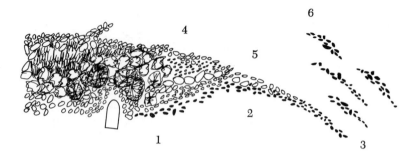

Figure 47. This point of land is fished from the shore. The reef extending out to the point is shallow for quite a distance out and filled with gravel and rocks, affording lots of casting locations. The text takes you through a typical bass-hunting expedition at such a location.

reef, we see that it shallows a bit on our side while remaining considerably shallower on the other side, where, at this season, with the water levels down about a foot below normal, gravel bars loom up from the deeper sections just enough to show us the pattern of the bottom.

Fortunately, the wind is momentarily "off" our side, and the surface is clear even from small ripples for quite some distance out from the reef. On the other, windward side, little waves are trying to accumulate some foam on the shoreline. There wouldn't be much sense in fishing the shallow, windswept side, so this morning we'll work the 1–2–3 side, hoping for a change of wind later. Tonight we'll have a good chance at the shallow side as we work again from the shore. It will be a pleasure to walk and wade instead of having to handle the boat, work the motor, and strain our arms with the paddle.

We'll wear boots. No need for waders, and besides, even at night waders can become too hot and heavy.

So here we are looking out over the expanse of blue water stretching out from our gravel beach. It is a full half mile to the other shore of the lake. There is no sign of life save a few minnows dribbling right on the shore, in and around the pebbles.

Shall we start by making a few casts with spoons, just to test any fish that might be there? Or shall we work some underwater plugs? Certainly fly-rod bucktails and streamers would be out of the question, as would surface plugs. Most of these rigs are better used at sundown. But for now what?

Live bait; you guessed it. We'll rig up with a slip sinker, as shown in the illustration (Figure 48) and also described in the

Appendix (*See* Appendix—The Merits of Bait-fishing). We'll just play the waiting game for a spell.

Later, if you become restless, you can cast a minnow with your soft spinning rod to keep active. It just might work!

We make our casts and wait. We hold sensitive fingers on the line so as to be able to feel the bait pull on the nylon through the sinker hole. We hope the cork will help keep the bait off the bottom and away from snags. And we pray that we don't get hung up. We anticipate that a bass—an old bronzeback, preferably—will come cruising by, pick up the bait in a lazy sort of way, and slowly but surely move out into the deeper water with it. We'll know the difference between the finning around of the live bait itself and a bass getting hold of it and taking off for parts unknown. It is interesting to conjure up visions of what is happening in a world into which we can only probe and never actually see.

Hey, that's just what's happening on your line. Look at it go. Something must have that bait for sure. Raise your rod tip slowly. Is that slight tension stopping him? No? Then wait about ten seconds and as he continues to draw out line and hit. Home run. A nice bass and he's off for the circuit run. Snub him! Set that hook. He may just have the fish sideways in his mouth without the hook being engaged yet. Now he's on for certain. Look at that jump and twist. Just like the magazine-cover illustrations. Keep that rod high now, with as much line as possible off the water. That's it.

You gave a fine show, but meanwhile, I goofed at my own stand. I became so intent on watching you that my own line has been spilling merrily off the reel, and I don't know how much line has gone out or what is pulling it. On my feet, with effort, I engage the bail of the reel and take up a bit of slack. Pressure comes from out there and I set hard. No action. Whatever it was has left the scene and my lead is lodged in the rocks. A few tugs and it comes free, but something is dragging with a slight struggle. Only a small rock bass.

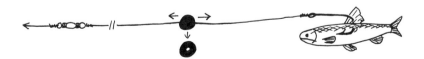

Figure 48.   The slip-sinker rig and the minnow entice a big bass through the grass.

Let's move out on the reef and try a bit of casting, now that you have at least had a taste of real action. We could stay here and probably kill a few bass, but I'm one for variety. On these trips it's my intent to try and expose you to the many variances of the water and the several ways of approaching and fishing a spot, so that when you meet the same situation on your own, you'll remember the thoroughness and purpose of every kind of move and decision necessary for you to connect with good luck.

Now back to the diagram in Figure 47. At 2 we can try casting our live bait near the shore as we walk along the gravel point to the end, where there is a deep drop-off. That's the place to try again with the slip-sinker rig. Fish often cruise back and forth out here, and unless some of the skiers and speeders come by, we should have some luck. While I'm waiting for action from my bait, I'll try for some white perch with a worm and cast as far out as my fly rod will pitch it.

Well, nothing happened to my live bait, but I caught three rock bass, one perch, and one catfish on the worm. They're all small enough to serve as trolling baits, so into the bait can they go, all except the rock bass, of course.

As we return to 1 we see a couple of boats approaching from downshore, apparently headed toward us and the reef. Let's watch them and see how they make out. They're slow-trolling. The first boat comes in close, about fifty yards from us, and we hail it. They have taken no fish and decide, after seeing our catch, to troll back and forth along the leeward side of the reef. They're trailing live bait on spoons, and within a half hour take three fish at just about the same distance from shore that we got ours on the slip-sinker-and-live-bait combination. They leave for lunch and, taking the hint, we find a soft bit of mossy old tree to lean against and munch on some sandwiches, washed down with some lakewater-fresh coffee.

It is a good day, with a light breeze on our side to hold back the mosquitoes, and it is cool and restful under these hemlocks. We watch two other boats troll by minus any action. They are evidently either too far out or not working deep enough, but we watch them without interrupting. Much can be learned in this way.

In the afternoon, the light from the sun glares at us and brandishes its rays into our eyes as it bounces off the water. We decide to take a look at the 4–5–6 side of the point and, since the wind has died down, the shallow side of the reef offers promise.

Beginning at a point inshore from 6, we wade out as far as

possible on the gravel bar, casting up and down the shore and also into the deeper water, throwing plugs, spoons, and even small spinning lures. But while we take a couple of rock bass and one pickerel, we draw a zero on bass. I even snap on a Jitterbug, but it gets no answer.

One trick left (if we are to fish this water at all successfully) is the streamer fly. With a slight headwind coming at us, it is a pretty problem to get the fly out very far, but on the third cast a walloping hit takes me off guard with a barrelful of slack on the water. It's a bass all right, and a good one. I'll retrieve. You try you streamer in the same spot and see if you can take him. Ah! That's the ticket.

After having those bass for supper, it's now after dark and we're back again, with a good feeling of steadiness from having fished the area in the daylight. We Jitterbug the deep side from 1 to 3 and get several halfhearted strikes but no fish. It is on the shallower side that we really connect.

Evidently the bass have gone into the shallows hungry. There seems to be a bass in about every ten feet of water, and taking them (or getting hits and misses) is fast action. Just for testing purposes we try the other, deeper side as we proceed, but nothing happens over there.

OFFSHORE GRAVEL REEFS

In this situation we have drawn the course of our trolling of an offshore gravel reef and its shallow and deep areas. In Figure 49, X's mark the spots where we either get good hits or actually land fish. Both the wind and the sun are from the direction of the arrow. Note that we take advantage of the shady side, little as it is, to run our lures. We fish the area at sundown and use a combination of casting and trolling.

Starting from a position outside, we troll down to 1, 2, and 3, close to the gravel bar. It is shallow water, about five feet deep at the most, with lots of underwater weeds. At 3 we are confronted with smaller gravel bars having deeper water between them, which calls for casting, as shown at 3, 4, 5, and 6. We troll through to the tip of the bar at 3 and turn out to retroll 2 and 1, ending our run. Our three fish are taken on a cast surface-diving plug at 3X. The second is taken from the bar at 5X, and the third on a troll just off the head of that bar, where we had previously cast over at 3. This

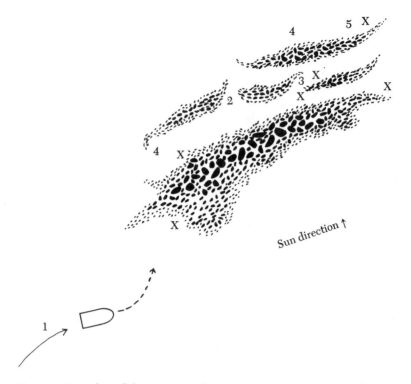

Figure 49. The offshore reef and bars—perfect water for trolling and casting, both day and night, although night is often preferred (see text).

fish takes a surface-diving plug with a perch finish. The other two take plugs I've painted black and white.

At night we take the same course, although we cast all along the 1–2–3 stretch rather than troll. We have hits throughout the area of the shallows, and take too many fish to register in a diagram. We fish slowly and carefully, resting the area thoroughly after each fish had been played and released.

Strangely enough, we take no fish by trolling or casting on the deep side of the reef this night, although I have records of many good fish being taken along this deep side late in the season when the water level was extremely low.

In this chapter we have fished a good deal of water under varying conditions. We could have fished it in many other ways, using other methods. Neither of us can say that we always did the right thing, or even that we did many wrong things. However, we did accomplish a great deal. We learned how to work together, to study the water and the conditions, and to use our boat and legs and gear and skill to the point at which we had a good time and took or connected with enough fish to tell us we were on the right track. And while what we discovered to be the right course of action was right for that moment, it was also a guide for the future.

12

MUD SHORELINE

We are looking out over some wonderful largemouth bass water. Mud shorelines are common to lakes that are not swept completely clean by ice-outs in the spring, a feature often encountered in lakes of the middle states and sometimes in the north. In these lakes, silt collects in shoreline pockets, a process that has been going on for perhaps thousands of years, unless washed out by sudden spring freshets or sudden melting of ice. The nearby forest holds the water drainage back, thereby producing a constant water level except in times of extreme drought. The gentle slope from the forest to the water is gradual and thickly covered by brush growth and grasses. The layer under the muck probably consists of gravel, some sand and, in New England or Pennsylvania, plenty of shale. Old trees and blown-in branches and leaves provide a constant supply of rotting material to add to the black ooze of the silt pockets. The resulting fertility of the shoreline contributes to an unbelievable ecology of plant, animal, and insect life. Most of the

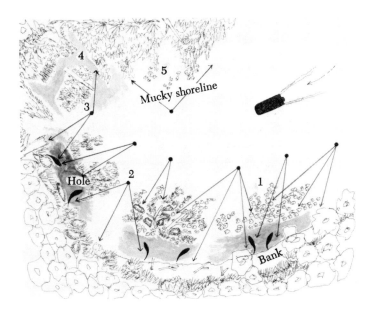

Figure 50. Mainly largemouth bass water, these mucky muddy shorelines afford hours of patient angling. You can always count on some bass being in here as residents. It is just a matter of getting to them quietly and making your casts count.

shoreline is also shallow, affording the denizens of the lake a quick warm-up in spring and gentle protection from the waves of the deeper, more exposed types of shoreline. The underwater weed growth is thick and, in the summer, often impenetrable. Turtles, frogs, flies, mice, and rats, and birds of all descriptions from the visiting heron to the nesting wood duck frequent this rich shoreline storehouse. The bass love the coves and intimate cut-ins created by the years of silt build-up, which provide natural and well-protected spawning areas for frogs and minnows, and they are constant predators of many other creatures in and around the lake, including small birds, mice, and rats. Most of the year, all day long and particularly at night, the bass are on the prowl, alert to the moves of the unwary.

Let's go after them. Although they are supplied with enough food to quell their appetites for a century, we know that they will strike at almost any lure we can throw and retrieve without a hang-up, if the conditions are at all working in our favor.

First, we must reach them. From where we are standing, we

can see a gentle curve to the shoreline. While it is possible to wade this kind of terrain and touchy bottom, it is really better to fish it from a boat either poled or paddled but not motored, since any wake will seriously disturb the entire area.

We can depend on the mud shallows throughout the summer months when other fishermen are about because none of them (and especially the average fisherman) will give such an area a first look, much less a fair try. Even the accurate caster, able to place his plug or bug to within a half inch of the target area, is going to have a short retrieve before getting hung-up or having to lift his lure off a snag.

So we proceed, using the diagram (Figure 50) for many examples of how to properly cast and retrieve our lures to the best advantage, and hoping that our hang-ups will be kept to a minimum.

Note that we have labeled the sections to be covered and that there are five that we have spotted as your "holes." These are not deep but are deeper than the inches-shallow muck and weeds; our bass will hole up in them with enough freedom to move about and pick up their food. But since we are going to count on the other characteristic of the bass—his cussedness and orneriness, and his delight in pouncing on a supposedly wounded prey—we fish with this in mind. We'll make him mad, not necessarily offer him a meal! Many of the bass caught in this kind of situation can be proved to be more than filled with food by examining their stomach contents. I've taken bass fifteen inches long with the tail of a hardly swallowed seven-inch perch still sticking out from the bass's mouth. It seems they're never satisfied.

At 1 we find grass and lily pads. The water is about a foot or two deep, and behind it the bank is seen to slope swiftly and abruptly down. On the very inside is water that is fairly clear, and the bass will rest in here under the shade during the day. Our surface plug with a weedless rig plops in under the overhang and sits quite still as the nylon line floats down. To keep from disturbing any fish in there (unless a bass has already struck!) we slowly raise the rod tip, bringing the line back up off the water and grass. A few turns of the reel tightens things up a bit and we begin the retrieve. Once it is in the clear at the outer edge of the grass we let the lure pause, for here, quite often, a bass will be found cruising along, just looking for a fight. Our last cast before moving on to 2 is made right into that corner where the grass and the snags meet around that hole. It would be surprising not to get a hit here.

Now to the next hole.

There are two approaches we can use for this. Actually, even though it appears to be more trouble, I like to work this area by easing the boat into that V where you cast into and work the previous grass flat over again while also casting into the hole. In all cases during this type of fishing be prepared for an instant strike from a bass, even before the line hits the water. They can be quick, even the heavier and sometimes well-fed old fatties. Pickerel also abound along these shores but usually take longer to hit, seldom smashing a plug the instant it hits the water in the manner of the bass. It is quite a thrill, if you have yet to experience it, when a bass smacks up the pads and belts that plug even before your line has fallen from the sky to the water. You'll find the bass in these confines unbelievably alert. Sometimes I think they sense something coming their way, even from the air, that to them must appear an unnatural phenomenon.

So we fish the hole. From our corner we can first work close to the boat, casting out toward the ring of grass, not into the bank. As usual, we work from the outside in, savoring the minutes until we make that cast to the real, diamond payoff. Our next angle would be from 2, with a final fling at the spot we just left and then into the actual backyard of the hole. There is a slight open slit on both sides of the grass point, possibly a channel, so when we are approaching 3 we angle some casts into it from below. Once we are at 3 it is a simple matter to work both sides of the grass. I'd pass up the muck shallow unless it is early in the summer. At that time there are a few open spots into which you can place a lure, hoping for that instant hit. But even then you're weeded up with only a few inches of retrieve and have to drag the mess back to the boat. Yet there are a few spots or places where the growth is thin enough to risk a throw even in the summer. The whole point of this fishing is the play for the instant hit. That's all you are there for. So many anglers pass up this type of water because "it can't be fished." They fail to see the merits of the cast itself, without any thought of a legitimate retrieve.

From here we proceed toward 4, with a pretty obvious lay for some nice casts into that channel, the first really open bit of water we've seen so far. It is enclosed by muck, grass, and pads but is deep enough for a retrieve with a floating-diving plug or even a light spinning spoon. If the fishing is done in midday, something that will cause a bigger fuss is recommended. Bucktails here would

be almost impractical, although they are staples in my tackle box
for a goodly number of conditions. However, all of the shoreline on
a lake such as this would be ideal for the bass bug, especially if
there is no wind and the angler does not mind getting hung up.

But do you know what we've missed? And it is surprising that
you or I didn't think of it. We have failed to work the open water
along the fringes of the weeds behind us and ahead of us when
moving into the clearer sections to take up our new positions.
Instead we have been concentrating on the inner shoreline, utterly
excluding this open water, which is bound to be almost as good
Of course it is fished by every angler, but if the day has seen no
others in the vicinity, it is at least wise to work it for a few casts.
On several instances I (or my partner) have taken fish here right
from the wake of the boat.

The next area, from 4 to 5, is thin muck, refuse, sparse grass,
and a few pads. It is ideal bugging water. A weedless bug is in
order, if there really is such a contraption. My design, as shown in
an earlier illustration (see Figure 40, page 116), is one of the best
I have yet been able to devise after quite a few years of trial and
error. Note that there are two wire hook protectors. These are bent
to fend off grass in front of the fly as it is retrieved. It may look like
something from outer space, but it works.

Ultralight spinning lures that have plastic tubing on the hooks
also work well here, provided you make fairly short casts and can
spot your open space with decent accuracy. These lures must be
retrieved relatively fast in order to keep them near the surface.
This requires standing up in the boat, holding the rod high, and
hoping. The only problems with these lures are that when a big
bass hits, the hooks are difficult to set into his maw, and when he
becomes snagged in the weeds you'll have to exert patience in
allowing him to swim out; your light line won't allow any horsing
or forcing.

I have seen these lures take scary bass merely because of their
speedy retrieve through a grassy area. There is something about
the motion of an escaping creature that triggers even the logiest of
bass. In fact, though, if it would be possible to sneak up on our
bass and get a look at him in his underwater lair, even in the comparatively clear grass beds, we'd see him ever alert to whatever is
moving about in the weeds, on the bottom or on the surface.

Much becomes obvious by now in your working of this type of
lake shore, particularly since we have, in previous chapters, encountered some fairly similar situations. Remember that many lakes

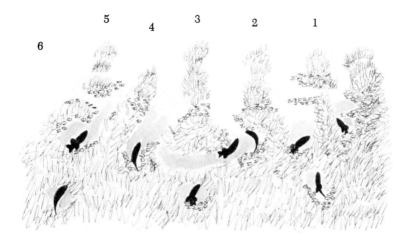

Figure 51. Another example of a muddy shoreline and grass. The indentations are the spots for concentration and spot-casting. This is excellent bass-bug and bucktail water, and good when fished at night.

will have much water of this type. You will be one of the few who will have the vision and patience to invade it. It is not easy fishing, but it will never be boring. It is for the patient and calm, not for those counting the minutes before heading home.

If you were to fly over this shoreline, you'd see many underwater indentations and variations along its edge. We'll fish these channels that some mysterious means has cut in the muck and ooze of the bottom, opening up the area for water circulation. It may be that nature is aware of the need for periodic and well-spaced drainage channels, even in a whole area that is under a shallow depth of water. Usually, grass hides these little "cuts," but the sharp eye of the bass and the bass fisherman discover them. These are, then, the "game trails" underwater that big fish use when they enter the shoreline in search of food, and in some instances, of cover from the rough wind-swept water, boat wakes, and other disturbances. They should be noticed and fished well.

From 1, with its inlet, we cast right into the open snakelike passages. The deeper water signified by the pads tells us that here is the potent spot for our first casts. Any bass entering the cut or leaving it will pass through the pads. Quite often bass wait at the mouth of such a cut to feed on the coming and going minnows, frogs, and large insects.

Point 2 is another example of the same thing, as is 3.

The situation at 4–5–6 is a little different. Evidently, long before the muck stage, the bank drop-off here went quite deep, and the area a bit out from it began to build up with silt and ooze, making the grass flat with its hole in the center. This is ideal forage for bass in that they have access to the hole from all sides and directions. Grass, such as here, as well as arrow-weed and other water plants usually indicates shallower water than is found around pads. On the other hand, there are plenty of areas with water at least six feet deep where pads grow but which are too deep for other plants and most grasses. This distinction helps you to determine the contour of the bottom and hence helps you to make the proper approach and presentation of your lures.

If you fish a lake with sharply contrasting muck and mud shorelines and broad expanses of beaches and gravelly shallows, your best bet will be in those areas. The barren water is good only in the morning and evening, for it services the bass that come in from the deep. Most bass found in the muddier shore areas are resident bass, fat and pesky to invaders. The cast that excites them to attack is as important to the angler as the lure that represents a type of food.

13

MAGIC ISLAND

There is something magical about an island, something that stirs the imagination, stimulates exploration, invites speculation and, in the case of the island shown here, that promises good bass fishing and at times good base catching.

I want to take you here for a real going-over of the entire area surrounding this bit of land in one of my favorite lakes in Maine.

We arrive in midsummer. The water level has fallen, as you can see, about two or three feet from where it was in the spring. During the winter and quite often until the end of April, the lake is frozen over.

I visited this lake one spring before the ice went out, for it contains, in addition to bass, some huge landlocked salmon and lake trout, not to mention some good-sized native brook trout.

I'll never forget being awakened one night during that visit by what sounded like thunder. I turned on the flashlight at the sound of the rumbling, wondering whether we were having an earth-

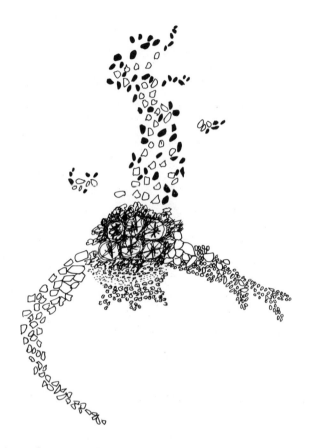

Figure 52. The magic island affords much good angling all season long. We fish the near side first (foreground) and then go to the deeper, back side for our exercise in angling.

quake, since thunderstorms had never before been experienced here that early in the year. Once on the porch I shivered in the low temperature, driven out there in the cold darkness by my curiosity.

Then I heard a C-R-A-A-C-K ! ! Then horrifying breaking, ripping sounds that were almost deafening. The vibration seemed to criss-cross the lake and then return again. Suddenly, comprehension dawned. I had read and heard of the strange, awesome sounds that ice creates when it is cracking up for the spring ice-out. In a very few days the lake would be clear and I'd be out there trolling for landlocks.

But now, several months later in the year, the lake is a clear blue under the softness of the summer sky. One would scarcely imagine the harshness of that Maine winter as we traverse the lake, bound for our summer bassing. The landlocks have gone deep, in company with the depth-loving lakers and brook trout that choose to remain down rather than ascend the rivers and creeks that run into the lake, several of which are fairly good-sized.

Smallmouths are the single bass species here. It is much too cold for largemouths. And even these bass were introduced to the lake, having been brought here some seventy-five years ago. The principal baitfish is the smelt. That's why the lake contains land-locks. But since the bass also feed on the smelt, we can use our tandem-hook salmon streamers for trolling, as well as double spin-ners with live bait. We can also cast big streamers and weighted bucktails. Stillfishing in the deep holes is effective with such bait, especially on a windy day, when casting is not only difficult but useless, since the shoreline of the lake usually becomes too rough.

On this, your first trip here, we are approaching the island from the 1 side first as we come up the shore. The morning sun is beating in on the lily pads and the little beach in the jaw of the island's cove. Note that the deep water to the left is similar to the shelf-type situation that we covered earlier. This island can serve us as a sort or review, since it contains many of the situations we have encountered earlier in this book.

Where you see the lilies, the lake shallows in gravel and coarse sand, deepening right next to the reef that extends to the left of the illustration. I've taken some fine bass from that little bit of deep run. It seems they like to come in there from the deeper water to either rest or feed. Approaching quietly now, having killed the motor, we pole right up to the first group of pads, and with the morning light at our backs we can see right into the water. Some minnows are dimpling the surface in the deep spot. Frogs are croak-ing. Flies and "darning needles" are in the air. Once in a while the trees wave a bit in the morning breeze, signifying the coming of a steady wind later on. We'd best get to our fishing quickly.

On our approach, we'll spincast the pads first, working them over with small surface plugs. The water is about two feet deep at its shallowest, offering good hiding water for bass. Again, I like my fore-and-aft spinner-plug with the perch finish for this situation. Your red-and-white surface floater will offer variety, and we'll see who connects first. Funny, this recalls a time when six of us were fishing here in Maine. The evening we arrived at the camp we set to work organizing our gear, and during the operations around the table, the conversation mounted on lure choice. So we decided to guinea-pig ourselves the next day, agreeing that each of us would use a different lure size, color, or type. This experiment went on for a week, and we found—as is always the case—that our presentation and manipulation were what produced results.

Rather than work into that deep run next to the rocks from the left (which would tend to drive any fish out into the deeper water), we'll cast a bit and then edge our way over to the right; then, changing to spinning lures that sink slowly, we'll work the point of gravel on the right side of the island.

Strangely enough, the pads aren't producing, so we'll cast a spinning lure, such as a small spoon, right along the gravel drop-off. Watch out. That cast went high in the air and you've got an excess of slack that's still streaming down from the sky. Get it in quick or your lure will settle much too deep. Learn to shoot those lures. If a bass ever hit that lure on impact, you'd hardly feel the hit and the cutting of the line. There. How about that? I'll drift you out into deeper water to play your first bass of the day. These northern smallmouths are a bit different than the bigmouths of your southern country, aren't they? Easy now, no horsing unless you want him to break you off.

I'll try to pick one up off that gravel bar.

No luck.

Let's try the trout flies. Bass seem to like them. We'll tie on some very light tandem-hook streamers (Figure 53) and shoot them into the deep cove water with the fly rod. It's as calm as a millpond in there. We'll approach carefully and quietly, for any fish can see us plain as day.

No. Don't put your fly right into the shore on the first cast. Work the edge of the drop-off first and fish into the deeper water later. That's it.

Now it's time for the long throw to the shore. Put it in right against the rocks.

There's a rise! He's on. Get that rod up and pressure him out of there, quick. What a jump! Smallmouths on a fly rod on a calm summer morning in Maine. What more could you want?

Ease him in now. Gosh, that fly is hooked only in his lip. Careful. I'll submerge the net and you guide him head-on, slowly, right into it. That's the ticket. Almost. He's circled out again, net-shy.

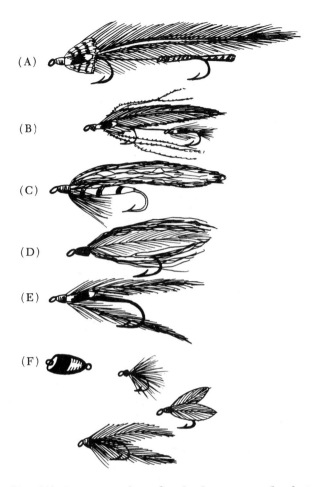

Figure 53. (A) Conventional tandem-hook streamer fly designed for landlocked salmon. (B) Smaller variety of tandem-hook streamer for trout and bass. (C) Weighted bucktail of conventional body size. (D) Bucktail-streamer combination, also weighted. (E) The split-wing, sparsely dressed streamer. (F) Popper diving plug with a choice of tandem teasers—either the bass bug, if the plug is to be fished on top, or the streamer, if the plug will be going far underwater.

Keep that slack line in your hand. Good; glad it was there. They make several dashes at the last moment like that; it's enough to drive you crazy. Okay, you can relax.

He'll look nice mounted in your office.

Here comes the breeze from behind us, headed right into the cove. That's good, because wait until you see what's on the other side of the island.

When there is little wind, I ordinarily fish either side of the two reefs until I get around the island to the hot-spot. The shore here drops gradually off into the deeper water. The bottom is gravel. We'll do some trolling here later, perhaps during the twilight hours.

I know you are anxiously eyeing the far end of the island, but we've got to try for a couple of good ones before we get there. As we proceed from the very tip of the reef on the right of the illustration, we head over some nice deep water. It is quite clear, and we can see the bottom about twenty feet below us. It is mostly gravel, with a few weeds and big exposed boulders. Out beyond, between here and the shore, the waters become even deeper and the really deep parts are good trolling territory. For now, however, we're going to throw some real long ones right into the shore and retrieve the lures slowly, letting them sink down deep and then retrieving them up again to the surface, right through any bass that might be tempted. Of course you may draw a strike from the rocks under those overhanging bushes. In fact you probably will, and on your first casts.

Boy, you put one right over home plate for a strike. You must have hit that old bit of bronze like a gong!

Up with the rod tip. Plenty of space to play him, so enjoy it, and I'll relax with a cigarette. Oooops, you lost him. You can't horse these Maine bronze backs, they come along at their own pace.

Try in there again, but farther along. You've got another. Don't be in such a hurry, your office is eight hundred miles from here and it doesn't matter too much if you don't make a sale on every cast; play this one easy and enjoy it. That's much better. Nice golden color in the net. Hard as a baseball, isn't he? More like a trout. And wait until you taste this guy. We'll have him for lunch if you like.

Now with that technique of shore casting and the deep retrieve, we can proceed to the billiard table of sunken boulders.

There it is just ahead, but instead of plowing directly into it, we'll skirt the edge and move around it at a good distance so we can try it first with a few spotcasts. Some really big ones hang out in there all season long. This is the one spot in the one lake where I've hoped to net a smallmouth over the five-pound mark but have never made it. Perhaps today. It seems as if they should go at least to ten pounds in here. Even during the August rush of speedboats they hold out. At night this is a real bass haven.

These spots between the big boulders are good. Notice the ample supply of weed patches in the water—perfect holding areas for baitfish and supply depots for the bass. A deep-running plug might hang-up here, so our choice is either a surface plug or a floating-diving wiggler. A true floater would be out, since the water is quite ruffled by the breeze. Try one or two casts if you like, but to save time I'd snap on a surface zigzagger. I'll square the boat to your casting angle. Don't try for the center of the cluster; sample the area like a wine connoisseur and savor every cast, working from the outside in. This often works on the fish that are near the outside, and can also draw a big one from way inside. If you were to cast well into the cluster right off the bat, the disturbance might kill your chances of picking up some really good fish.

That was a good hit and he meant it, but the barbs didn't connect.

Put your next cast between two of those sunken rocks. Let the plug float for a few seconds and pick up your slack. Now jiggle the plug by raising the rod tip ever so gently. No action? Begin your retrieve very slowly, and when the plug comes alongside another boulder slow it up a bit or even stop it. Now give it a twitch and retrieve quickly for about ten feet. That's it. That bass came from a boulder about fifty feet away. Any bass nearby had already been attracted. All they wanted to see was the object making away from them. You have to tease sometimes.

Stay with that technique while I put you in a different cluster of rocks. I'll pole here rather than paddle, for less disturbance. I'll bet you have fished with few anglers who do this. Most of them will rely on the motor, stopping and starting it, having forgotten that paddles and poles exist. There isn't one in a thousand bass fishermen that even carries a pole in his boat, and they wonder why they often come home fishless. A Maine guide is lazy; he's so used to poling that it seems like an effort to sit down, fuss with the motor, and pull the cord for a mere change of location. It may all be in the head, but pole or paddle quietly and you're bound for more action.

Let's put the bait to them. This is a great spot in which to experiment; we have enough bass in here to feed a mob. It's just a matter of enjoying it in as many ways as we can.

Rig up a slip-sinker rig and single hook. Now for a pair of big, juicy nightcrawlers. Ah, some really squiggly ones; the best kind.

Okay, throw the works out just short of that first big boulder;

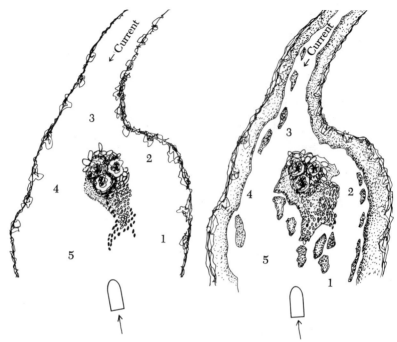

Figure 54. The island near the inlet is a real hot-spot for all kinds of fish, especially smallmouth bass if the lake is in a northern clime.

Note our course around the island and the casting and trolling moves. Work this island as many times as you can on an outing. You can learn much from returning to the same area at different times and under different conditions, including water-height conditions. You will then learn to vary your tactics and really discover the subtle changes that happen here.

Figure 55. The same island as in Figure 54, at low water. Starting at 1, we throw a couple of casts to the flats on the right shore and then concentrate on the island flats to the left. As we proceed toward 2, we work both shores, placing our lures right to the edges of the bars. At 3 we can work the entire circle of shoreline including the inlet. At 4 we can drift, possibly with live bait, and cast to both the shore and the island with the spare rod until we come to 5 and those lower flats.

you might even pick up a big trout. I'll put one between the rocks and our position and see who connects.

Remember that it's midday and bright even down deep. If you feel the line pull, let him run with the bait. Quite often smart bass will run a bit and drop the bait, unless they are very hungry. They will then pick it up again, mouth it, munch on it a bit, spit it out, and then suck it in again. Don't strike too soon or you will interrupt their savoring.

Whether it be at high (Figure 54) or low-water (Figure 55) conditions, one of the most potent areas of a lake is the inlet, especially if there is an island near the outflow.

During the high-water part of the season the current from the stream above carries with it baitfish and other small fish that drift down from the stream, along with aquatic insects. As the water warms up in the lake, the fish seek out that cool water from the stream.

Obviously, the current brushes by both sides of the island or reef, as the case may be, and also washes the shores on both sides of the outlet.

If the entering stream offers sufficient current, I like to fish this section above the island, starting well up from the actual lake and drifting down slowly, dragging with an anchor if necessary and making casts to both shores as far as I can reach with a spinning rod. I also point a number of casts to the upper tip of the island and work both shores of the island as I drift down. When well below the island where the water is generally deeper, I like to try live baitfishing as a rest from casting. I also know that it will produce good fish, especially along the edges of the rocks as shown in Figure 54.

At low water I follow the same routine, but since the water is much shallower or at least somewhat more shallow and there are sandbars and ledges exposed, as shown in Figure 55, I tend to try the shallow zigzag-type lures and in the morning and evening the surface poppers and surface running plugs, to avoid snags as well as attempt to draw the attention of big bass to the surface. At either water level, a good idea to start with is to troll slowly around the island. If two are aboard, one can cast to the shoreline while the slow trolling is going on. This gives more thorough coverage of the area.

If the wind is coming from down the lake and up toward the inlet, work in close to the top side of the island. If the wind is coming down the stream toward the island, work below the island along the gravel bars.

Subtle fishing, this style of live baiting. Worth practicing, for you'll use it when all else on the action side fails you. Few anglers care to slow down long enough for this. They prefer to wear their arms off casting, for it is fun to make good casts and there's a particular fascination in watching the lure as it travels back to the rod. But bait catches fish, and don't you forget it.

Troll through this stretch of bass hatchery in the golden hours of twilight, dragging tandem streamers. Come out here in the dark of night with bass bugs. Drag minnows and spinners 'round and 'round, over the shallows, through the deeps. Feast your eyes on the sky, the old dead pine monarchs that still hold out above the green second-growth spruce and fir. Come here in the early fall when the birches begin to turn. Try it in early summer when the goldeneyes parade their youngsters along the grassy shores. Get out early in the morning when the loons cry. Fish it on a gray day that is solemn, dreary, and cold. Try it on a muggy August afternoon when the winds are down and all is still enough to hear the cackling of geese upshore, or the conversations of the mallards up an inlet. Pick out a clear morning when you paddle or pole along the shore and watch a bear coming down for a drink. Select a foggy morning when earth and sky disappear in front of you until an old windfall comes into view, and beside it a doe with her fawn come to the waterside for a drink.

The unhurried, quiet approach fits into the mood of the wilderness; it is just as if you were the first and only person left on Earth and it is all yours. That's the big part of fishing: the feel of the water, the rocks, the snags, the scene. Action? Necessary, of course, and it will come to you as you learn, little by little, to become one with the picture.

Then back at camp, in front of the fire. A savored drink. Good companions who also caught fish that day. A tasty meal. That's bass fishing.

14

SHORE SNAGS

On lakes where the ice line breaks up the shore in the spring, there aren't likely to be many shoreline snags unless they are of the kind that go adrift in storms or are swept out by a high-water freshet and settle into rock clusters after being driven ashore by the wind. In lakes where there is no appreciable springtime ice break-up to scour the shoreline, however, snags are found to carying degrees, particularly along in-curves and indentations of the shore. Many lakes of this kind are shaded by overhanging big trees that fall into the water as they grow older or are killed by elevations of the water level. These are usually old monarchs that form the basis for lakeside detritus and driftwood. Quite often there is also a deep hole under the main log at such points: just the place a big bass would choose for his hangout.

It is just such a situation that we will fish now. We have picked one on a very popular bass lake—one that is heavily fished—our reason being the likelihood of a good bass inhabiting that hole. If so, how is this possible, with so many anglers "taking bass out of the lake"? Well, fortunately for us, most anglers don't take bass out of there but merely give the area a superficial flip or two with lures, not daring to penetrate the snag for fear of getting hung up. The angler of the other extreme will pound the living daylights out of the area, a process that we like to think is equally unrewarding, since overcasting can scare bass.

As you can see from our chapter-opening illustration, the two main trunks of this old tree spread out in a wide "V," with accessory branches almost weaving together amid the other underwater branches. It looks somewhat like a picture puzzle as we approach. It being mid-July, this snag has probably been cast at by every angler who has fished the lake this summer. But even if many bass have been taken from here, nature seems to stock it regularly, which means that the big bass must do a good bit of moving around in order to find a spot they can call their own. There is reason to take up residence here. Wherever old wood is found, there are insects, and insects to feed on the insects, and mice and birds and frogs and toads and turtles too. Minnows and other lake fish will also enjoy the snags and shade of the old tree, all making for a steady food supply for Mr. Bass.

If you fish this at the wrong time, when the "for rent" sign is up, you'll get skunked. However, give it a positive try anyhow, so that when you leave you can safely say that you believe that there were no fish there at the moment. Leave little possibility for guesswork. It is worth all the time you spend, not only in sharpening up your observation, but also in perfecting your casting and learning a bit about the lures to use.

The added attraction of fishing such a spot is that you are no longer hunting for a bass. Simply assume that he's in there, somewhere under that bunch of branches.

Now let's get down to the business of enticing him.

What would you throw in there? How must you approach such a snag?

Should we start with underwater lures, throwing them in there as closely as possible and then retrieving? Or should we start with a surface lure and bang right into the heart of the water? What about approaching, from a close-in angle and working well out from shore to do our casting? Would live bait, cast free of weights and corks, be a better solution and make the bass come out to us? How about small bucktails, cast as if we were fishing for trout in

Figure 56. This is a diagram of the snag pictured in the chapter-opening illustration. It is quite a place for bugging at night, twilight, or dawn. The moves seem obvious, but if you're eager to take your time and fish it patiently, you will see countless angles of presentation that will allow you to place your lure where it counts—way in there. At first it is a horrifying maze and you think you'll get hung up. But look at it quietly and you'll see the openings for casting. The bass symbols suggest good spots to drop a lure.

the snag of a stream? Or would bass bugs flipped in there delicately with an accurate arm do better?

Yes, there are lots of questions about fishing a spot like this. But now, in high summer, we can use all of these approaches if we like, and any one of them could work wonders.

Okay. How would you like to start?

How about a surface plug to the very edges of the rocks and snags?

We'll approach the snag from the right, since we've arrived near it from that angle. Now don't go throwing the lure right in close at first. Let's cast our plugs along the brushy shore to get the range and to tempt any fish that might just come out to us. We'll save the best for last.

We do this as a sort of test of the area. If there is a bass out there beyond the snag, or if we can attract one from way in yonder, so much the better. The chances are we won't but it is better to start this way. So let's use the diagram to fish this snag.

For the sake of orientation, the 1 area is upshore, the 2 area is the hot-spot, and 3 is the downside. We are starting out at position

1. Your spinning gear is in order. Use the medium-weight rod and a Jitterbug, Hula-Popper, or any surface floating-popping plug. The technique for onshore fishing is to put that plug as close in to the land or snag edge as possible, just as we have done in earlier situations, such as casting right to the edge of the lily pads. Logic has it that if there is a bass in there, he's there either because he's a resident, standing by for a baitfish or insect to float or skirt by him, or because he's just come in there scouting for trouble. So your first casts go right to the shore. If you don't get a strike instantly, leave the lure alone, gradually pick up the slack, gently move the lure, and let it stand still again. Then begin a series of pops back toward the boat. If the angle of the sun allows you to see into the water, you may spot a bass or other fish following the lure almost to the boat.

Since two of us are fishing, we can use different types of surface lures, just to offer the fish variety. I'll try a bucktail with the fly rod, but since the line disturbance will be more noticeable with the fly rod, I'll follow your casts.

Before we move on to the meat of the problem, we'll switch to underwater lures. You can cast a spoon and I'll work a small Colorado spinner. Even if all this fails, our prize fishing is still to come.

In approaching the main snag, it is best to move out from the area to a convenient casting distance. With little or no wind we can let the boat drift us to and fro in the general area. And with a wind coming down the lake, we can either make our casts as we drift by or we can anchor. In this instance, I prefer to anchor at point x, below the area marked on the diagram, since we'll be spending a bit of time here. We will then proceed to y and finally to z. Now all this may seem childishly simple, and it may (to the nervous angler bent on covering a lot of water) appear as if we could spend much too much time here. But let me ask you: What better kind of situation could you want? It is well worth the time spent.

That's pretty tricky water for bugging, so let's stick to the spinning rods for the present.

You take the first crack at it. Careful! If you overshoot, you've had it, so shoot the lure hard and stop it by snubbing the line to drop the lure directly down to the spot you select. I have indicated where to drop the lure by drawing in several bass in Figure 56. These, of course, are arbitrary and are merely shown to offer you a series of possible casts. Since no two snags are ever alike, there is no perfect way of planning how to go about fishing a spot like this. However, when you encounter similar situations, try and remember our deliberate routine, and you will find that you'll fish the snag much more thoroughly.

Because no two snag situations are ever alike, you must also simply go for broke and risk the hang-ups. The worst that can happen is that you will have to go in to save your lure and forget fishing the snag anymore on that day. Alternatively, you can fish your lure with a very light tippet that will be heavy enough to bring out a fish but will break if the lure is snagged. After losing some lures this way, you can boat in later and take up the collection!

Try the surface lures first, and as the underwater obstructions come into view you can decide whether it is possible to put a sinking or at least a floating-diving plug in there. Also remember not to retrieve too fast. I've constantly warned you against this in the book. Use the lure to its utmost in attractiveness. Realize and utilize its built-in possibilities.

In fact, one reason that there are so many plugs and lures available to fishermen is that fishing conditions vary from one minute to the next, and no set rules can be laid down to fit all circumstances. I can recall that when the lure manufacturers first began to demonstrate their products at the sportsmen's shows, the lures were pulled around and around in circular tanks to illustrate their action. This was not only a good sales gimmick, but also highly educational, for the customer could not only see the different colors and types of lure, but also, most importantly, could watch different lures go through their antics right before his eyes. And by slowing down or speeding up the rotation of a lure he could note at just what point its action was best.

I've found that the only way to get the most killing action from lures is to fish them at the speed that brings out the lust of the fish. We do not definitely know whether a fish strikes a lure from hunger, annoyance, or a subtle combination of both.

So study the diagram and fish this snag thoroughly, bearing in mind all the elements we have discussed here.

After a bass is hooked in such a situation it is yet another problem to get him out. Suppose you hook a bass in under a snag and he starts for cover. The only thing you can do is hope and yank back hard on the rod to keep him from diving in farther. Usually, keeping the rod tip up as high as possible will keep the line from fouling on lower snags. Also, since a bass in this situation will hit almost instantly when the lure touches the water, the stop cast is important because it leaves little slack to be taken up, letting you strike back quickly.

If you strike and pull back on the strike of the fish, you'll have a good chance of bringing him out before he gets any ideas of heading for an underwater snag. You're living dangerously, so be resigned to it; the excitement is worth it even if you lose every fish you hook in this type of problem.

Another and sometimes the only way of getting a strike from a bass and pulling him out of a snag hole is to cast a floating lure just outside the snag—aiming for a target area of less than five inches and not making the mistake of retrieving too fast. The trick is to leave the lure there for some time motionless. The bass will see it, don't worry about that. Just make him curious enough to venture out to it.

After casting the plug and letting it sit, retrieve it very slowly. You'll be surprised how many snags it will slip by. Mr. Bass considers the plugs as intruders, and so will come out to them. If you fish in this way, it won't be so necessary to risk penetrating the heavily snagged-up situations.

Remember also that the bass in this sort of situation is headed out toward the open water, just dying in wait for something to come by his nose. He's on a constant hair-trigger alert, which makes him doubly vulnerable. However, it is one thing to make him strike and quite another to creel him. Those first seconds are vital. You must move him out immediately.

I am sure you can recall many of the snag situations you have fished before angling here with me. I remember one that I came across while fishing the shoreline of one of my favorite New England lakes. Most of the shoreline is snagged, and it usually takes me a week to cover the half mile properly.

I was gliding along slowly in a canoe, trolling a surface-darting plug that would float when I stopped to cast to the shore with my other rod. I was casting small floating-spinning plugs and marveling at my accuracy. Spinning was new in this country then, and I was finding out that the experts' statement that "spinning was nowhere near as accurate a method as baitcasting" was pure tommyrot. I could bounce those plugs off rocks, tickle the edge of the sand or mud shore, flip one over a fallen log, or even drop one precariously over a branch without swinging back over the line. I'd then pull gently and the lures be on their way. I caught several bass that evening. It seems they were right in close to the shore or hiding under the snags.

Had I cast even three feet beyond the snags, or three feet short, they'd have paid no attention. Success seemed to hang on inches.

My canoe made it possible to glide by without disturbance. I love a canoe for this reason, and fishing alone is about as quiet a setting as one can have. The only ripples that went out from the sides of that little craft were made when I cast, or by the paddle when I gently stroked the water to push a bit farther along the way.

Right under those bent-down birches there once lived a big bass. I'd seen him and tried for him often. He would rise to a plug but miss it, and then snub any offering that day or the next. I took several anglers to the spot and they too were sloughed off by the old bronzeback.

One memorable day I approached him from the side, slipping the plug mere inches from the floating tree and the shore. I saw a swirl and quickly withdrew. Then I cast to him from the other side, putting the plug about a foot between him and the rocks. That did it. He's now mounted on my den wall. It takes billiard precison, a strong fish sense, and much luck to land a snag-hole bass after he's hooked!

These are the spots most anglers pass up, thank God. If it were not for the casual fisherman, we would never have any decent fishing. Long may they thrive.

And as if it weren't enough to warrant praise for getting them out of the snags, one of the worst and sometimes most exciting times with bass is when they, like pike, come up to the boat seemingly tired out and ready to give up, only to dash under the boat and hang you up in the snags that lie underneath. This little trick usually throws even the tried-and-true pro. But if he's fly fishing, he's got little slack line handy, while the spinfisherman, considering the bass to be almost licked, has steadily tightened his drag. Then it happens.

A bass did this to me only a few seasons ago at this exact spot. I'd tricked him into striking a weighted bucktail and he gave me the devil's own time, finally breaking out into the open for a fair fight. A few minutes later he came straight for the boat and I readied the net. My spinning rod was bent in the magazine-cover arc and I looked just grand there, holding it as if a photographer were aiming. But the bass kept going, right under the boat, heading for an old sunken snag that I knew was there. All of a sudden I turned into something clumsy and confused, trying to guide the rod tip around the stern of the boat and motor and catching the line on the gas-tank cap. I took an oar in one hand while still holding my pose and the bent rod and finally got the line free. The bass then decided that he'd double back, and under the boat he went again, this time toward the bow. That meant I had to stand up in the craft—a precarious maneuver at best—and heft my rig over my partner who, by this time, had taken the other oar and the net and put them well out of my flailing path. The only kick missing from this story is that the fish didn't wrap the line around the anchor rope or the old snag. The reason he didn't was that the anchor line was securely tied and stowed under the bow hood!

How that fish remained on the hook was a mystery. He fought valiantly, and I think I did too. We were both tired when it was over, and it was a question of which one of us really got taken. He pulled all the tricks. I knew the answers to some of them, the most important being to quickly relax the line when the fish went under the boat, so that he would stay deep rather than surface and become snagged in the propeller or rub the line on the rough edges of the boat bottom.

Yes, bass fishing is fun, even when the action becomes a bit grim. And its exploits are good for laughs for many years afterward. The fish and the spots they hide in are tucked into the crevices of memory, to be dug out once in a while and given air.

PART TWO

RESERVOIR BASS FISHING

15

IMPOUNDMENTS

So far in this book we have fished together in a number of quite varied situations found in all kinds and types of natural lakes. Many of these same situations are also found in reservoirs and other types of impoundments. But you'll note, as we go along, a difference in fishing impoundments that varies from slight to quite a bit, depending upon their age, size, the season, and the drainage or fillage schedules maintained on these bodies of water.

When we consider that the "natural" lake has been in its present form for perhaps hundreds, if not thousands of years, we can readily see that the biological and ecological set-up in these bodies of water, from the most minute form of life up to the final game fish, follows a generally steady picture, barring natural changes due to floods, fires, and other considerations such as gradual weather changes.

As a result, the food supply and fish population of a lake are likely to have maintained themselves normally, and the fish are likely to have become particular in the way they grow and act because of their heritage and forebears. It is quite often noticeable that bass of the same species and from the same lake can vary in shape, markings, weight per length, and especially feeding habits.

The lead-in streams and outlets are well established in a lake. Spring holes are steady suppliers of fresh, cool water, and the ecology around them has become equally well established. The plant growth around the edge of the lake and in the water itself is also part of the steady picture.

But the reservoir, particularly a new one, presents quite a different picture. The fish that are there may well be those that lived in the river or streams that formed the basin that man chose for a dam and an impoundment. In most cases, however, stream fish are not necessarily good survivors, nor do they thrive well in a new body of water. Moreover, after the reservoir has formed and a certain amount of the natural ecological background has been established, new species of both bait- and game fish can be introduced.

After a while, angler surveys are made to ascertain the size and condition of the new arrivals, and a report begins to take shape on the suitability of the reservoir for sustaining food- and game fish. As the reservoir "matures," the cycle of rise and fall of the fish population varies, from a quick increase in the numbers of small fish through a longer period of fewer but larger fish. This cycle can take as long as ten years to complete.

It is during this period that drastic changes take place in the reservoir. As the food ratio becomes established and the natural plant growth begins, the reservoir produces a great amount of food. Fish stocked in the water at this time grow big and strong very quickly. But eventually, the game-fish population reaches its peak, and a war develops between the potent and climax growth in the food supply and the fish population, whose appetite is insatiable. The result is shown in records of stunted fish, although for a while the fish population remains large.

The next phase is that of a sudden decline in the number of game fish, since they begin to feed more and more on their own kind. With unnatural losses from ill-timed drainage of the reservoir (especially during the spawning period), too much chemical poison control, oversilting, or what-not, the "good fishing" quality of the reservoir is rated low. There are still good fish in the reservoir, but they are fewer in number, although in some cases, and especially with the more delicate species such as trout, the fish completely

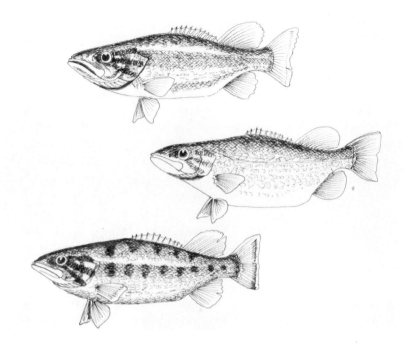

Figure 57.   Shown here are three bass, all smallmouths and all the same length. The drawings indicate just how much variation in the weight and strong features in the same species of bass there can be from one lake to another. The three fish were taken within fifty miles of each other, a week apart. Note that the top fish, taken from a lake where there are lots of medium-sized bass and few large ones, has a head that is large in proportion to the body. The body is slim and lacking in deep or characteristic perchlike bars. The second bass, fat and plump, was also taken from an open and natural lake. It weighed twice as much as the first bass, yet is of the same length. Note also a deeper coloration, although the typical bar marks of the smallmouth are lacking. The third fish, taken from a reservoir, is a compromise between the first two. Note the even development and normal lines, deep bar markings, and generally good appearance. All three fish were spawned the same year and were four years old when taken.

disappear. As an example, once the cisco herring or smelt are gone from a lake or reservoir, so go the landlocked salmon, despite the possible abundance of minnows, fall fish, or other coarse baitfish species.

Therefore, stocking and maintaining a "new" lake for top productivity is not an easy task for conservation departments, even when natural functions and water levels are not severely tampered with or changed abruptly. The problem is somewhat like the need for understanding the balance of nature that the aquarist faces with a home aquarium: there are very defined and unbreakable laws that must be followed; otherwise there can be and usually is trouble.

Anglers making reports of catches accurately and honestly can and do help the authorities maintain and even improve the fishing in a particular reservoir, provided, of course, that violent changes in water levels or "unseasonable" water-level variations do not occur. For after all, the first purpose in building an expensive dam to back up water over costly land is to save water, either for drinking or for power; sportfishing and recreation are secondary considerations.

In the past few years growing numbers of municipalities and private companies have become much more cooperative in letting the public fish their "private" waters and in allowing state fish and game authorities to operate within the framework of local policy. Additionally, with increasing angling pressures, powerful local, county, and state rod and gun clubs have prevailed upon the holders of large water impoundments to "let them in." As a result, and since the drinking water from them has to be filtered, chlorinated, and treated with chemicals anyhow, many water supplies have been opened to fishing. The recreational activity on a lake or reservoir does not interfere with the water quality, despite old wives' tales and rumors to the contrary. The time when people looked askance at boats and human activity on or even near a reservoir from which their drinking water was to come now outmoded, although such feeilngs still dominate the holders of the water supplies, particularly those owned by the public.

In cases where a lake has to be treated with various poisons in order to keep down weeds and the overgrowth of certain algae, conservation departments generally keep in close touch and work with water-company authorities to avoid killing off the natural ecology, which supports the game fish and the health of the lake itself. Even those solely interested in producing raw water, no matter what the purpose, have recently begun to understand the importance of this.

None of these problems or attitudes are involved in the case of power companies using a lake or reservoir for power or irrigation, such as the TVA Lakes, although with the steady demand on water by a growing population around the power circuits that feed local communities, this water is also used for human consumption. Yet at the same time, because of the nature of the structures and the need for security, public access limitations are still very high, and in some cases a lake or reservoir is not open to the public for any reason.

Often, the public itself, when invited to enter the private land of a water supply, is not as clean or respectful of such an allowance as it should be. Poachers are an added problem, as are vandals, and are treated as trespassers. Then there is also the matter of insurance. If a person is hurt or his property damaged on private lands, he can sue the owner for a large sum of money and in many cases collect it.

But times are changing, and many of the problems of today will be solved if and when man becomes interested sufficiently in his fellows. A few years ago, most if not all of the reservoirs for drinking water were not open to fishing, much less boating and other recreation. Today that picture has improved considerably and is getting better still as we progress. This means more good fishing for more people, especially those who live within the immediate areas of controlled lakes and reservoirs. Watersheds are also coming increasingly to the attention of their governing authorities, as well as sportsmen and conservation groups, thus bettering the flow of good clean water and, in many cases where auxiliary upstream dams are built, ensuring the flood-free, gradual downstream dispersal of run-off waters.

All of these developments are making it possible for the angler to have better fishing right near his home. I know of several reservoirs within a hundred miles of New York City, for example, where you can catch three-pound rainbow trout, five- and six-pound largemouth bass, and equally large smallmouths, pickerel, and a host of panfish species. It is better fishing than I have found in most wilderness lakes, yet the reservoirs are pounded very heavily all season long. Moreover, the streams between them, which are highways for the lake fish that travel back and forth at various seasons of the year, are also loaded with fish by seasonal stocking. Some of the biggest brown and lake trout seen or heard about have come from these reservoirs and streams.

The reservoirs themselves are very old, more than fifty years in some instances. Others farther up the line are of more recent vintage. They all feed into the huge pipe of water that supplies New York City and some of its suburbs with billions of gallons of water every day of the year. A very active conservation department operates on these reservoirs, in conjunction with the thousands of local sportsmen in the clubs under the jurisdiction of the Southern

New York Fish and Game Association. Sport is insured here for generations.

From the sportsman's point of view, the history of these bodies of water may be of interest and can serve as an example for municipalities yet to open their doors. The original owner of much of the land that comprises the New York City water supply was quite a fisherman, and when he deeded the property over to the city for this purpose, he included a clause that the lakes and streams opened to the fishermen of the state through individual permits, just so long as the privilege was not abused. To this day, the water company and the fishing public get along very well. There are no motors allowed on the reservoirs, and seasonal and other state laws must be obeyed at all times. A limited number of specific types of boats are permitted and must be off the water at the close of the season before the winter ice sets in. As a result, the fishing is fabulous and is a godsend to those locked up much of the time in the city. They can fish to their heart's content of an evening or for a weekend.

As I mentioned at the beginning of this chapter, the vast difference in fishing for these bass and other game fish from those in natural lakes can, when known and followed, help the angler to increase his totals and thus have more fun. Let's scan a few conditions, rather than situations, and mark some of the points to remember and the problems we'll meet in reservoir fishing.

16

SPRING:
HIGH WATER LEVELS

The accompanying illustration is typical of a northern lake-reservoir in the high-water season. Note that there are no rocks in evidence along the shoreline. The brush and seeds and trees are wetted at their feet by the water penetrating far into the weeds. The bass come into these areas under the cover of the brush to do their feeding and stay in them just as long as there is water to float in. At such times, fishing anywhere but in the brush will yield few if any strikes.

The important point here is to cast those small one-eighth- and one-quarter-ounce lures, surface plugs, and bugs right in under the trees to connect. You'll get hung up more times than you wish, but that evil is necessary when those fish are feeding so far into the brush. Let your floating lure sit still once it is in position for a few seconds, and then pop it gently. In the case of a spinning spoon or small plug, it is best to begin the retrieve almost before the lure hits the water, since it may snag on an underwater bit of brush. Fishing under these conditions demands hairsplitting accuracy but will pay dividends. Some of the biggest fish in the lake will show themselves up in that brush. However, when the level descends, that's the last you'll see of them, except possibly at night.

While no definite or never-changing rules of water levels in relation to season can be set down, there is the usual pattern of high levels in the spring no matter what the climate belt of a reservoir. Take, for instance, the reservoirs, mentioned in the last chapter, of the New York Department of Water Supply. Most of these gain their run-off water from high hills and the Catskill Mountains of central New York State. The ice break-up on the lakes takes place in March, and in April the run-off comes down from the mountains. During winter, lakes have been at a low stage because of drain-off and freeze-up. When spring comes, the water levels rise from a low or medium-low to a level that usually goes over the banks no matter how much is drained off for use at the other end of the pipe. All of this happens while a natural flow is maintained below the dam for the outlet stream to survive and maintain itself. This means that the brush and grass of the "shoreline" is sometimes covered with several feet of water. The fish come into this area to feed, and it is here that good catches are made long before the spawning period. And while this is of only academic interest where the bass season does not begin until July, it is of theoretical concern here in order to understand the year's cycle.

In May, when the bass spawn, the reservoir has returned to a "full normal" level and, barring an extended spring dry season (or sudden freshets from the feeder streams), it maintains a good level during the spawning period, a blessing to the bass. This is what can be considered as a general "high" period. With luck, the shoreline water is not disturbed until summer, after the bass fry have had the chance to grow big enough to care for themselves and, when necessary, follow the water level down as it gradually leaves their parental home.

But while the taking of bass early in the year is illegal, unlike fishing for panfish and trout, there are many fishermen who angle for bass with barbless hooks and return their catches. There are also the poachers.

With still good luck and a normal early summer rainfall, the reservoir can remain at its high level during June and July. During these months the bass fishing and panfishing is excellent, and has, as we have said, been far better than I have found in many natural lakes of the same locality. Many shoreline snags abound along the edges of the reservoir, in which fish can hide. Muddy sections, gravel bars, and rocky and bouldered shores offer the angler literally hundreds of hot-spots in which to fish either from the shore or from a boat. Night fishing will really come into its own as the season progresses.

Because there is plenty of forage, the techniques to be used in a reservoir are a bit more sophisticated than those in a lake. Since the bass are not over hungry beyond the demands of their everyday needs, they are not susceptible to artificial lures but seem to prefer bait, either cast, drifted, or on a weightless leader in fairly shallow water, fished not too far from shore.

It might be well to mention here that very deep reservoirs can present a delusion to the angler. It is quite useless to troll in water that is more than thirty feet deep, since bass do not go down any farther. Most reservoirs are hollowed out, with quite steep sides particularly near the dam, and even the best spots can be handled conveniently from the shore. Of course bass also frequent the center waters of the reservoir, but only at a depth that is conducive to their liking with regard to temperature.

It is often quite a sight to see bass feeding on the surface way out in the middle of a reservoir at sundown; one would think that they would be heading for the shoreline, where the best and most food is to be found. A hatch of flies, such as the big mayflies, will sometimes cause them to surface out there, or a passing school of small white perch will also draw them to the center. But by and large, the edges of a reservoir are the places to fish, casting to the shore and fishing deep right along the bottom as it approaches the correct temperature depth.

The moment the water levels begin to fall the picture changes. Trolling is then done farther out from the normal shoreline, and it will take longer casts to hit the desired deeps, where a rocky bottom supplies the bass feedbag. Islands are also excellent possibilities.

Good bass fishing will also be found where the water has penetrated into coves and over flat and marshy lands among the main shoreline. With lily pads and grasses beginning to grow into mid-season maturity alongside these onshore feeding havens, the fish congregate in them and can be lured with artificials cast well into the tangles of growth and underbrush. It is tough, hang-up type

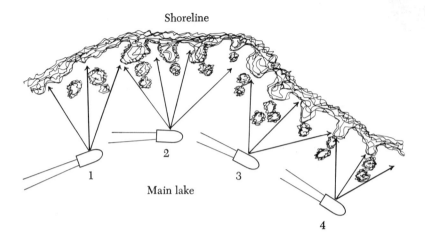

Figure 58. This diagram, in which the water is at its high level along the shore, shows you how to mix trolling with casting. Remembering that casts must go well into the brush, the trolling is done as close as possible to the shore. Four rods are needed, for when you stop to cast, the one-quarter to one-half-ounce trolled lures of the floating type will remain on the water behind you. Then, when you stop, you take up the casting rods and go to work. In the approach to (1), note the trolled lines lying behind the boat. Three casting spots are indicated. Trolling continues as you proceed to point (2) and cast both behind and in front of the boat with the boat quite near the shore. Trolling to (3) you have a half-circle of good shoreline to target into with your casts. Troll again to (4) and cast to the point of land.

Later, when the water is at midlevel, you can work this shoreline either from the boat or by walking along the edge. At the very low dry-season level, you'll have much easier times, but the fishing will be largely at night.

of territory and a general headache for the angler, but working it properly can be quite rewarding. Trolling and casting in and around the shoreline rocks and underwater boulders half hidden in the land grass and pond grasses is good too. The deep water can be skipped until later, except for baiting and deep trolling.

In the late spring, many bass like to go down the lake outlets and up the main inlets to the lake in June and July. They travel here as much to follow the baitfish as they do to seek out future fresh and cooler water. Brush-choked feeder streams where the water levels are still high offer tempting spots for bass to "lair up"; casting a fly-rod bug or a brace of bucktails can score under these conditions.

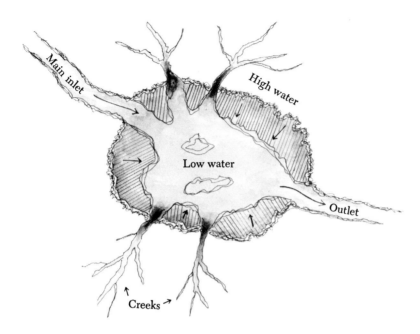

Figure 59. Typical high- and low-water reservoir boundaries.

This high water often carries with it a cloudy condition, since much sediment and earth is dislodged from the shoreline in the spring; more so if the reservoir is a new one with much silt run-off. Much of the water coming down pipelines from lakes and streams in the reservoir drainage area above also carries its share of silt, clay, and mud, and it takes quite a while for this material to precipitate to the bottom of the reservoir. To a certain degree, silt is a help to the ecological factors making up the well-balanced reservoir. However, too much, especially during the spawning season, can be a hindrance to the young fry that are being hatched and cared for. The cloudy conditions are also no help to the angler; he must remember that bass cannot see any farther in the haze than he can, and so should make more casts over a given spot than would be required under more clear conditions. Because of the cloudiness of the water, the bass is not as particular as later in the season; he seems to take it for granted that your lure is something to eat and so makes a pass at it.

Since the water level penetrates the shoreline, or at least meets the natural high-water mark of the shore, much food in the form of blown-in insects, frogs, snakes, turtles, and other small aquatic life-forms feed the bass. This argues for the use of a myriad of artificial lures cast right into the shoreline brush, rocks, and dead-wood snags. Even in the bright light of day, the bass will be in there, laired up as well as just visiting to gather their meals.

Add now the fry from sunfish, crappie, bluegills, perch, bass, and a host of fall fish as well as minnows and other coarse fish, and you can see that the pantry is filled with goodies, a potent reason why your bass is not always prone to grab at your lure the instant it hits the water. The combination of good food, high water conditions, and cool temperatures argues for good fishing, and it must be emphasized that your time will be wasted unless your lures are placed right in the midst of the natural food supply.

During June and early July the parent bass continue to hang around the nesting areas, where their offspring linger in the weeds and growth near the nest holes. They still maintain a feeling of guardianship over the nest as their home, and consequently will strike with abandon *only in these areas*. This condition will extend into August, again depending on the steadiness of the water level.

Sudden summer rains will wash in much food all along the reservoir shore, and it is the fortunate angler who can be out after a long and hard night's rain, particularly where little creeks draining into the reservoir temporarily rush with excess water. Good feeding locations for the bass and good fishing spots should be worked with live bait, particularly angleworms.

It is a good time of the year to be about, and one can be thankful that water skiers and other boaters with their fast motors and speeding wakes will not invade the premises. The only ones about are those dedicated to the same quiet approach to angling. One can feel quite alone on a "fishing only" reservoir. It has the quality of a wilderness lake and should be respected and the laws of trespass obeyed, lest the privilege be taken away. A fishing trip on an "open" lake will immediately reveal the vast difference. There is a delightful peace to a body of water that is neither shattered by the roar of racing motors nor sliced by disturbing wakes.

17

DESCENDING
WATER LEVELS

At low water the island shown here looks quite unnatural, poked up on its mound of gravel. Interestingly enough, there is a spring on the island that gives water during dry periods.

I have beached my boat on the island at night and have preferred to cast from shore, particularly on a night when there was no breeze to hide the wake and action of my boat. I have taken most of my fish at the hot-spot just on the far side of a line you can imagine drawn from the island to the shore.

Those not accustomed to seeing such an extreme change in water level as shown here may find this unsettling. It is also a shock to the bass, which is why an understanding of the lake's conditions is a must if we are to catch bass, especially at low water levels. During the early season and again in the fall, the level is up and the water penetrates into the island, under the brushline right along the rocks. The normal water line gives good fishing, since the rocks and shoreline are still near the overhang.

Summer spells added drainage by a city on a reservoir's water supply. There is also less water coming down the pipes from the chain lakes and streams above. Phase 2 is about to take place, and the complexion and mood of the ecological balance are about to go into a descending level in terms of both water and food supply, with a consequent reaction by the bass. The fish, sensing the change and actually realizing it, pick up and move out of the very shallow and mucky waters to which the water level formerly allowed them access. They are now in the "real lake," not the flooded land areas, and with their departure the pond and lake grasses and plants that are growing in profusion, as well as the minnows and other underwater life including crawfish and a host of insect nymphs and larvae, can now fortunately develop in their natural conditions to maturity.

The bass fry and little fish that have been spawned follow the descending water levels and find new homes and food supplies in the sands, muck holes, and gravel at the bottom of the reservoir. The bass locate new lairs and feeding strips near big boulders, holes in and around old stone walls, rock piles, and other man-made heaps of rubble that were left when the lake was first filled. These locations, particularly old square stone barn and house foundations, old roadbeds, and other abandoned sites now harbor the biggest bass. Knowing these locations from a map of the area printed before the reservoir was created can be of great help. Out in the two-hundred-foot level, however, there is no food—which is why deep trolling below thirty feet for bass is a waste of time; few minnows ever dive below fifteen feet, and the bass should therefore be trolled or baitfished at somewhere near this depth. The most obvious place to do this would be near the bottom, and usually close to the shoreline, unless the map shows definite shallow underwater ridges in the main body of the lake.

The hot-spots to fish will be found where there were streams and drainages into the small body of water that was once the only water in the valley, but again only if these are not down too deep. Even without a map one can easily see many of these contours begin to appear as the descending water level gradually reveals them. As the level falls, natural land grasses grow to the edge of the water, mixed with pondweeds that are seasonally left in mud or shallow water. These harbor insects and offer fodder for all forms of wildlife. The bass stay close to these locations and find a readily available food supply (particularly at night) in crawfish, grubs, and worms. Here too are old tree trunks and snags that have fallen in and become waterlogged. With the falling water level these once again become exposed to the air and can be identified as having been there for several seasons because of their silver-gray color. It is under, in, and around them that bass hide. They are the spots for properly cast surface lures. Where the waters are shallow and many snags are to be seen, trolling is it.

It is best to fish these snags as always when the wind is blowing away from the shore, leaving a vacuum of air and a minimum of woves, for, as you remember from our earlier situations, bass will not be active in roiled up water, particularly when it is shallow. Early-morning and late-evening, and, of course, late-night angling is excellent here at this time of year. Break out the small surface-disturbing popping and popping-and-diving plugs, and the bass bugs.

Generally the clarity of the water is better at this time, arguing for the use of more specific colors of plugs and spoons. Although it might be an arbitrary choice, I prefer natural-colored plugs with fishlike markings such as those with perch finishes rather than the bold-colored, conventional red-head and white-body types. The bass can see for a greater distance, their food supply is still generous, and they are not yet voraciously hungry, as they will be when the water levels really fall later on. This also calls for more care in casting and more caution in boat handing. Bass-bug fishing can now begin to come into its own at twilight and at night, especially as moths and larger insects abound.

At almost any given location along the shore you can start out blind and try several types of lures until you find the one that connects. Live bait is the ticket in the shore-side deeps and particularly near rocky shores that promise rocky, craggy bottoms. The bass are in the peculiar mood that comes from having much food to choose from and are seemingly interested in almost anything that moves. But while they cannot resist killing a bait, their stuffed stomachs discourage the actual swallowing of the food itself. I find that an actively retrieved plug or spoon or, quite possibly, a spinner and live minnow or worm rig, will often take their attention and make them strike merely to kill. When they're in this state, the mere grab will hook them before they decide to spit out the food.

It is not necessary to use a boat at this time of the year. With the water level down about five or six feet, there is ample shoreline that has become solid enough to wade or walk. Of course, there will be muddy and silty pockets, and you have to be careful lest you fall into a kind of quicksand—a point that requires that you do not fish at night over this kind of territory. It is quite okay to work during daytime the shore that you expect to fish that night, but do not go into strange reservoir shorelines at night unless you know where you are headed.

When fishing from the shore, you can cast in a wide arc and, especially in a cove and using a bobber in the shallower sections, work a live bait (*see* Appendix: Basic Bait-Fishing Techniques) well out beyond any creek or spring that may lead into the cove. Quite often it is possible to wade out for some distance on a point or a gravel or sand bar and work the deeps that extend from it. This sort of area is perfect for night casting of surface plugs or fly-rod bugs.

With the water steadily descending, the bass become less and less dependent on land foods. They must now feed almost exclusively on the food and baitfish that actually live and breed in the water. With the middle and late summer at hand, the pondweeds and grasses in the gullies of gravel and mud that both contour the bottom of the reservoir and lie near the shore have grown up to contain minnows. There is little cover from trees during the day, and no shade. The water temperature is higher. The bass hole up in the deep more often now, and a live bait is best drifted weight-free over the deepest parts of the drop-offs, but again not below the thirty- or forty-foot mark. The midlake spring holes are now hot-spots for daytime angling. Only at night will the shoreline offer up its best prizes, and it must be worked from the shore rather than from a boat, since many of the shallows prohibit entrance to the inner coves. But remember, take caution in wading "new" shorelines.

This is bass-bug time, and surface popping lures are best cast at night when there is no moon. Hazy, muggy evenings when there is absolutely no breeze produce magic. You can stand still and listen for rises of feeding fish down the shore. When they are heard and seen they should be targeted, for it is really more fun to cast over feeding fish than to merely cast vaguely all night long; it has the element of the hunt in it, and the rewards are often greater.

When the water levels become very low, the bass have less territory in the reservoir in which to wander. Generally the bottom contour toward the middle is flatter than it is along the banks, which also leaves fewer lairs for the bass. Now they have only the choice of the spring holes, a few old stone walls, or piles of rubble and stones in which to hide during the day. At night they are forced to feed over the flats and in the gullies in between. During the day they just seem to sleep it out. With less space and the same number of bass, more pressure is on the natural food supply, and the fish hunt more usual. This augurs well for the alert night fisherman. The water is anything but clear, so trolling of artificials is not usually recommended.

Night fishing is it if you want to hook really big bass, and many of the biggest ones will be congregated over a smaller area of the reservoir. Fish for them near the deepest parts, within the forty-foot level. About the only place where there might be good daytime angling is in the inlet, if any amount of cool water is coming through. With water levels approaching the low of the season, the least amount of rain will stir things up, and at those times it is best to be about, preferably fishing from shore. One prize lure for this work is the eel or large plastic worm, dragged over the gravel slowly. It is the ace killer when all else fails.

18

LOW WATER LEVELS

Late season is the lean time for the reservoir and its inhabitants. The level can be at its very lowest. In fact, without recent rain and with a prolonged dry season at hand, the reservoir is bared over most of its acreage. This condition kills much of the natural weed growth and insect life that has been unable to follow the water level down as it descends. This is a good research time for the angler, however, for he can now learn the secrets of the bottom contours and see just where the springs and deepest spots are located. The drainage lines, established when the area was merely a small stream, now exhibit those contours, to be remembered when the water levels become higher. Trolling over them will be more productive than merely dragging lures across the reservoir without any knowledge of what is underneath.

As for fishing, remember that at this extreme low any change is noticed by the bass and is more dramatic.

A good rain brings relief. As the fall rains begin high up in the mountains, the portals leading into the reservoir carry in life-giving water. The baitfish, general ecology, and bass come back to life. The air temperatures are cooler for a greater length of time from morning to twilight, and the nights are almost cold, causing the water temperature to gradually decrease. The bass no longer need search out the deep spots to keep cool. As the waters begin to rise a bit, shore casting again comes into its own. During the day, live-bait fishing can be productive over the deeper sections.

But do not forget that the city is hungry for water, and while there will be natural rise in the water level from the storms, there will be an artificial and unforewarned drainage by the city. With so much water coming in and going out, the natural condition of the reservoir is upset. Experiment. Notice the shorelines. If the water has even been falling ever so little, the fishing will not be as good there. If it is rising, the chances are that the bass will tend to be active right on shore, particularly at night. As the levels gradually begin to rise, things get better all around, and fishing returns to its theoretical "good."

19

RISING FALL
LEVELS

It is now late summer or early fall. Rains are coming more often and heavier, both locally and high up in the mountains. The water levels begin to rise, offsetting the drainage by the city. Bared stretches of sand, gravel, and cracked mud are gradually being covered with a fresh supply of water. Life begins to come into the reservoir and refreshes its inhabitants. Fishing can be more productive in all its forms now: trolling, still- and baitfishing, plug and lure casting, bugging, and in the inlets, even fly fishing with big bushy dry flies.

This last type of fishing is excellent where a good river enters the reservoir. The bass congregate at the mouth and ascend as far as they can for a breath of cool water and some insect diet as a relief from the drab days of the low-water season. Besides the big dry flies, now is also the time for braces of gaudy and fluffy wet flies, and of course my favorite streamers, two at a time. Night fishing along the shore and especially in the newly flooded gullies would be my choice.

When the reservoir is again about half full, the lower temperatures and clarity of the water are exhilarating to the bass, and they increasingly tend to hug the shoreline since much food abounds there. Later, as the level of the water returns to the edge of the reservoir, fishing can be good near overhanging trees and old snags. The reservoir is almost back to the normal level that we experienced in spring and early summer.

The bass now take up lairs in the snags, and from now until the cold of fall, the fishing will approximate that in a natural lake. Live-bait fishing, particularly drift fishing in about twenty feet of water in a gully previously spotted during the day, can yield a good mess of fish for a quick supper. It will not be necessary to spend the night out there. One need only work a few hours in the late morning or early twilight in order to connect.

It is also a beautiful time for the angler. The foliage is turning into its fall dress. The air has a cleanness and a crispness—a welcome relief from the murky and humid days and nights of summer. The mornings are often chilly, as are the sundowns. There's not much time left for this season.

More or less the same conditions as we've just discussed hold in the reservoirs used as power sources. The only difference is the day-to-day drainage for power, which remains a constant flow except for a slight period during summer, when plant production and electrical needs are less. Because the water levels do not fluctuate from drainage as much as they do in the water-supply lakes—unless there is a serious drought—power-supply reservoirs approximate natural lakes even more than do drinking-water reservoirs.

Quite often, motor boating is allowed on power-supply reservoirs within certain confines and away from equipment and drainage areas, and many more fishermen pound them. As a result, there is not the quiet that is found on the drinking-water reservoirs. However, as elsewhere, this overfishing is a boon to the angler bent on catching fewer but bigger bass. The chances are that he will achieve this by deep baitfishing and deep trolling, saving the casting to be done when the vacationers have left for the day. And he'll get his big ones on live bait even at night.

The power impoundment, then, as opposed to the drinking-water reservoir, is becoming of prime recreational value to communities. Much local revenue comes from those who travel sometimes hundreds of miles to these bodies of water for boating and fishing. The TVA lakes and such impoundments as Lake Mead in Arizona are among the best examples of such reservoirs, and the future seems to point to many more. In such locations, the auxiliary dams and their smaller lakes way up the feeder streams also attract recreationists.

Yet while every new impoundment has offered a hundred times more recreational facilities and better fishing for a greater number of enthusiasts than was available before its creation, every dam that has ever gone up has, in the record, had a history of fierce and frantic opposition from sportsmen's groups and nature-loving associations that want things to remain *status quo*. It is attacked by the very ones who will prosper from it, including the local citizenry. And while it true that it would be nice to keep nature as it is, we must begin to realize that our very presence on the earth imposes changes in nature that, in this case and considering the greatest number of people, are for the better.

Way up in mountains where logging and other operations are going on and rising waters flood the woods, you will find the deadwater backflow and its characteristic dead trees. The first dam builders, the beavers, have been experts at this for centuries: behind every beaver dam is an area of brownish stumps and trees that are dying or dead. You can spot a beaver pond from a plane miles away, almost an eyesore in the green carpet of the living forest.

But venture in there and fish those stump-studded shores, even if artificial stocking has not been done. The natural brook trout or bass population has swelled and taken over the old snags. Lunkers live there, and it is a pesky problem to extricate a fighting smallmouth from those twigs and branches. Some of the finest smallmouth fishing I have ever had has been in lakes or ponds of this sort during their first few years, when the fish reach their peak size and before their growth decreases because of too heavy a drain on the food supply. You are fortunate if you strike one of these lakes at the right time.

20

RESERVOIR DRAIN
FLOWAGE PORTAL

The streams that join the main lakes of a reservoir system are another prime bass-fishing territory. The flow of these streams is kept fairly constant. The spring floods that normally come are held back, and in the dry season that formerly exposed their banks to the deadly sun, they are instead given a steady and cool flow of water, usually from a portal at the bottom of the dam. There is some fluctuation in their conditions, of course, but generally speaking these streams are more constant than natural ones and thus better fish holders with consequently better fishing.

The connecting streams between established reservoirs such as those of the New York Water Supply system have these qualities as well as a great variety of fish that use them as their "roads" from lake to lake. When the local natural trout streams have all but dried up, these connecting streams, with their steadier flow, offer all-season sport, and many of them contain good-sized smallmouth bass.

One of the best examples of the validity of the concept of controlled flow over natural flow is the Esopus Creek in the Catskill Mountains of New York State. About halfway up this fast-moving mountain stream is a portal emptying from a tunnel that has been bored through a mountain. This drains the water from Gilboa Reservoir. In the spring the main stream is heavy and full as a result of natural conditions and remains natural below the portal when the portal is closed. But the minute the Ashokan reservoir, which lies below the Esopus, needs water (generally in May and June, and certainly in July and August), the portal is kept open, and a large flow of water from the reservoir above joins the main stream. Above this the stream is but a creek, while below the portal it is its normal size, making it about the only stream in the area with good fishing during the dog days. We'll deal with fishing these flowage streams in our next section, on river fishing, but the mere discussion of them sets the stage for what is to come.

21

FARM PONDS

There is one more growing source of fishing enjoyment, especially for bass and panfish angling, and that is the farm pond. On many a farm there is such a small "water hole" for the cattle. With the demand for new lakes and new fishing resources becoming more pronounced, farmers have begun to build these ponds not only for the cattle but for clubs and recreational groups as well, in most cases making them available on a fee basis for public fishing. Often, the farmer can reap more financial benefit by letting anglers fish a ten-acre pond than he can from his farm produce.

PART THREE

STREAM AND RIVER BASS FISHING

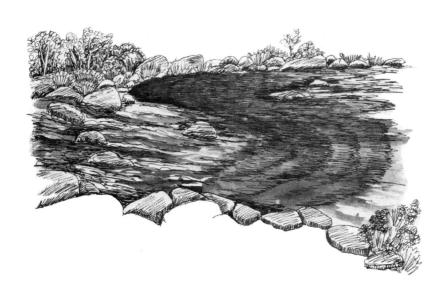

22

STREAM AND RIVER BASS FISHING

My blood chills whenever I think of the first time I encountered a smallmouth bass in a river. I'd fished for about twenty years before that event, and everything from giant, seven-hundred-pound tunas, thirty-pound muskies, pike, Atlantic salmon, marlin, sailfish, bonefish, and a host of other fish had fallen to my rods in many parts of the world.

If you have never sampled a river smallmouth, come with me and take my part in the experience, for the event, as it happened, offers a fitting introduction to this chapter for you who, I trust, will take my writings and run with them to the nearest river or stream that contains this fighting species.

In this instance, I was fishing for brown trout that live in a large pool on a fast-rushing Catskill river in New York State. During the late summer season some of the big brown trout inhabiting the reservoir that the river enters migrate upstream, and one of their holding pools is the famed Five Arch Pool, for those who know the river.

You can stand on the bridge over the pool and look downstream for almost a quarter of a mile at broken water that seems to be swallowed up in the heavily wooded mountains; but where the stream turns sharply there is a deep hole below the bridge that is almost a backwater. The main current rushes hell-bent over smaller boulders and rocks to later flatten out in this deep hole. The far side below the corner is a hot run for trout. Mixed foam and solid water part at the rocks to make wakes and bubbly strips that extend well below. Watching these wakes for a few minutes gives the illusion that the rocks are traveling upstream.

On the particular evening I fished this pool and the corner hole, I was alone. Previously, I'd fished it for several evenings, trying for what I assumed would be a big brown trout.

In late August, When I was fishing, there are no scheduled fly hatches on the stream. Only sporadic mayflies, stoneflies, and even caddis flies come up and out of the water just at dusk, mingling with the many-sized land-bred insects. As soon as the sun has set, while light still glows from atop the mountains, the air suddenly cools over the river and the insects and swallows seem to pour forth. This is the truly magic time on the stream. The trout that have been lying deep in the pool or right at the lip of the rapids under the foam remain uninterested in any offerings. Now, however, they begin to show themselves: great tails, wide dorsals, big snouts. All move along the surface film as they begin to forage. There is about a half hour of light left.

Quite naturally, I was fishing dry flies that night. My rod was a very light and fast six-and-a-half-footer, and I had a leader tapered to 4X with a thinly dressed light Cahill pattern "bent on," as the traditional British writers are wont to say. Even though the river was fairly low, I could wade only to within forty feet of the lip of the pool and its backwater corner. On my side the current was fast, though the pool water was quite a bit slower. I'd cast the heavy water, but now, in order to get any kind of a drift before the center current would take the bellied line and whisk away the fly, I had to send the fly over the pool water and the run and land it into the target hole. I made several casts on which the floater had cocked and drifted for a foot or two but had then been sucked unceremoniously under. I wished I had brought my big bucktail rod but hoped that a big brown would give me the test on lighter gear.

I really pushed those casts and stretched to my toes in order to keep that slack line up. Several times, big browns had risen to my floater, but thus far, nothing—not even a small trout—had nipped at the Cahill.

Now take my place. Make your cast right into the corner, as far as you can reach. Up with that rod. Gather in the slack so it won't drag the fly. That's it. Nice lay and good drift down. Pick it up now before the line drags, and put that fly right back in there again.

Fish throwing spray in your face? He took it as if it were the only fly on the entire menu. Down he goes under that fast water. He's up again and into the air. Hey! That's no brown trout! Look at him tail-walk. That's a *bass*, by golly!

Your rod is bent in a nice half circle. Play that bronzeback from the reel if he takes off in a run downstream, and keep that rod up. Another jump, this time a slasher as he flip-flops over the surface. Tighten up on him to turn him. Careful, that's a mighty pesky fish for such a light leader. Hurry with that slack. Another jump! He had about two yards of slack on that play. Gather it in. Now you can fight him out in the center of the pool. Don't let him fool you, he's far from licked. Quick, submerge the net hoop and lead him into it.

And you were hoping you would tangle with a big brown trout. Man, that little smallmouth on that light gear gave you the battle of your life. No brown would fight like that and for so long a time. Looks nice shining there in the meshes. Firm, cold, brave.

Now you've raised the curtain on a career of smallmouth bass fishing in streams that will rival anything you've ever done short of Atlantic salmon fishing. That smallmouth made any trout, no matter how big, look like a sullen perch. And he took a *dry fly* on a gossamer leader and a very lightweight rod. What could be sweeter?

From today on, follow me from river to river under all kinds of circumstances and settings. We'll catch some mighty fish even though most of them will be far from record breakers. But some of the ones we'll take will be mountable and worth a ten-liner in the local press. Instead of putting our rods away at the end of the trout season, we'll fish harder (if this is possible) than we ever did during May and June. Perhaps we'll even come back, to the Five Arch Bridge Pool, but we'll cover the map first.

If you'll indulge the guide, we'll use only very light spinning gear and lures and a fly rod—either a stout stick for distance and power casting, or something similar to this little, light-but-stiff six-footer.

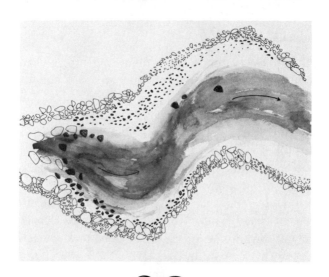

23

THE HEAD
OF A RIFFLE

Unless the stream is a small one that rushes all season long, it will not be too cold for smallmouth bass to be there naturally, as a result of stream breeding. A large stream (or small river, if you will) that used to contain trout before the banks were bared by floods and before the springs in the mountains dried up because of fires or the overharvesting of timber will hold good supplies of sizable bass, both large- and smallmouth, the latter particularly if there is a large, cool lake below.

There are many such rivers in the eastern and central states that have always been famous for their bass fishing. Rivers of like size in the north that used to be known for their trout fishing are now excellent for bass and other warmer water game fish.

Then there are some stream-rivers such as the Beaverkill, Esopus, Neversink, and countless streams in Pennsylvania and New Jersey where both trout and bass live together.

If we were to fish one of these rivers and work the heads of the pools during midsummer, we would have to take our chances on trout, but interestingly enough, we would work that pool head exactly as if we were fishing three months earlier for trout. With the water warmed up, the bass head for the bubbles and the faster, aerated water, much as the trout do. The two kinds of fish now feed with one another and on the same foods: blown-in insects from the surrounding forests and fields, nymphal life, and freshly hatched insects. In July and August the regularly scheduled hatches are largely over. The only mayflies or caddis flies, for example, that would be hatching are those late in development. In some cases there are repeat hatches of the earlier insects. Crawfish, worms, and minnows, and an occasional frog, mouse, or bird would comprise the total potential diet for our bass.

This broad menu leaves us with a large choice of lures to be thrown with light spinning gear or the heavier fly rods. It does not rule out the use of big plugs and spoons, but somehow, especially if you are trout-oriented, you prefer the light touch, sinking to the heavier lures as a last resort. It seems so wonderful taking a bass on a dry fly rather than on a monstrous plug or spoon. That last you can enjoy on any lake. What a thrill it is to have a bass bounce a small bucktail into the air, even if he doesn't grab it.

Even nymph fishing *à la* trouting technique, dead-drift style, is quite an experience when the quarry is a really big fish that fights, as we have shown, much harder than the usual trout.

Let's take a typical section on a large eastern river (as on page 204) for our try and see just how we would fish it. When you come upon the same type of situation yourself, try and remember our program. We'll work up with the fly rod and then down and across with the spinning rig.

Note that the pool is laid out in a sort of lazy "S" shape after the fall-away from the fast water. There are two shelving riffles here with deep runs beside them, a large, deep, center stretch, and a long flat at the end.

In the July sun of a hot day it is easy to see that there are no fish in the shallows at the tail of the pool. We can't see the deep bottom there, but we can imagine what's under that fast water near the head of the pool: bass, in this case mostly smallmouths, but there will also be some largemouths, probably in the center, since they are less prone to stick their noses into fast water unless absolutely necessary. There is an occasional slight breeze riffling the water in spots. It also serves to cool us under blazing sun from above.

We are wading now, up along the side, and just as if we were trout fishing, we will work into the deep water gradually, or over it with our flies—say a brace of large wets or very small bucktails. For variety, you can tie on a big Wulff dry-fly pattern, preferably of light coloration, so that its reflection will be seen more easily by the fish below. If you haven't got a Wulff, try a fan-wing, either the staid old Royal Coachman or a Yellow Sally. I've come to the conclusion that fish see bright whitish flies better in bright light and darker flies in darker light. Certainly the popularity of the white fan-wing, no matter what the shank dressing, has become legion.

After I tire out the wets, I'll push a small bug over that center part of the pool. I'll also work right behind you, alternating casts and drifts to give the fish a choice.

Next we drift the flies from an up-and-across cast as far as we can and then retrieve to work again in due time, following up to the actual runs of foam at the head of the pool.

There's a hit on your Wulff. That was a chub.

Something took a sock at my bug. Probably a perch or bass. It certainly wasn't a bronzeback.

Now we begin to get into the payout area, as the lines of faster water run between the quieter stretches along the riffles. Drift your fly down one of those flats in between the white water. I'll follow with the bug.

There. Nice fish. A smallmouth. Look at him go.

Now for another cast with the bug. I'll skitter it across from the flat and into the white water again. That should bring action. Do this often on this kind of water.

Since we've had action in the middle of the day on floaters, we won't need to rehearse our baitfishing techniques. Farther on we'd bait up, hooking a live minnow or chub by the lip, casting it right into the foam, and allowing it to drift freely in the current. On slack line this is always a gamble, however, for the bass can take and unhook the bait without your knowing it.

Speaking of bait, here's an angler coming down from above. Let's see just how he does it. This ought to be a good show. He has a long fly rod, and that looks like nylon monofilament on it. By golly he's got a cork on that line. Let's watch.

Out goes his cast. There goes his minnow in, and now, a second later, his cork. Let's follow the cork down the current until it reaches the center of the pool. Look! It just pulled under with a plop of water amid some bubbles. There you are, watch that water erupt and look at that big bass take to the trees. That didn't take long.

I'll remember that rig and you do likewise. I'll bet it would murder early-season trout, especially if that minnow bait was weighted to bounce along in the cold rocks of the bottom.

I can recall fishing this stream on my return from a business engagement. It was very early in the morning, about a half hour after sunrise. Tired as I was I couldn't resist making a few casts, even though I did work from the shore only, not wanting to bother to get into waders.

I used a trout favorite of mine, two small bucktails, and in five casts took three bass; not large ones, but just enough to feed myself and the proprietor of the local diner. He's a prolific fisherman and thinks I'm a nut to fish for bass in a river when all the local talent has taken to the lakes. And when the going got rough during the trout season and no one was catching anything, he would always laugh at me when I broke out my small plugs.

"Trout won't take that hardware," he'd say with disgust. "Too big. You'll scare all the fish into the next county."

Maybe he was right, but a lot of plug-caught trout ended up on his counter.

Plug the heads of pools in the late summer. Work the slow streams mainly where there is a current break, particularly where the stream bends and there is a generous backwater or deep section below the rapids. That's where the bass will lie in wait for you. And while the trout may not react, the bass will.

Save the flats and the lower sections of the pool for late evening or night fishing. Make those flies dance and work them as bugs. You'll lure big fish from the deep, even though they may be lying quite a bit upstream in the pockets.

24

DEADWATER RIVER

Winding its way in a meandering mood through the forest country, the river barely shows signs of life or movement. Yet there is a current there, however weak, and as a result of this slight flow the bottom contours are shaped well for the residing, holding, and feeding places for bass, both large- and smallmouth. During the winter months the river is much higher and quite fast. When the ice goes out, a torrent carrying great chunks of ice bores downstream in a frantic movement toward the lake below. Ice from the lake above joins the ice that has broken free from the frozen river, gouging out current lanes that can hardly be seen through the amber water, and only a few tiny surface current indications tell us anything about these lanes as we troll along the river's length.

We are aboard our little craft and the motor is purring gently as we troll long lines behind us. In our wake, down deep, is a large silver spoon. On a shorter line is a slipping-sliding type of weighted underwater plug that sinks down, and, at our trolling speed, works under to about five feet beneath the surface. The river is very clear of refuse and grass for this time of year. As we progress "upstream" we pass many inviting hot-spots along the banks. Once in a while a shelving riffle, gravel shoal, or muddy backwater presents pond lilies or grass, a sure sign that a bass-feeding station is at hand. Once in a while a big boulder creases the surface water, even if its top is as much as four feet under. We can bet that there is a bass or two behind it, and possibly some trout, too.

Trolling, generally, is what I have always considered a blind sport. Whether for big tuna or fingerling trout, it is for strong backs and weak minds. In the tradition of the dry-fly trout-fishing purist of the last century, trolling is like wet-fly fishing: "chuck-and-chance it" angling.

And for most anglers that's just about what it is. Throw the works overboard and drag it through the water with the hope that something will grab hold, even though the odds are against this. Besides, a lot of people like to think that they have carefully mapped a plan in their brilliant minds, and that it will work. General Burgoyne tried that sort of thing not far from the scene of this watershed when he lined up his soldiers and marched them through the forest. The Indians simply hid behind the trees and it was all over in short order. Maybe he should have trolled! Learn to observe and adapt to the situation.

Yet fishing this river is not simply a matter of hiring a guide to mind the motor and unsnag your lures.

Let's look at the water in Figure 60 for a minute. Today (or at least this morning) only a slight breeze ruffles the surface. But I've seen this river blowing up a storm, with whitecaps all but swamping the biggest of the river craft. Even a whisking downwind can be dangerous. At other times it can be glassy, and the memory of a moose upside down on the mirror is something to remember. I was fishing here a while ago on one of those calm twilights when the sun goes down gold against the black silhouette of the woods. The river is a richer yellowish-orange-gold then, and flat as a sheet. For those few instants, the whole scene lacks depth yet feels boundless. That evening a fish rose to ring the water ahead of me. It might have been only a chub. I was working a big Wulff dry fly, since a few small bass had been seen jumping for flies. Hardly even hoping for a big one to take hold, I'd rigged with a size 14 fly on a 4X leader. Yes, you're right, it was one of those moments in life when

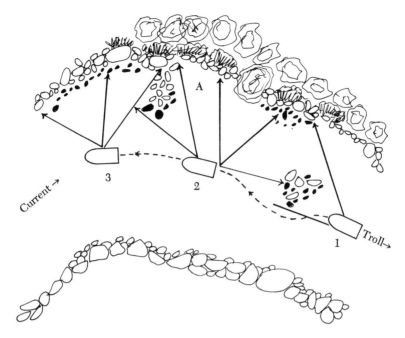

Figure 60. *A diagram of a curve in a river. Note the three boat positions and the angles of cast to the shoreline with its rocks and underwater boulders. This area can be worked easily, without too many casts, as you progress upstream.*

you know you should have your head examined. Had I used my so-called gray matter I'd have fought a good fight, but in this case that big bass really shook this veteran. He took me all over the river and on that light gear, especially the light fly instead of a heavy plug or spoon. He really tricked me and splashed up the water. It would have made a great movie.

But now, on a blue-sky day, it is pleasant in the sun, the breeze gentle and somewhat cooling. A few clouds float in the sky, but they don't seem to interfere with the direct rays of the sun that pierce the beer-colored water. Mixed with the reflections of the sky, the stretch ahead looks like a ruffled purple robe. In the fall the reds, yellows, and golds of the trees make this scene really sing. That is another good time to fish, and hunting is fine in the birch groves for grouse and in the alders and swamps for the first batch of migrating woodcock.

I've worked this river many times and know the guides, who

are aware of every whim and pebble in it, and who know almost every bass—especially the ones that have gotten away from their city customers.

Today, let's be different.

Starting at the bottom of Figure 60(1), we are trolling. A cluster of rocks catches our attention. A big one could be in there, so we move slowly. I reel in the short troll and cast the plug into the rocks. Nothing happens.

At this juncture we are faced with a decision. Shall we continue to troll close to point 1 or elect to do something else, like casting over along the partly rocked and graveled shore of bend B? With the sun slightly shading the bend, we choose the latter, and both cast alternately to the shoreline. We can troll the point on the way down, and not too far upstream is another point we can work. We have plenty of chances to connect on this river.

Coming together at a point above A we can again troll separately close to the deep curve water along bend B, or we can troll to point 2 and cast into the rocks there. We elect to troll, even though the sun is beating down here. We are lucky. Both of us pick up a fish, if small ones.

Let's circle the next bend. We'll work it to a froth and see if we can stir up some action.

No luck. But we have had a look at the river for future times, especially this coming twilight. Trolling and casting either side are in order, and we should pick the side in the most shade and with the most appealing rocks and holes, especially if there is any amount of bank overhang.

Now this short trip on a bit of this long river hasn't been too exciting. I have taken you with me as an observer of the many ways to work a river by trolling, casting, and troll-casting. It is possible, and at most times advisable when the shoreline is suitable, to do both at the same time.

As I look back over the years, I can start a list of the best lure types for such a river and the best ways I have found to fish them. The first year I fished this river I had a box of Trix-Orenes. They were the hot lure that year and I murdered the bass with them. I had tiny-sized ones for the fly rod and a big one which I weighted well ahead with splitshot. Yet I have tried this lure here since that time, and for some reason have never again connected.

For June fishing, when the water is cool, I like to stick more to the surface, using one-eighth-ounce spinning lures, tandem-hook streamers, small Indiana spinner-and-worm combinations. Once in a while a hatch of mayflies will come off around eleven in the morning, or perhaps, if the day has been unusually warm, at about three o'clock. I have even taken some nice bass on size-14 dry flies. But remember, the hatches in this northern country are of short duration; a burst of flies sometimes starts and finishes within a matter of five minutes or less. During the summer, when the water is down a bit, warm, and slow, I prefer to deep troll most of the time, even risking hang-ups. I almost insist on bait on at least one of the lines. I take a lot of trout that way too. In the mornings and evenings, especially in the logy and slack sections of the river where the water almost backs into a whirlpool, floater plugs, and especially the small Jitterbug, are my choice. I like the darkest patterns for this amber water. Any dark plug fished on the surface is better in my opinion than the lighter ones. It must be the black contrast in the beery water that gets the bass.

Twilight in the summer, when the wind subsides, is another "best" time. I can't tell you why, but it seems that on a windy day, particularly when the wind has been really streaking up the water, the bass seem to wait until things calm down a bit. Not that the wind has any effect on their watery life, but just let it subside and they seem to perk up and dimple the surface, smacking at invisible flies and bugs. They like action then, and any surface plug pulled along fast will draw them into one angry dash. I've seen as many as three bass head for a lure from different directions and practically kill each other to get there first.

Knowing the river and its bottom is the entire secret. Of course you can see the good spots along the shore, and once in a while an obvious snag or gravel bar shows itself, but there is more to it than that. The true pattern of the river must be known from experience. Often, if you look down as you glide along, you'll note patches of rotted tree branches and leaves that have been caught between the rocks. Those are bass feeding grounds. There is no way to know about them other than by spotting them under you. The next time around you'll fish them. This is why, as we said at the beginning of this book and at points throughout, it pays well to hire a guide who knows his stuff on this kind of water. But while there was a time when good guides were common in the north woods, the generation of today prefers to make money in the city and stay home watching TV. Few youngsters carve out a career in the woods unless they really love it. If you can find such a person you have a real prize, to be cultivated over the seasons.

Many good bass waters are also found in Georgia, and, as we

have seen, in Florida. But while stretches in the St. Johns, for example, come into this category, you can be skunked on these waters unless you know the secret of the bottom. You must also know the bait story. In the case of the St. Johns you can troll your head off and possibly cover a carload of bass every fifty yards without ever getting a strike. But let a downstream drift of shad minnows enter the bend and the place looks like a machine gun target being blistered. The entire river is afire with spray and leaping fish, some of which must weigh over the fifteen-pound mark, jumping as crazily as trout fry to the hatchery man's handout.

Boy, can you connect by casting at those moments.

But learning the river is half the battle. Learn to "see" it, "feel its pulse," "sense" where you should be and where your lures should be cast. Trolling, just like casting, is really an art, and the curving river is the canvas on which to paint your picture of success. To be one with a river is to be one with its composition and the living things in it, and although you will never acquire the same sense of oneness as the guide or woodsman who lives by, on, in, and with the river, you can develop this sense to a high degree.

Fishing this kind of a river downstream is like meeting a new friend. The technique, mood, problems, and solutions are different than when you're fishing it upstream. True, the current itself is of little import—barely enough to move the boat, but the current is there and life is moved by it at a continuous pace that is felt by the bass and that must be observed and put into action by the angler.

Drift fishing is the basic method for downstream fishing. So let's take a look at the same general bend of the river and see just how we would fish it going downstream.

If there is a wind blowing, the way to keep the boat in the right angle and position for shoreline casting is to drag anchor, with the stern pointed downstream and the bow up; this way, the riding is also comfortable.

Since your lures will be presented largely ahead of or beside the boat, you will be putting them right at the noses of the fish, much as what happens in stream fishing. In a lake where there is no current, the fish can be resting or feeding in almost any direction or angle to you. The point here is to concentrate on the cross-retrieve—retrieving *away* from the shore. In the case of a forward cast to a spot ahead of you, however, retrieve slowly, waiting for the boat to catch up and then retrieving the lure across the path of the current. As you float downstream near one shore or the other, you will spot many windfalls along the banks, shady spots under big old trees, and rocks and clusters of boulders that stop the current along the edge, offering slack water and comfortable harboring areas for baitfish and big fish.

You will also see ahead of you the oncoming gravel bars and drop-offs. With the sun on your back you can look into the water. The smart cast is directly ahead of the boat into the area you want to fish. The retrieve as you drift down on the lure has to be a bit faster than it would when you're casting upstream against the current. Here the boat movement plus the current has to be taken into account.

Make up your mind that if you fish the bottom of the river properly you're going to have to make a trip to the tackle store for fresh terminal rigs and lures. If you slide over this water fishing too high, the bass underneath will seldom give you a tumble.

Drift fishing with a live worm? Use a single hook and no weights. Drift the worm overboard on plenty of slack and just let nature take its course. You can use two rods for drift-fishing in this manner while you cast to the shorelines or to the edges of drop-offs. You can also fish only one drifting bait with a very small sinker, put it down, tie a floating plug on the other line, and let this line out a considerable distance behind you while you and your partner cast with the other two rods.

Incidentally, when fishing downstream, both surface and underwater darter plugs are useful. I usually carry two rods for casting so that I don't have to take time out to change lures, even with the very quick snap-on clips. With all this going on, you won't have time to see that hawk gliding lazily in the sky over your head. Your eyes will be on the shifting of rigs.

When you drift down on a "V" formation of current and see a split riffle, it is a good idea to lower your anchor and hold there for a while, casting in a fan-out pattern first and, when the casting activity is finished to your satisfaction, dropping over a nice, succulent nightcrawler rigged on a single hook and slightly weighted about three feet above the hook. Drop it overboard; do not attempt to cast it. It will drift downstream, deep into the hot-spot. That's the time to watch the hawk, if he's still around. If there is a bass there at that moment you'll see it and get it. As usual, let him take it for a good run before setting the hook.

You've had a busy morning. At twilight you'll be able to simplify your fishing by using surface plugs for casting and that old standby, the bass bug. Cast both directly onto the shore to represent anything live that has crawled, flown, or been knocked into the water and is trying to get away. If you glide by a shallow gravel beach, tie on a streamer fly and jerk it noisily and actively in the center of the beach and out toward you and the deeper water. I've often taken big bass this way, and they are much more fun on the fly rod than on any other kind of rig.

25

SLOW, DEEP, STREAM OR RIVER FISHING

It is most fortunate that we have bass in the lower reaches of many trout streams. We also have them in streams that have slowed up or that contain water that is too warm for trout. In the Catskill mountain stream I spoke about at the beginning of this section, the smallmouths ascend from the reservoir below when they want to find cooler water. The lower reaches of many rivers, down to the pollution band, contain good bass. Earlier in the season they are seen below rapids, at the heads of pools, and in broken water, feeding on insect hatches with other game fish. Later they are found mostly in slow, deep water. But as summer progresses the fish seem to move upstream and in the extreme dry and hot weather are found in the faster pools.

Let's fish another one of my favorite spots, a long pool on the Ten Mile Dutchess County River in New York State, a stream typical of those in the midwestern and south central states. In August, fly fishing for stream bass can be excellent, for none of the fish have been overly worked. Few are big—the largest I've seen was under the three-pound mark—but they are full of fight. Actually, I never knew they existed in the river until I'd gone there for a bit of late-season trouting, since I'd heard that some of the browns and brooks come into that pool from below and that some even drop downstream in the dry periods when there is too little water in the tributaries.

For about three hundred yards this pool is flat and glassy. Large trees overhang both the road side of the stream and the opposite bank. It is an easy pool to fish from the shore, accessible by rollcasting without getting your feet wet. You can also wade in at almost any point and work the several rocks that protrude well out of the water. The main current is in the center, flowing over sandy stretches of gravel. At this low period the deepest part of the stream runs to about six feet, with most of it ranging about three feet deep. Those deep holes, particularly behind the large boulders, are where the bass seem to hang out, and if there is any insect-hatching activity, that is where they are seen rising.

We start at the tail of the pool just to see what's going on, but our prime objective will be the biggest rock just below the rapids that start the pool. Between us and that big rock are smaller pools that we can fish, for past experience has shown us good bass in and around them.

It is late afternoon, with hardly any breeze; there are insects buzzing in the air but no hatches.

Although it might seem most unorthodox, you are carrying two rods; one is a very light spinning rod, since river fishing does not involve the need for heavy tackle to extricate fish or lures from the weeds. The other rod is a staunch, nine-foot fly rod capable of throwing very large dry flies or light bass bugs into a generous wind if necessary. Perhaps you'll also cast a worm, a hellgrammite, or a small minnow. You can work the spinning lures in a down-stream direction and the flies upstream and across. The two kinds of gear will let this laboratory pool show you the ropes in this kind of situation.

First, the fly rod and some big dry flies of the Wulff design: thick bodies, plenty of hackle, and hairy wings. A dark one is tied on first; the white-winged ones are reserved for the bad light that will come at dusk. Take up a position below some rocks and make your first casts—random ones—just to get the leader straightened out and the line wet. You get and miss several strikes. These are chubs or fallfish. They'll destroy a box of flies in an afternoon. But in order to interest the bass, you have to work through them. The trick is to keep snapping the fly away from the chubs while at the same time hoping that a bass sees it. You also have to know the difference between a bass strike and a hit by a fallfish. Actually, the chubs call attention to the fly and so attract the bass to you and so are of some benefit amid the confusion. Maybe there is a bass behind that first rock. Cast to the right-hand bend there and let the fly dance slowly by the rock. If a chub hits, let the fly float anyway until it is well past the rock.

There! That's no chub. He's still little, but look at him fight. Worth twice his weight in trout.

While you're resting the water in that vicinity, try the spinning rod and a plain old Colorado spinner on the rocks below. Make your casts in the standard fan-out pattern. Maybe you'll pick up a good fish. It would be a shame to skip that water just because it's behind you.

Shoot one under the old tree that overhangs that glassy stretch on the opposite bank. Another! That's no chub either. By golly, it's a trout.

Now let's fish the deeper water up near the center of the pool. You can't wade out very far, even in the slower current, but a long, salmon-type cast will get you there where it pays, right in the center current that shows a very slight ripple as it passes over the bar. It looks shallow, but it isn't. Curl your cast upstream of the rocks so you have a long drift from the upstream position of the line; then, when the line begins to drag, pop the fly, if a trout or bass hasn't already hit it or a chub nudged it.

There's a chub rise. He's hooked. But there's a bigger splash right under him. The chub got hooked and the bass got him. Now that's first class live-bait fishing if I ever saw it. That's no baby bass, either. Better get him out of the rocks.

Now see if you can wade out along the bar near that center run of current and boulders. Take the spinning rod and work some weighted 8X bucktails. Better still, how about a weighted marabou streamer?

Try the marabou fished across and downstream. It should connect. At least the chubs won't bother it.

That didn't take long. Your first cast produced. One thing about bass in relatively slow water is that they're not too selective. As a result, one would think that an obvious pool such as this would be fished out. The reason it isn't is that few anglers bother to fish this stream once the early part of the trout season is over. The bass fishermen usually take to the lakes. True, the bass here are small, as we said, but by golly they're a heck of a lot of fun. I can take you up to Maine and to larger rivers for larger and more pugnacious fish, but this backyard stream can show you a thing or two about these river bass. Also, I have always maintained that the size of a fish is a relative thing.

There are thousands of meandering rivers in our country that abound in fair-to-good bass fishing for both large- and smallmouths. Some of them can be fished from the shore, others from the boat, and still others or parts of them waded trout-stream style. I prefer to wade most of the time, for I can really become one with the situation, take my time working over a given stretch of water, and try different lures and retrieval techniques.

Let's fish a slow northern river for a change of pace. The river winds in gentle curves through flat land and is rocky and snagged right to the shore. Only on occasion do you find a current break and the suggestion of a faster current. It is all good water—alder-fringed shores, large rocks on the banks, gravel bars, deep holes, and runs in the center. Perfect spinning water during the day and excellent for dry-fly or bass-bug fishing toward nightfall. Float down this in a canoe, slowly, and fish it hard, plunking your lures right in there under the snags. Drag a few spinning lures immediately below the boat and work a brace of small-size streamers in across-stream and drift-below techniques. You might pick up a good trout in the offing.

Many large northern rivers big enough to hold large boats also tend to have their share of bass, along with walleyed pike, pickerel, and a hot of other freshwater fish. On the East Coast, in the mid-South states, and west into the Ozarks, float fishing on the slow rivers is a well-established game, and experienced guides take you for trips lasting as long as two weeks, camping with you along the way. You can bass-fish yourself to death on one of these trips, catching more fish than you ever have in your life. That's one thing about the bass: if he's there at all, he's there in numbers. And if you catch numbers, the percentage of big ones is bound to be greater. Bring along a plastic bobber for use with your fly rod, as well as your light spinning gear, and keep plastic worms in your tackle box, as well as taking live worms; for the really tough going, some take plastic eels.

As for general technique, I've found that with these lures, with spinning spoons, and with spinners-and-bait, as well as with my favorite size 8 to 10 bucktails, a slow and deliberate retrieve is best in the runs. In this type of water, bass don't seem to be in as much of a hurry as trout. I also like to alternate technique and equipment, switching quite often from the fly rod to the light spinning rod and then back again.

In my book, evening on a slow river seems to be reserved for fly fishing. Perhaps this is because I am also a trout fisherman. (See also my *Tactics on Trout,* Scribners, 1983, in paperback.) In my early bass years, I fished exclusively with the baitcasting rod and used bigger plugs and spoons. Only during the past twenty years or so have I learned the killing qualities of blending light trout gear with bass-fishing needs in order to better enjoy both large- and smallmouth fishing, especially in waters that are slow and easy. Yes, the heavy tackle is almost indispensable where there are snags, weeds, and bigger fish. Not that the big bass are lacking in the slow, curvy streams. They're there. But it is amazing how the light gear will kill big fish if you give it a chance and are prepared to lose a few lures. And fishing with it is better than knowing that every bass you hook can be overpowered. When you know that a bass can throw even deeply embedded treble hooks, you also know you are not always guaranteed a creeled fish no matter what tackle you use. On the other hand, if you are not careful while fighting him on light tackle, he can file your leader on an underwater rock if you let him, no matter how well you think he's barbed.

But, suppose you fish the Ten Mile River, or the late summer slow water in Maine, or perhaps work an Ozark flat trip or possibly drift down a barge-carrying river and nothing happens to your artificials?

For such times, learn to swim a worm, live or artificial, or if not a worm, a hellgrammite or crawfish with the claws removed, or even a live minnow. If you like, stick to surface-worked live baits; there is nothing like a cricket or grasshopper rigged to the hook with an elastic band. If the water is deep, troll with a spoon for weight, letting the live bait travel free-style behind it. If you're floating down the river, let the bait to bump along deep by holding the speed of the boat down so that the current swings the bait well out and downstream of you. If the going is bad, break out the pork rind, either real or phony.

Many of the slower rivers have long stretches where the river itself is lost in an interweaving of snags, inlets, sloughs, long promontories of grass flats, lily-pad backwaters, and a generally very indefinite shoreline. Only the center current can be found by watching the water as it graces through the reeds and grass. Wherever the water is not moving it is off the main current. It is along the edge of the main current that the bass hide, for they can rest in the peace of comparatively slow or actionless water and watch the bait go by. The trick in fishing this water is to make the bait drift by the right places and in the right way. Remember that the top of each curve feels the current. At the bottom of the curve there is the likelihood of slower water or even a slight backwater that forms a deeper pool or run.

These are live-bait holes, if you have the sit-still patience. The only way I have learned this patience is to anchor above one of these spots and quit wearing out my casting arm. It is well known that in rivers such as these there are big bass to be had, and it is up to us to take them out. So go the bait course, and if you have to bring along a nonpolitical book, preferably some poetry.

26

Sloughs

The hurried float fisherman bound for the next exciting pool or run ahead of him downstream usually skips by the deadwater sections off the beaten path of a river. That is why there are big fish to be caught in these spots. But fishing in these locations demands care, time, an exact execution of casts, and luck in avoiding hang-ups. I learned that these are the holding lairs for the really big fish from a guide who, once he was aware that I could spot cast with accuracy, poled me into one of them. Boy, did I connect!

Let's go, then. There is one up ahead of us to the left. See the water belly into the weeds? Look at that rock- and snag-strewn shoreline at the opening. Hardly a place for a poor caster.

We won't go bouncing in there hell-bent. Instead, we'll pinpoint a few nice casts with the spinning rig, throwing a jointed surface-diving plug right at the upstream entrance to that backwater, right in front of the rocks. The current will carry the plug down a bit in the wake of the rocks. There should be a good one in there.

No? That's strange.

Try a cast to the lower side of the entrance, where that other fallen snag is and those two rocks. Place the lure between them and retrieve slowly. We'll drift down lazily so you can urge that guy out of the snags and into the main current.

Now let's go inside. Again, we won't go casting our half-ounce lures to all points of the compass at once, covering the water like a mechanical fan. We'll pick our spots, remembering that casting out toward the inlet of the slough is very important. It's clear that surface plugs are called for. If we fished it in the evening, I'd prefer bass bugs, rollcast from the bow of the boat (with you holding the boat in a T-formation, or right angle, to the target).

27

SPRING BROOKS INTO LAKES AND SLOW RIVERS

It is late summer. In another month the birches and alders will begin to rival the maples in their shades of red, gold, and orange. Etched against them will be the darker spruce, pine, and other softwoods. Right now, the lakes and streams are low, and the connecting streams also. The bass and other game fish seem to be at an all-time low in action. Even trolling the deep fails to produce for us. We've been at it constantly, under the damp fogs of dawn and the piercing rays of midday, without results.

I have an idea. Across the way from our campsite is a broken shoreline that's indented in several places by little brook outlets. While we have been concentrating on the deep spots, we've probably neglected the best locations for bass, and where even some trout might be under the conditions.

Those little brooks, hardly noticeable now, still bring fresh water and some coolness. In the springtime, they are real brooks and burst forth through the burned stumps and relics of old trees that have fallen every which way across the outlet, hiding the source of the brook from all but the eyes that know that location.

It is hot today; there is hardly any breeze at all. Once in a while a perch rings the mirror, but nothing more. No bass on the feed or signs of action from any game fish.

Let's try the spring brooks, even though they are loaded with snags and are most difficult to fish. We must have a bass or two for the camp larder, and our action department is somewhat frustrated. We have almost forgotten the feel of a striking fish, and it is bad news to lose this awareness!

We'll glide silently along the shore and cast side by side in close sequence, putting our lures right into the shore. We'll need the practice for the time when we come into the focus of the inlet and several others downshore.

Actually, our tactics are obvious. We shoot half-ouncers from our upstream or upwater direction right to the edge of the outlet on our side. Then we cast to the opposite side and retrieve a quarter-ounce plug right across the entrance, letting it pause a bit. If this doesn't produce, we'll take up a position directly out from the angle of the inlet and shoot some long casts with quarter-ounce spoons right into the pocket, hoping that we don't overshoot and catch a big log. Better to rig the plugs with light leaders so we can break them off if need be, instead of having to enter the area and ruin it.

WELL, IT SEEMS THAT WE'VE COME TO THE END of our fishing trip together. We've covered a lot of miles seeing many streams, lakes, sloughs, backwaters, impoundments, and some tricky waters.

We could go on and on—and will, in our separate ways. Meanwhile, I've gotten to know you pretty well and you have become accustomed to following directions. So we can both hope to go on the water again with a bit better know-how, now possessing sharper powers of observation. Seeing nature as it is and consequently having some sort of plan of action to help catch a few bass will increase our enjoyment in our search for entertainment and add to the size of the stringer we take home.

APPENDIXES

It quickly became evident in writing this book that there was a need for a kind of off-water classroom where discussions and descriptions of tackle and its use in operation could supplement the actual fishing techniques found in the chapters. This Appendix also details the different methods and combinations of tackle that would be too specific to discuss under the various fishing situations. These are here illustrated in diagram form and explained in detailed captions that can be read and viewed along with the text of the Appendix, and perhaps reviewed while the reader keeps a thumb in the section of the book he is reading at the moment.

TACKLE TALK

There are generally three types of tackle used for freshwater fishing: baitcasting, spinning, and fly-fishing tackle. Trolling and stillfishing can be done with your choice of any of the three, but the fly rod is least suited for trolling unless light baits or small flies are used. Bass can be caught with any kind of tackle that is legal, using any method at almost any time of the year. They are the most impartial "takers" of all our game fish, showing far less feeding fastidiousness than the trout. They require lighter tackle than that used for pike and musky fishing.

In selecting tackle, the beginner is warned against shopping by price.

In years past most fishing gear was available only at local hardware or legitimate tackle stores. The men behind the counter depended upon personal contact and repeat business for their success. Today, however, tackle counters and lavish rod racks are found in all manner of discount houses and price-cutting establishments, and there is a lot of cheaply priced tackle that looks good. As a result of this price trend, many manufacturers produce tackle that will sell at a bargain price but that will not necessarily perform well.

Beware.

I sincerely hope that you will not object to my making it a practice throughout this book, in all but very specific instances, not to mention a specific brand name of lure. For one thing, it dates the book. Fifteen years from now, when your youngster reads it, the lures I'd specify might no longer be available. Another reason for not mentioning brand names is that with so many lure manufacturers trying to get your dollar for their similar lures, the picking at the tackle counter is often frustrating. There are many lures available that do virtually the same thing. When I started out bass fishing, some thirty years ago, I was the biggest sucker for brand-new creations, one after the other, as they came out on the market. This was especially true when plastic lures began to replace wooden ones. Over the years, however, the choice of lures has become a sort of sleight-of-hand to me (and I hope to you)—something that comes from some kind of inner indication when given a specific situation. It is the tendency to go for type and action rather than label and style.

Let's face it, there are only a few basic types of action in all the lures on the market. So, given two lures to fish with, both almost identical in purpose and action, I would certainly hesitate to suggest that your choice is wrong. For my own part, I have found it foolish and needlessly expensive to try and collect all of them. I like to simplify my lure selection and concentrate on finding out what the bass are up to!

What you can count on when shopping is both imported and domestic tackle with an established brand name. This is quality merchandise and it will cost you more to buy it, but it will be less costly in the long run. Also, try to buy your tackle at a legitimate tackle store, for the men there want your repeat business and will work with you in building the proper outfit. Many such stores also have repair shops and other services, including a sort of comradely spirit of sharing techniques and where-to-go information.

BAITCASTING TACKLE SELECTION

The term "baitcasting" is actually a misnomer in this day and age, since "bait" at one time meant only meat or fish. "Lure fishing" might be a more accurate term grammatically, since baitcasting tackle is used to cast plugs, spoons, spinners, jigs, and lighter lures for bass and other game fish.

In baitcasting, a level-wind reel (Figure I) is used.

The spool of this reel revolves four times with each revolution of the handle. The line, usually silk or braided nylon or Dacron, is threaded evenly on the spool by the vertical frame, which travels back and forth across the front of the spool as the line is reeled in.

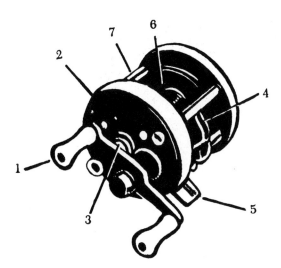

Figure I. A typical baitcasting reel with an adjustable drag. Some reels have a star drag, similar to the bigger saltwater reels. (1) handle; (2) head; (3) drag-adjustment button; (4) level-wind mechanism; (5) foot (attaches to rod handle); (6) line spool; (7) pillar.

The control of the spool's speed of revolution, commonly called drag, is maintained by a button-type screw-in plug on the reel's side plate or by a more quickly adjustable "star drag" on the base of the cranking handle. Further control of the cast is achieved by thumb pressure exerted on the reel spool as it revolves on the cast.

If the spool travels faster than the line pulls on it, the result is a backlash or "overspin" and its inevitable line tangle. You can have visual proof of this effect by merely reverse-winding the reel for a turn or so. The reel must be back-wound in order to eliminate the line reversal on the spool.

The way to avoid a backlash is to always control the outflow of the line by resting your thumb on the top of the reel spool, as in Figure III. This is described later, in the instructions for casting.

The rod used in baitcasting is generally about five feet long, with either a straight or an offset handle. It can be made of bamboo, steel, or solid or hollow glass. Long, flexible rods are generally selected for lighter lures and appropriate lines. Shorter, stiffer rods are designed for heavy-lure fishing under rougher conditions, such as in heavy weed beds and lily pads, or for trolling.

Lures of all manner of weight can be used, but the matter of balanced tackle with which to cast them long distances with accuracy and ease is very important. The relationship between the weight of the lure, the action and relative speed of the rod, and the weight of the line should be such as to allow delivery of the lure with definition.

While it is quite impossible for you and me to visit the tackle store together and for me to help you pick out a set of balanced

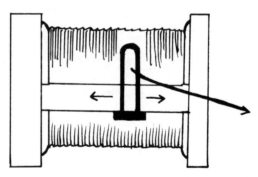

Figure II. The level-wind mechanism. The vertical bar travels back and forth across the front of the spool on the cast and also on the retrieve, keeping the line spooled evenly.

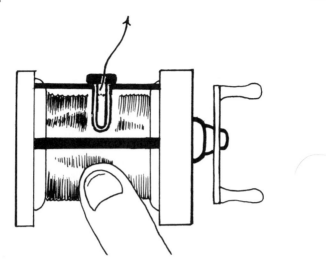

Figure III. The thumb shown in position for line control on the reel spool. Note the high level of line on the spool: not too much nor too little.

tackle, I can and will give you some general guidelines, with generous margins, that can at least help you with what to start to look for in the tackle you need. In making these suggestions I have consulted my own tackle, that of other bass anglers, and the highly refined recommendations of the tackle companies. My recommendations are merely to show a relationship between rod, reel, line, and lure weights that must be considered if you are to find an outfit that will cast well for you. For further help, a competent tackle retailer can be of as much help to you as a good friend who has had to go the route before you.

In choosing a balanced baitcasting outfit, your personal body and muscle reactions will be called into consideration. Those who fish fairly softly and don't cast as if they were trying to tear down a mountain are in one class. The strong-man type will demand quite another set of gear. The needs of the moment must also be taken into consideration. If the casting in a particular situation does not demand great distance in a strong wind, one set of needs is represented. Tough fishing conditions, where heavy weeds will be encountered, will require another.

Here are four samples of balanced tackle designed to cast their specific lure weights well. You can use these rather general specifications as your guide.

Baitcasting Tackle Specifications

REEL SIZE	ROD LENGTH	ROD ACTION	LINE TEST	LURE WEIGHT
Small	4' to 6'	Soft	4 to 8 lbs.	¼ to ½ oz.

This outfit will deliver small- to medium-size lures adequate distances for most shore casting and boat fishing situations in which the angler can come close to his target area (generally within 60 feet). The rod is not designed to horse out big bass from heavy grass or weedbeds, nor is it to be used to hoist a bass over the side; for this, a net should be used. The rod is also good for stream fishing, since it is not too heavy and will handle well the light lures used primarily in stream casting. Additionally, this outfit is good for stillfishing in fairly shallow water and when very light or no weights are used with bait.

REEL SIZE	ROD LENGTH	ROD ACTION	LINE TEST	LURE WEIGHT
Medium	5½' to 6'	Soft-Med.	6 to 8 lbs.	¼ to ⅝ oz.

This is a trifle heavier and more versatile outfit that allows a bit more distance with the same lure weights than does the first outfit. It is also good for light-lure and near-surface trolling and for stillfishing with weighted baits.

REEL SIZE	ROD LENGTH	ROD ACTION	LINE TEST	LURE WEIGHT
Standard	5½' to 6½'	Medium to Stiff	6 to 10 lbs.	½ to ⅝ oz.

This is a distance-casting outfit, and one that will control a cast into the wind and offer a better rod for extracting fish from weeds. It is also good for deep trolling, and bottom fishing, and is versatile as a saltwater outfit as well.

REEL SIZE	ROD LENGTH	ROD ACTION	LINE TEST	LURE WEIGHT
Large	5' to 5½'	Stiff	10 lbs.	½ to ¾ oz.

This is good for trolling heavy baits, deep fishing, and casting heavy lures long distances. It is also big enough for most pike and musky fishing.

BAITCASTING INSTRUCTION

We can assume that you have bought a set of gear that is balanced, such as a medium-action glass rod with an offset handle, a level-wind, multiplying reel of good quality, a spool of nylon braided line of, say, eight-pound test, and a practice plug. If you do not have a practice plug, use any one of the fishing plugs you've purchased, removing the hooks for the time being. If you lack a plug, use any weight around the house that is the general size of a lure and weighs about a half ounce.

Figure IV.   All tackle ready to go in position.

We can also assume that you've reeled your line from the factory spool onto your reel spool, threading it through the level-wind slit before tying it to the spool and beginning your winding. As you view the full spool now, the line feeds off the top of the spool as the reel rests in its groove on the top of the rod. The rod guides are lined up to receive the line, and the whole rig looks like the illustration in Figure IV.

Now thread the line through the guides and pull it about a foot and a half out beyond the rod tip, and tie on your practice plug.

You are ready to learn the routine of casting. We will start with the *vertical* cast. Tie on your weight. Stand up. Pick up the rod in your right hand with the reel up, and place your thumb lightly on the reel spool. Your thumb is going to do all the important work from now on, for it will control the line on the cast. Tighten your thumb a bit on the line so that the reel spool does not revolve in response to the weight on the end of the line. Hold the rod parallel to the floor. Now gently ease the thumb pressure on the line and spool but not entirely remove it. The weight of the plug will pull downward and the plug will hit the floor.

Just as it does this, or a split second before it does, learn to tighten your thumb pressure on the line, so that the spool does not overspin and release more line than is necessary for the lure to drop to the floor. If you did not stop the spool from revolving, you now have what is called an overrun, the beginning of a backlash. To correct this, strip out line until the overrun disappears. If you do not do this but merely reel in for another try, the overrun will interfere with direct and easy line flow on your next try. In order to have the line wind properly and under even tension onto the spool, switch the rod to your left hand, place your right hand in front of the reel, grasp the line, ahead of the level-wind bar, between your thumb and index finger, and squeeze gently, maintaining an even pressure as you crank in the line. We are going through this operation now, before you make an actual cast, so that you can establish your handling of the rod, reel, and line and avoid problems later.

Now try the whole sequence again. If you have succeeded in

stopping the reel spool from revolving when the weight hits the floor, merely grasp the line as described and reel in. Making the cast is merely an extension of this procedure. Now, just for practice, try a very slight waving of your rod to and fro sideways, allowing the plug to pull the line from under your reel thumb in the middle of the rod arc.

If all went well, you have had no backlash.

Reeling in is a simple proposition. Do not reel the weight in too close to the rod tip. Leave at least a foot of line in between. This extra length helps the action of the cast, for the swing of the lure activates the rod top, which in turn will send the lure on its way during the cast.

Before advancing to the cast itself, perform the routine we have just been through several times in order to get the feel of the tackle, the rhythm of the combination, the various changes of your thumb position, and the changing of the rod from the right (casting) hand to the left (retrieving) hand. It is better to master this routine before becoming involved in it during the act of casting.

You're not ready to go fishing yet. There are many needed refinements and some more subtleties to come.

In order to direct the plug to a specific target, you hold your rod in the ready position and actually point to the target. This lines up the swing of the rod. You also use the pointing action to begin flexing the rod. To start your cast, swing the rod down to the target. As soon as the rod bends, flip it up. Sometimes it is useful to false cast, swinging the rod up and down, clarifying the direction, and flexing the rod for the cast before the actual haul-back. If on the cast the lure seems to go to the left or right of the desired mark, you can change its direction by pulling the rod back, angling your arm in, and bending your forearm either to the right or left as the need may be. Try this a few times to get used to it.

Another thing that must be controlled is the slack in the cast. If your cast is traveling in a high arc, you are allowing the line too much freedom on the thumb release and also releasing too soon on the forward swing. Adjust these two factors. If the plug travels too low and splashes in the water in front of you and far short of the target, you are releasing too late and applying too much tension to the thumbing. Correct these problems by practice.

There is not much you can do about a well-executed but underpowered cast that falls in line but short of the target; however, you can control a wild cast that is going too far out. This control is especially needed when you are fishing from a boat and want to land your plug right at the very edge of the shore or bounce it off a log or rock. To control such a cast, you'll have to become familiar with this range problem and, upon seeing that you are going to overshoot, be able to gently snub the line with your thumb. If you do this too fast, the lure will fall much too short of the target. If you don't snub enough, you'll overshoot. Again, practice.

One of the most important tricks to learn in baitcasting is instant control of the plug the second it hits the water. Bass will bust you up or at least confuse the issue if they hit a split second after your lure has touched the water and you are not ready. Being ready requires that at almost the time your lure is about to hit the water, you have made the changeover of the rod to your left hand, grasped the incoming line with your thumb and index finger as described earlier, and started to retrieve the loose line in the air. If a bass then hits the plug the moment it hits the water, you're in business.

When fishing in and around obstacles such as rocks or trees, or in a boat where other anglers are near you, the *sidewinder* cast is recommended, although it has to be made most carefully. The arc of this cast is made parallel to the water rather than perpendicular to it. The problem here is that the direction to the target must be found more definitely for proper timing of the release on the forward swing than is the case with the vertical cast. A few swings in the false cast will build up the feel of the rod's action, and if you will try this cast over a short distance at first, you'll be able to master it for the times you'll need it. The *underhand* cast is another trick cast that can be used if trees or other obstructions prevent the use of the usual vertical or the horizontal cast. It can be done best with a short rod, unless you are tall. To start this cast, you begin from the ground, and as the rod flexes upward you release the line quickly but keep it under control. It is merely the reverse of the vertical cast.

In the retrieve, it is important that the line be fed onto the reel evently, under slight tension. This must be done even though you are reeling in and the pressure on the rod as you manipulate the lure may vary greatly. Always control that incoming line, even when fighting a fish, and it will "lie right" for the next cast. If you feel any unevenness, there is no reason why you cannot draw out that portion of the line and reel it in again properly.

Other improvements in your technique will become obvious, but this much instruction will get you on your way.

BAITCASTING LURE SELECTION

If you were to own only one of each kind of plug and lure that has been invented for bass fishing, you'd have to have a pretty big trunk to hold them. They come in all sizes, shapes, and colors, each packaged most attractively. This point argues against most of them being necessary. Not that they are not all excellent plugs or that any one of them would not entice a bass to strike at one time or other, it is just that—as we have noted—there is a great similarity among them. Some anglers I know do own quite a collection of lures, and they catch bass. There are probably just as many who own but a few basic types with plenty of back-ups in case of loss. If you have a collector's personality, you'll probably spend a fortune over the years on bass plugs and varied types of lures. Some even come with directions on just how to catch all the big ones. The chances are that if you follow the directions you'll connect with some whoppers.

In truth, lure selection and the more important lure use develop automatically after you have become almost part bass yourself. The real test is in making a bass that you know is hiding under that stump along the shore take the lure that you throw at him on your first cast.

From the recommendation of lure types rather than specific plugs or brand names that I have most often followed in this book, you can then select the specific lure in that category, snap it on your line, and cast it out. It would be foolhardy and in fact useless to list all or even a few of the plugs within a specific plug-type category. As I have mentioned before, bass are not anywhere near as choosy as trout. Learning to use the required type of plug and fishing it properly are far more effective than constantly changing plugs of the same type merely because you think the bass is that selective. You need only remember that the bass seldom, if ever, feed selectively on any specific type of food. They are willing to settle for anything that is moving, particularly if it looks as though it is wounded (such as a popping wounded-minnow plug) or helpless in the water (such as a fluffy bass plug). Color, form, and even size are much less important than the illusion of action.

Figure V shows several of the basic baitcasting lure types. A selection of these based on design, function, and action should be included in your tackle box inventory.

Now to a discussion and identification of the three basic types of lures. As you read, study the illustrations in Figure V.

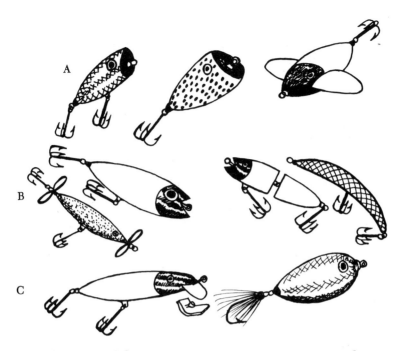

Figure V. Typical bass plugs. (A) Surface popping type. This is a floating lure designed to be cast to the target, allowed to rest, and popped or otherwise made active on the retrieve. The action here is one of a stationary rather than a traveling disturbance over the hot-spot. The lure is not taken from the water on the retrieve until reeled close to the shore or boat. (B) Surface wobbling-diving type. This is also essentially a floater when left stationary. When popped or retrieved it dives and zigzags underwater, deeper as it is pulled faster. Some of these plugs have adjustable metal fins, as in (C), that permit the diving action to be regulated by the angler. (C) The sinking-diving, zigzagging plug that sinks when left stationary after the cast. It has the same action as (B) above, except that the action imparted by the angler happens on the pull and consequently on the "upward" course of the lure. (See sample suggested casts and retrieves in Figure VI.)

The surface action of a floating lure depends entirely upon your manipulation of it once it has been cast and has landed in the target area. If left alone, it will just "sit." It is up to you to make it alive and interesting to the bass. Floating lures are basically designed to cause quite a rumpus on the surface once you activate them by reeling them in, popping them with the rod tip, or with a combination of both line control and rod-tip action. If you retrieve a floating lure too fast it will lack an enticing action and appear merely as a stick or clump of weeds being retrieved. If, however, you pop the lure and pause every foot or so in your retrieve, and repeat this process out from the shoreline or snag, the bass, if he is there and the slightest bit hungry or excited by it, will surely show some interest. He might swim up to the plug, possibly nose it a bit, and even make a halfhearted grab *at* it only to refuse it. Then again he might pounce on it like a puppy snatching a butterfly. Hunger might also be his motive, and usually is the activating force behind the striking willingness of most bass. They might have full bellies, but they will kill food and cram it into their mouths even if they later spew it out. They are not alone in this characteristic. Striped bass, bluefish, and a host of other fish with voracious natures have this common attribute. All we have to do is to present a lure to them in such a way as to appeal to these reactions and they will come forth.

Along with the popping plugs there is another division among the floaters: the floating-diving plugs that dive in a zigzag course when pulled through the water. Some will merely zigzag on the surface while others will go under and down in direct proportion to the amount of speed or pull applied by the angler. Floating-diving plugs can be popped on the surface, allowed to pause, and then be pulled under in a more versatile show of action than a strictly popping lure provides. However, they can be used only where there is a stretch of water that is free from subsurface snags and grass. The floating-only plugs are a great deal less prone to get hung up than the floater-divers, simply because we can see their path of retrieve and so can guide them past or through most obstructions.

Study Figure VI and the next time you are out fishing try and duplicate these retrieves and note the action and path of your lure.

SPOON- AND SPINNER-BAIT COMBINATIONS

This class of lure can be handled effectively with either spinning or baitcasting tackle. The same demands of casting are needed as with a surface lure: the lure must be put on the target with a minimum of slack line to keep it from sinking down too far and too fast before the retrieve can begin. In deeper water, this is of course a lesser problem. It is also important to know the action inherent in the lure itself. In most cases there is little that can be done to add to this action, since the lure is quite a distance away from your tip and the action you apply to the tip, and is well underwater. However,

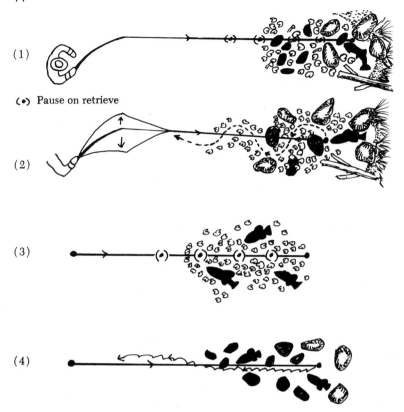

(1)

(•) Pause on retrieve

(2)

(3)

(4)

Figure VI. Shown here are four types of typical retrieves for the bait-caster fishing still water, either in a lake or in a stream. They can be varied and combined. They are diagrammed for either surface, surface-diving, or floating-diving plugs. Here they are as seen from above. (1) The direct cast, possibly to a rock or snag. The plug is allowed to rest upon landing and is retrieved in a zigzag action that is built into the lure itself. All you have to do is to retrieve and pause as indicated. (2) The cross-retrieve, done by sharply angling the rod so that the path of the lure is angled to cover more territory and to get around floating snags, pads, and grass. (3) The direct pause and retrieve, which is used most commonly with a surface lure that is popped, allowed to rest, and then popped again. (4) The direct retrieve, which allows the built-in action of the lure to supply the attraction.

some spoons and spinners are built to zigzag up or down or sideways, and a mere slight pause and pull is enough to activate them properly. Too fast a retrieve can negate some of their attractiveness. The proper speed can be learned by a few trials with each particular lure.

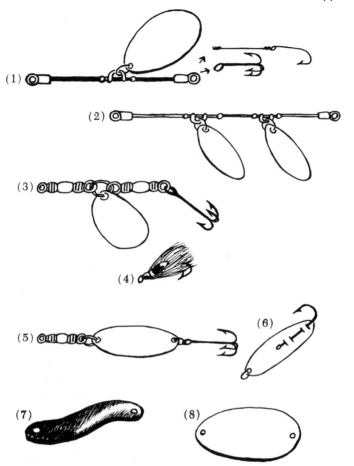

Figure VII. Typical spinners and spoons. Spinners and spoons are exclusively underwater lures because of their weight, although they can be held to the surface by a high rod position and faster retrieve than that usually applied to plugs. They are designed for murky water and deep lakes, where their sparkle will draw fish up from the depths or from pockets and holes. They are particularly effective in the summer months, when the water is warm and the fish tend to be logy.

Spinners. (1) Single spinner for detachable hook or fly hook. (2) Colorado-type spinner with single blade. (3) Double-blade spinner (Indiana type). (4) Spinner lure.

Lures. (5) Typical or original "spoon" lure. (6) Medium spoon with embedded hook. (7) All-purpose two-colored spoon. (8) Deep-trolling spoon.

Keep these lures shiny. Keep polish and soft steel wool in your tackle box for on-the-spot use. A wide assortment of spoons in all weights is necessary. Also, since sinking lures like these are often lost to snags, have plenty of back-ups.

A completely separate category of lure, the lead jig, which has absolutely no built-in action of its own, has to be line- and rod-manipulated; otherwise it is an almost dead thing being dragged through the water. If retrieved too fast, spoons lose their appeal, and if retrieved too slowly will offer nothing much of flashing interest. Here again, then, the way to learn how to work a given lure is to experiment with it before you go fishing. The same goes for the Colorado Spinner, with or without bait, and for the double-bladed Indiana and its fly or bait. If you do not experiment and see the lure under the real conditions in which it will be retrieved, you cannot possibly know how to work it properly.

There are two interesting experiments you can try. The first is to go to a swimming pool or some clear-water part of a lake where you can cast your lures and watch their action. After the cast and allowance of some time for the lure to sink, you begin the retrieve, giving the lure some action by vibrating the rod tip or even hauling the tip back in a wide arc and then letting it drop forward suddenly, creating a slack that will allow the lure to head downward and sink only to be lifted up again when you repeat the process. You will notice that most of the action you apply is absorbed along the way, and that little of it enlivens the lure. If your rod tip is fairly stiff, the results will be a lot more noticeable. You will also "feel" the dampened response of the lure in your hand. This is why, when fishing with springy rods, the smaller, lighter lures are far superior to the heavy ones. The bigger, heavier lures are designed for shorter, stiffer baitcasting rigs. The best combination for spinning is a rod with enough stiffness in the tip section but a relatively limber middle section—perhaps a fine point in rod selection, but nonetheless important, since the object in buying the right tackle and proper lures is to create a harmony that you can feel and an activity of the lure that will affect the urges of the fish.

Another test of rod-tip action and its effectiveness can be made by tying a bit of cloth to your line about two feet from the rod tip after you have cast a lure its normal distance (Figure VIII). By working the rod tip, reeling in, and releasing line while you watch the movement of the cloth, you will know what percentage of the action you apply is being transferred to the lure. The longer the line, the less the action will carry down to the lure. The lighter the lure, even though it is a sinking type of lure, the less will be the effect. To fish a spoon or spinner to its top efficiency is to know the results of your actions.

Remember this technique when trolling also, particularly with the lures that are to be fished fairly deep. There's no point in your exercise of the rod and line if it is not being transferred to the business end. Also, too much trolling speed will reduce the lure's effectiveness.

SPINCASTING

While I have it second in the description and discussion of the three tackle types, spinning is not necessarily second in importance. Since its introduction in America back in the 1930s and more extensively in the 1940s, spinning has consistently threatened to replace baitcasting. When it first came in, many angling experts predicted doom for the old tried-and-true, since the new gear seemed to do the job much better and offered a wider scope of lure weights and techniques. Moreover, spinning required less learning time for the beginner, since the reel practically eliminates the danger of backlash and line tangles due to faulty operation. The closed-face or spin-cast reel, different from the open-face reel, is almost automatic, and its use can be mastered very quickly. (Both spinning reel types are discussed later.)

Shortly after its introduction, despite the fact that baitcasting rods and lines had become steadily lighter and sportier in response to the demands of the light-tackle advocates, the still lighter and more flexible spinning rod, with its very light line and smaller lures, began to take over. It was found that a mere four-pound-test line was sufficient to land a monster bass, where a ten-pound line had

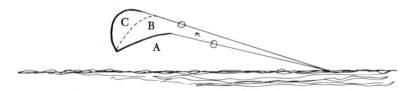

Figure VIII.   As suggested, tie a piece of cloth onto the line. Hold the rod in typical "fishing position" when trolling. If you twitch the rod from position (A) to position (B), the line has not moved at all. It must be twitched to (C), which will move the cloth about one foot and the lure a little less owing to line take-up. On this short troll, such twitching would be sufficient to activate the lure, but at twice the distance out, the line would absorb most of this, and more pressure and greater rod pull are therefore needed.

been used (somewhat nervously) in baitcasting. Besides this, big plugs and heavy spoons had been taking decreasing numbers of bass under almost all conditions, especially in the overfished waters of suburban lakes, ponds, and rivers. Then too, the same tackle used for trout fishing could be employed interchangeably in spinning and even employed in saltwater small-game fishing. All the angler needed was the one outfit to meet all light-tackle situations, or so it seemed.

However, baitcasting has since made a return visit to the store counters, and the demand, especially for newer, imported equipment is big.

Basically, a spinning reel consists of a spool of line facing "end out," rather than across the rod and at a right angle to the outgoing line, as in the baitcasting reel (see Figure IX). As the cast is made, the line winds off the end of the stationary spool as needed, and consequently no backlash is possible. Without the need for thumb tension on the line or the distance-cutting friction of a revolving spool, lighter lines and lures can be cast farther with just as much or even more accuracy. Best of all, unweighted live bait can be cast much farther because of the softer tip action of the longer spinning rod, with less possibility of flicking the bait off the hook.

The reel has either manual or a full-bail pick-up (such as the one shown on the open-face reel in Figure ix) and a drag control that must be accurately adjusted to a pulling force well below the pound test of the line. An antireverse device is employed when one wants to play a fish with the drag while using the reel handle only for retrieving line. This feature is excellent for trolling, since the drag, rather than the reel handle, will be activated when the lure being fished hits a snag or is struck by a bass.

However, light-tipped spinning rods and low test lines have one serious drawback in most bass fishing, which is the lack of sufficient power to set the hook on a strike or to horse a fish from heavy weeds or fight him out quickly from tricky snags. This is why, under tough fishing conditions, and especially in spots where there are bound to be some big bass, a fairly stiff tip is recommended —one that is stronger than the tip of the light-action spinning rod that would be selected for most stream trout fishing.

As in the baitcasting section, some guiding principles for spinning-tackle selection are given below. These indicate necessary factors for arriving at a balanced outfit that will cast well and accurately and that will meet the angler's personal needs. These

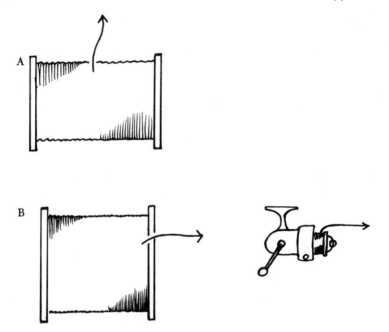

Figure IX.   From your tackle manual. (A) The spool from a level-wind baitcasting reel. The line rolls off the spool as the spool revolves. (B) The line is pulled off the end of the stationary-spool spinning reel as the lure is cast.

recommendations are general only, and offer a wide range of choice, but should be a guide and starting point in selecting the proper tackle.

Spincasting Tackle Specifications

REEL SIZE	ROD LENGTH	ROD ACTION	LINE TEST	LURE WEIGHT
Ultralight	5' to 5½'	Soft	4 to 6 lbs.	⅛ to ⅜ oz.

This is not an outfit for general bass fishing; it should be used only in fishing for small bass and panfish in a pond where there is little chance of bigger fish being caught. It is to be used with very light line and small lures. It can also be used sparingly in open, snag-free water for sport, when the angler will accept the loss of fish gracefully. It is good for small bass in streams where trout-type small spinners and weighted flies are used.

| *Medium* | *6' to 6½'* | *Medium* | *6 to 8 lbs.* | *¼ to ½ oz.* |

This is still considered to be a light-action outfit, capable of handling light lures for stream and lake fishing for bass of up to 4 pounds. It will handle the weeds well but is not intended for horsing fish. Its medium action is designed to handle live bait well on the cast and for trolling with light lures and bait.

| *Medium to Large; Freshwater* | *6' to 7'* | *Heavier, with a fast or stiff tip* | *5½ to 6½ lbs.* | *½ oz. to baitcasting sizes* |

This rig will be good for deep trolling. It has a stout rod for working 10-pound fish in weedy and snag-filled water. It is big enough for most pike and muskie conditions other than casting such big live baits as chubs with heavy sinkers.

In the outfits given above, the variation in rod actions from a stiff to a soft tip makes a great deal of difference in lure choice and the handling of lures.

SPINCASTING INSTRUCTION

Open-faced Reels

Spincasting is much easier than baitcasting. The touchiest parts of the action that must be learned are mastering the swinging of the rod and the line release. Let's deal with the open-face-reel outfit first.

You have purchased your new tackle. Attach the reel to the rod. It hangs down below the rod rather than perching on top of the rod as in baitcasting.

Reel the line from the factory spool to the reel spool in the manner shown in Figure X.

If you don't do this properly, you will have twists in the line. One way to untwist the line when fishing from a boat is to let out the entire length behind the moving boat and let the pressure of the water unravel it. You can also stretch the line over the ground, and pinching the line between your fingers, travel from the reel almost to the end of the line, allowing it to build up twists until you are near the end. At this point the twists that have collected will spin out. Monofilament line will also twist as a result of the

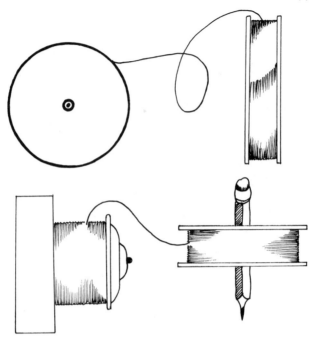

Figure X.   Reeling a line from a factory spool to your reel spool.

faulty casting of revolving lures or the use of wrong rigs in trolling. Both of these types of terminal tackle should be attached with swivels, and both the swivels and the line checked occasionally.

With the drag set very light on the reel, draw out about two feet of line and then, by turning the reel handle, close the bail. The line is now under the control of the drag, and you will have to pull it out in order to thread it through the guides, leaving about two feet of line beyond the rod tip.

The very first step in spincasting is that of opening the bail, which allows the line to fall freely from the end of the spool. To control and stop this, the tip of the forefinger of the rod hand is hooked under the line and brought up so that the line is pressed against the cork handle of the rod. The bail is then opened and snapped into the open position. With the line now controlled with the index finger, the cast from this point on is controlled similarly to the cast as described earlier with a baitcasting outfit (see page 232). However, instead of the thumb being the controlling finger, this job falls to the index finger.

The steps from here on are quite similar to those in baitcasting, and it might be good to review that section first.

With the line now controlled by your index finger, and the reel ready to cast, point the rod parallel to the ground in the direction of the proposed target. Before making a cast, let the line slip off your index finger. The weight of the plug will make it fall to the ground, pulling sufficient line from the reel, but no more. To retrieve, you merely start cranking the reel, automatically closing the bail, which in turn gathers up the line and distributes it evenly over the spool. Try this routine a few times to familiarize yourself with the functioning of the reel. As you pull the line from the reel spool, you will note that it comes off in wide coils, and you will see that the reason for the large circular guides mounted well away from the reel is to keep the line from slapping the rod or bunching up as it passes through the guides.

To make your first cast, let the plug dangle a foot and a half below the rod tip. As in the baitcast, this length of line helps to activate the sensitive rod tip when you begin the cast. Next, point the rod toward the ground (with the reel set in the bail-open position and the line in your index finger as before) and flip the rod up sharply, noting that the lure whips up. Now just as quickly flip the rod tip down again. You are building tension on the rod, which will provide the spring for your cast. Continuing your movement, increase the action of your rod by starting low again, then flipping the rod up, and at the same time raising your forearm to a ninety-degree angle. Sense the pull on the rod. Now try again by raising the rod to the vertical position and swing down once more. With this you will have almost the entire swing needed for most casts other than the extended power cast. Get used to the feel of this swing, and when ready, release the line about halfway down on the forward swing. The lure will sail out in front of you. If you release it too late, it will plop down quite unceremoniously in front of you; too soon and it will sail up in a wide skyward arc. Try again until you can get that lure to travel almost straight out, with but a slight elevation above a horizontal line parallel to the ground. Retrieve as I have described by merely starting to crank the reel handle. That's how it's done.

To refine the cast and gain better control, you should plan to "feather" the edge of the spool with your forefinger right after the line release. By gently feathering the line you can control the length and speed of the cast, a necessary control when casting a lightly hooked live bait or extremely light lures. To control the distance of the cast and stop the lure in flight, merely place your finger on the spool edge and gently press down on the line. If you stop the line too quickly on a powerful cast, especially when using a light line and a heavy lure, you'll risk snapping the line at the knot or swivel and having the lure fly free into the trees.

Again, practice.

The sidewinder cast in spinning is performed in the same manner as the vertical cast, only the rod is swung along a horizontal path rather than a vertical one. Care must be taken to release the line at exactly the right second in order to deliver the lure to its target.

To learn the range of your gear with the weight of the lure you are using, mark off distances from twenty to one hundred feet and try to cast to these points, learning the timing of the swing, the line release, and the control of distance by feathering. Once you have learned this you'll be able to cast to those shoreline rocks and snags and land your lure to within fractions of an inch of the target.

When actually fishing, it is a good idea to plan to overshoot just a bit but to stop the lure by feathering just before the lure hits the water, closing the bail as you begin to retrieve. In this way little slack line—or at least less—will remain in the air to settle down on the water. It is during those few seconds that a bass can strike. If he strikes on that slack line, the chances are he'll bust you up or that you'll miss the strike because of a late hit back.

As with any method of fishing, however, spinning makes its demands: well-balanced tackle to fit the situation and hairsplitting timing and accuracy. The fishing techniques are almost unnumbered.

Many are given in the illustrations here in the Appendix and throughout the book, and should be studied so that you can remember them when you go fishing next time.

Closed-face Reel

The closed-face reel is a variation of the open-face spinning reel with added refinements and more varied uses. It is the simplest spin-fishing reel to use. You rig up with the reel (when using a baitcasting rod) in the same above-rod position as the conventional baitcasting reel. Large guides are not needed for the line flow, since the line comes out of the center of the cone on the face of the reel (as shown in Figure XI).

Figure XI.   The closed-face reel.

To release the line you merely press the button on the rear top of the reel. To reel in you simply turn the reel handle. You use the same controls for casting as with the open-face reel, except in this case you feather the line as it comes out of the cone.

This closed-face reel can also be used with the conventional spinning rod with its large guides, in which case it is mounted below the rod, and it can be used with the fly rod, where it is recommended for short cast, live-bait fishing, such as with un-weighted minnows. In this type of fishing the monofilament line is well controlled by the reel, and the limber tip of the fly rod has an action that is even softer and slower than that of the most soft-tipped spinning rod. The only limitation of the open-face reel is its size. It is not made in large line capacities, nor is it geared to play heavy fish with a strong and sure drag control.

SPINNING LURES

If you thought you were confused (and perhaps delighted) by the great number of plugs, spoons, and spinners available for bait-casting, make a return visit to the store and check on the basic styles of spinning lures. They run the gamut from the very lightest of flies to the heaviest of plugs, spoons, and lures that spin, in weights all the way up to the "heavies" used in conventional bait-casting.

But again, the choice of a given lure for a specific situation in bass fishing is a matter of chance, hunch, theory, or, in rare cases, knowledge. Some anglers have found in their bass hunting that they tend to carry a greater variety of lures when they spinfish than they would for baitcasting, perhaps because the lures are smaller; there are always those few standby lures that will take fish when most others won't. However, fishing a lure with confidence is much more important than the design of the lure.

You can generally break down the types of spinning lures into the same basic categories that apply to baitcasting lures: plugs, both surface and sinking; spoons, both large and small, for trolling and coasting, and jigs for both methods; and the fly-and-spinner combinations and heavy bugs, weighted streamers, and large wet flies.

In building your "hope chest" of lures I suggest that you look at the local tackle counter for up-to-date lures for specific uses. These types should be bought in various weights and colors, with at least two or three backups for stock, since you'll be losing them regularly, or at least much more often than you would with heavier tackle.

I use the Jitterbug as a surface-disturbing lure, a Hula Popper for popping, a floating Pikey-Minnow for both subsurface work, and surface diving, a jointed one that sinks for subsurface work, and the old fore-and-aft spinner plug for both floating and sinking casting and for trolling. As for spoons, I use the Daredevle; and for spinners the Colorado or twin-blade Indiana, with or without bait or a fly. If the bass refuse these I generally go home. My collection of revolving spinning lures and mini-plugs is quite wide, however.

With an outfit of the proper weight, baitcasting and spinning plugs can be used interchangeably. Most spinning plugs from one-eighth to one-half ounce are smaller than their baitcasting counterparts, to activate the lighter tips and slower actions of spinning rods, particularly ultralight rods. Spinning spoons range in weight from the standard heavies of the baitcasting sizes (one-half ounce) down to fly-rod mini-weights (one-eighth ounce), and should therefore be selected for tackle balance as well as for fishing conditions.

These lures can be deadly when fished properly. The tendency is to retrieve them much too fast. If speed is needed to keep them up from the weeds or off the bottom, use one of a lighter weight and fish it accordingly.

FLY-FISHING AND BASS-BUGGING

Even the beginner at any kind of fishing, be it for bass, trout, or small saltwater game fish, is likely to know something about spinning gear and fly-fishing tackle. But when it comes to bass bugging with a fly rod, an entirely new set of conditions, tackle, and technique are necessary, even though the basic casting of the bass-bug fly rod is similar to that with the conventional fly rod. Below are the basic requirements for a bug-casting outfit for bass.

Rod Selection

The correct bass-bug rod must meet a set of specific needs and is not always easy to find in the tackle store. In addition, the personality of the angler must be weighed into the selection of the proper tackle. For example, a strong man over six feet tall who wants to cast a bug seventy-five or more feet requires the stoutest rod made. A short person who goes at the sport a bit easier and recognizes that it is smarter to move the boat in fifty feet closer than to try a long cast does not need that same rod. Most of us can be cataloged as being somewhere in between.

Before we can really select the best bass-bug rod for our size, spirit, and needs, it must have defined attributes. These are several in number.

In order to cast a bug accurately, directly, and a sufficient distance even into a wind, the rod used for casting it must be able to handle a weight-forward (bullet) tapered line of the GAF or G2AF type of classification. This line has a short, flat, nontapered front section followed by a sharp taper to a heavy section of heavy line and a sudden drop back to a flat running line, as shown in the line illustration. This type of line is not false cast in the manner usually used with a double-tapered line; it is heavy and designed to shoot a leader and a bug for a grand joy-ride out there to the target.

If the action of the rod is too fast and stiff it will be an abomination to cast, a veritable backbreaker. If the action is too soft and the rod has a soft tip and a stiff midsection, it will not keep that line high in the air on the back cast. If the whole action of the rod is too soft, it will not deliver any distance or accuracy. The subtle rod taper that is needed is one that goes from a strong (but not stiff) midsection to a tip section with graduated power that does not fizzle out toward the last two feet.

This is a general description of what I consider to be the proper type of action. That same set of specifications, increased for the strong angler bent on distance, can also be found. For the lightweight angler not bent on distance, a scale-down set of specifications is available.

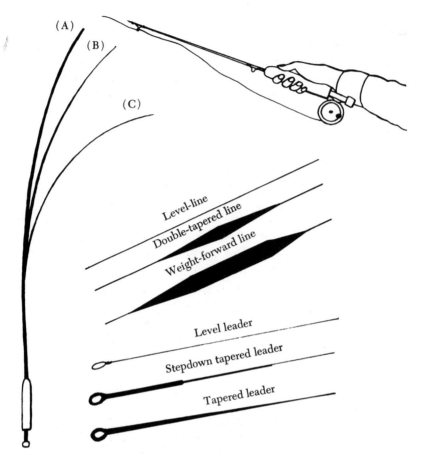

Figure XII. The bass bug tackle set-up. ABC shows the relative tapered power of three nine-foot standard-taper fly rods. The heavy rod (A) has the even action and relatively stiff tip needed to cast and to pick up fluffy bugs or heavy flies at a long distance. The three lines shown— level, double-tapered, and "bug" or "weight forward" or "bullet taper"— are required. The three leaders shown are the level, used for short casts and ranging from four to six feet long; the step tapered, which is hand tied to premeasured lengths to balance out your cast for a particular situation, lure design, and weight; and the factory tapered, to which a heavier butt section or a lighter end tippet can be added.

Ultra-long-distance casts, described by many experts as being necessary, have no merit as far as I'm concerned. Sure it's fun to make those long casts, but if the idea of bass-catching is uppermost in your mind, it isn't necessary to reach way out there. It is a very simple matter to move the boat in a few yards or to wade out (or in) closer to the target. There are many trout fishermen who are distance minded and own tackle that casts a dainty fly great distances. But whether they catch more trout than the angler who fishes closer in is a good question.

The next requisite is that of being able to pick up that bug once it is cast to the target. Now a heavy, fluffy bug and a long line create a lot of drag on the water. The rod must be able to overcome this with ease. True, it is seldom necessary to pick up the bug at the full extent of the cast; when the angler wants to pick the bug up for a new cast, it is generally retrieved for at least half the distance out from the rod before the actual pickup, to make the job easier. Also, most bugs are heavy and wind resistant, and the angler should select only those that balance with the rod rather than selecting the rod to balance with the bug. The perfect bug need not be designed so that it is difficult to cast; many of those on the tackle counters are much too fluffy. Therefore, select only those wind resistant bugs that will sail through the air well on your own rod. This is something you must discover in relation to the speed of your casting on the fore-and-aft swings. Often, a cork-bodied bug with no feathers or hair, if popped properly, will take just as many bass as a fluffy, difficult-to-cast bug. Remember, the characteristic of the bass is its irresistible attraction to a surface commotion, no matter how it is made. That commotion should be as near to him as you can get. Therefore, the main point in bug casting is to be able to present the bug *where you want it to land*. This fact is more important than the bug's attractiveness. An attractive bug that is cast far from the target will probably be ignored by the bass.

Another requirement of the proper bass-bug rod is that it have the power to set the hook when the bass hits the bug. Soft tips are out; there must be an instant pick-up or retrieve of the slack line immediately after the cast is made. Also, if the bass hits firmly, and there is no need to hook him, the first and most important requirement is to head him out into the open water. The first thing he'll do if he is hooked near a snag or in the weeds will be to head back farther into the weeds or down under. Therefore, you must have control of him at that moment of the strike. This is why the conventional trout rod, even though it might cast a small bug well at short ranges, will not fulfill the needs for bass fishing. Nor will a fairly stout-action Atlantic salmon rod.

Then there's the problem of wind. Some rods, particulary of lighter design, will cast a bug well in a calm situation, but when it comes to bucking a wind, either from the side or head-on, will fail miserably. Extra power, then, must be available. Generally, the rod length should be a minimum of nine feet and a maximum of ten feet, and the rod should preferably have two sections for a better division of action.

CASTING THE BASS-BUG FLY ROD

The conventional casts used in fly fishing are necessary to know in bug fishing for bass. Additionally, you'll discover that your direction will have to be sharpened for that longer cast; more power will be needed on the high back cast to keep the bug high, and a powerful drive will be needed to direct the bug in a straight line to a point a few feet directly above the target area. Mastering of the double-haul cast is a must, and requires further refinement of the use of your entire arm, in fact your entire body, right down to your pivoted feet. This symphony of motion will come as you learn the art of bug casting.

For those of you who have fished with a fly rod using small conventional flies, bass-bug fishing will not be hard to master, since the tackle is only bigger, stronger, and heavier, and the casts will be of longer distances, utilizing the double-haul. For those fishermen who have fished in salt water, bugging will be a bit easier in many ways.

The techniques of bug casting are given in the following sections, for the beginner as well as the experienced flycaster.

The basic and simple fore-and-aft cast requires that the line be cast as far behind the angler as it will go in front of him. This action requires a certain timing in the movement of and force applied to the rod, with additional pulling by the line hand on the line as it comes from the reel and enters the first rod guide.

Try this action now, with the rod rigged up and about twenty-five feet of line stretched out on the grass or water. To add more tension and power for a longer distance cast, strip in an arm's length of line from the rod guide during the beginning of the pickup, and release it when the line rolls forward in the air over your head on the forward swing of the rod. Try this several times and notice that the stripping in and releasing of the line add more power to the cast. To use this power, simply lengthen the amount of line for the cast.

Since a weight-forward tapered line is used in bass-bug casting, it is not necessary to false cast a long line in the air. Once the proper amount of line is being false cast, and power has been built up by stripping in line in the double-haul fashion, the cast is made, and running line previously stripped from the reel is literally pulled out of your hand by the force of the cast. On the next cast, do not try to throw all the line that went out on your first cast. Instead, strip in the extra line that was pulled out by the force of the cast. With this line either coiled in your hand or laid in coils neatly at your feet, strip off additional line from the reel for a cast that will go out farther than the last one you made. Now false cast as before, but on the forward throw exert more pressure on the rod, and while doing so strip in line, further increasing the tension on the rod. As the line goes forward, release it and let it run freely. If all goes well, you have mastered the double-haul, and with practice can deliver a big dry fly or fluffy bass bug sixty feet away.

The subtleties of the double-haul will appear as you learn by doing. You'll discover that you must keep your wrist stiff on the backswing and not allow the rod to pass beyond the vertical position, or the line will fall down quickly behind you and the cast will not go forward properly.

Keep that backcast high and refine your timing so as to deliver a wide bow on the fore-and-aft casts, so that the line will unfold properly on the forward drop, turning the fly over properly for accurate targeting and maximum distance without slack.

Learn to know just how little of the line is false cast so that you save your energy and build up rod strength properly for the release of the running line. And as you retrieve the bug in short pops back to the rod, remember the length of line to be cast before making your pickup for the beginning of another cast.

In the case of conventional trout flycasting, the leader is generally selected, rather than the fly itself. In this case, the fly simply goes along for the ride. But in bass bugging, while the same general formula exists, the added weight of the bug, including its air-resistance factor, must be taken into account in selecting a leader of proper length and weight. Both the bug and the leader must be considered in choosing a specific leader for the rod, the line, and the particular bug type that will be used. Since there will be a variety of bug types used, leaders that are specifically designed for them should either be labeled as such or permanently attached to the specific bug. Then, instead of merely changing the bug on the leader, the bug-and-leader are changed together so that the balance of the outfit can be retained.

With some rods (and some fishermen) a six-foot level leader

or, for example, a ten-pound test leader will cast a light bug very well, particularly one that is fluffy and wind-resistant. However, that same bug on a longer leader tapered to a fine point would not only whistle and spin in the air but also would not land straight out as desired. By the same token, a tapered leader should be used with a less wind-resistant bug of equally light weight. A heavy bug requires a proportionately heavy leader, either tapered or level, depending again on the action of the rod and the power and timing that are characteristic of your usual casting. These pronouncements are, of necessity, general. Start by using a level leader with different specific bug types. If you find a good combination, forget the tapered leader. If a taper is required, then use it, cutting back on the thin end as needed.

BASS-BUG FISHING

In almost every chapter of this book I have described methods of bugging in our hunting for bass and have detailed many of the types of water and fishing conditions where the bug can and should be used as a matter of choice. There are standard requirements to be remembered.

First of all, the bug is a small object in comparison with the usual popping plug. It will cause less commotion on the water, and should therefore be placed in a pocket in the pads, in an open stretch of water between the grass stems, right next to a rock or old stump or windfall, or right on the beach. It is not a lure to merely cast haphazardly anywhere on the lake. In the offshore water where bass are seen to be feeding or chasing minnows, the bug can be cast as near as possible to them, allowed to sit there on the water, and patiently retrieved.

PLAYING THE BASS IN BUGGING

While a section on striking, playing, and landing bass follows, there are a few specifics required in the handling of a bass on a bug rod that should be detailed here.

First of all, the bass will probably take the bug in difficult water: snags, pads, grass, or shallow water with refuse. The bass-bug fisherman has a distinct advantage in the use of the long fly rod, in being instantly able to raise that rod tip up sharply in order to quickly get that long line off the water for better control of the fish and to get the fish away from snags. The fish must be headed out

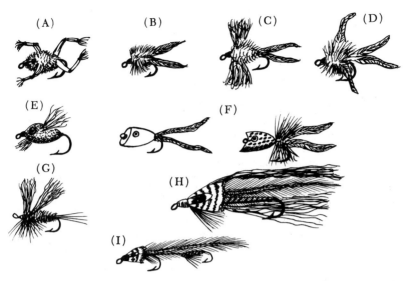

Figure XIII. (A–E) Various hair and feather bugs and flies. Small sizes can be cast with the trout-fly rod, but only for short distances. These are good for stream bass. (F) Cork-, wood-, or plastic-bodied plug-bug. (G) Trout-type, Wulff-type dry fly. (H) Conventional streamer-bucktail that can be cast well with the bass-bug rod. (I) The tandem-hook streamer, equally effective as the streamer-bucktail, can be skittered like a bug on the surface in a fast retrieve.

immediately from its lair and the slack line of the cast must be instantly gathered. From this point on, line control is a must.

The angler should also be able to gather in all slack line and coil it in the bottom of the boat or canoe, in an area free of any kind of obstruction. When wading, the habit of dropping the slack in coils away from any grass or snags must also be developed, for when that bass decides to take off in a fast run, all that spare line had better be available to whisk through your line hand and into the rod guides in an unobstructed way.

You'll seldom have the time to crank that line back onto the reel during the fastest part of the action.

BIG WET FLIES

As you may have discovered from your reading so far, big wet flies, streamers, and bucktails are among my favorite lures for bass. Few bass fishermen use them with any regularity, simply because it hasn't occurred to them to master their use on this species. The only reason I have had success with them is that they have been so productive for me on trout, and logic projected their use into bass fishing. For me they also served as an introductory phase to my use of bass bugs, since they are fly-rod lures.

These flies can also be cast well with heavy trout and light salmon rods (or eight and a half to nine and a half feet in length). With such rods, casting distances of up to sixty feet can be achieved with a double-tapered line, using a tapered leader with a tippet of no less than four-pound test.

RECOMMENDED FLY AND BUG-FISHING TACKLE COMBINATIONS

While I am almost reluctant to make specific recommendations as guidelines for selecting a bass-bug rod, there are basics that can be set down for your consideration. I suggest that you start by looking at three combinations of rod, reel, line, and leader. After you have sampled these, you will be on your way to deciding just what you need to fulfill your personal requirements.

Bug-fishing Specifications

REEL SIZE	ROD LENGTH	ROD ACTION	LINE TAPER	LEADER
100 yd. cap.	8½′	Medium	HDH	7X to 3X tip

The rod in this outfit is capable of throwing big wet flies and streamers. It can also cast bass bugs of light weight and little air resistance up to 50 feet.

REEL SIZE	ROD LENGTH	ROD ACTION	LINE TAPER	LEADER
100 yd. cap.	9′	Medium, with a stiff tip	GAF	Tapered; 6′ to 4 lbs.

The rod here is a bit more powerful than the one in the first outfit if the tip action is not too soft in a step-down taper. The extra length allows a broader arc in the cast and affords better pick-up and striking power.

REEL SIZE	ROD LENGTH	ROD ACTION	LINE TAPER	LEADER
100 yd. cap.	9½′	Strong mid-section and fast tip		Level; 6′ of 6 lbs., or tapered from 10 to 6 lbs.

This outfit has a strong rod capable of casts to sixty feet, using a reasonably designed bug without too much wind resistance. It is excellent for casting three big streamers or bucktails and also good for long-distance salmon and light saltwater flycasting. It handles light spinners and small fly-rod plugs too.

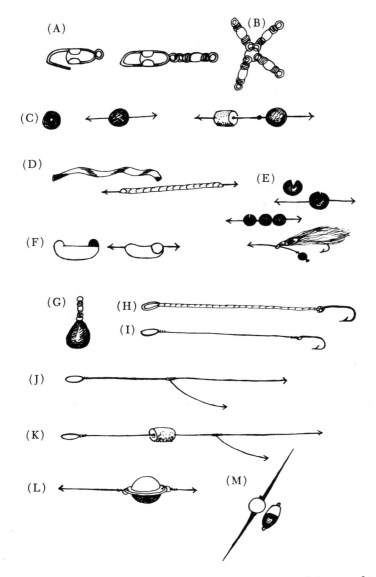

Figure XIV. Terminal tackle items. (A) The snap, used for attaching lures and rigs; also shown with the swivel. (B) The three-way swivel for multiple rigging. (C) The slip sinker, which is either round or oval-shaped; the line goes through it. (D) A wrap-around lead strip, also shown wound on a line or leader. (E) The splitshot (BB shot), shown open and clamped on the line. (F) The clamp-on sinker with pinch ears, shown on the line. (G) The ringed sinker, either round or oval-shaped and usually attached to the end of the line. (H) Plastic-covered metal (sometimes braided) leader. (I) Hook tied to leader material (nylon or metal). (J) Tippet tied in barrel knot to main line. (K) Simple cork with line running through it for adjustment. (L) Plastic bobber for float. (M) Stick bobber with rings for attaching lines.

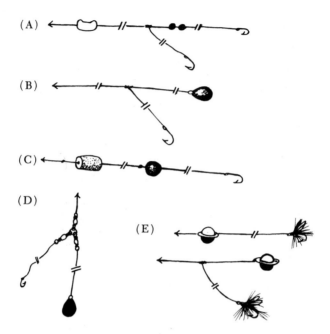

Figure XV. Terminal tackle, as rigged. (A) Simple two-hook rig with splitshot or clamp-on sinker attached (for casting, trolling, or stillfishing). (B) Single hook with sinker on terminal (for casting and stillfishing). (C) Slip-sinker and cork bobber and single hook (which is cast out for still-fishing). (D) Three-way swivel for weight and single hook or lure (for casting, stillfishing, or trolling). (E) Plastic bubble ahead of terminal fly or lure and also tied in at the end (for casting).

TERMINAL TACKLE

Often referred to as the "business end" of your fishing equipment, terminal tackle must be selected and used with as much care as your rod, reel, and line. Yes, you can catch bass with a bent pin, a rock for a weight, and a piece of driftwood as a float, but there are better ways that are more enjoyable and more productive.

In order to accumulate the proper terminal tackle for catching and holding bass, remember that the mouth of a bass is rough and bony, that its scales are rough, and that the spikes on some of its fins are sharp. This means that thin nylon leader material will often be cut quickly. Heavy nylon leaders and, for most fishing, nylon-encased metal leaders are recommended, since they will be fished where there are snags and sharp rocks. True, big bass can be and are taken on dainty dry flies tied to the traditional gossamer leaders, but you seldom hear about the ones that get away.

In addition to the ready-made metal leaders, there are swivels and snap-swivels for attachment of the line to the lure or to a hook. These help to eliminate line twist and line tangle. The snap swivel offers a quick way to change lures or terminal baits without having to cut line or untie knots. Sinkers and bobbers are made in varied shapes and sizes for their particular task: bottom and stillfishing, casting, and trolling. Bobbers, plastic bubbles, and floats are designed for keeping a rig off the bottom. They are attached at various points along the line, as you will see in the illustrations that follow. Study these and their captions.

THE MERITS OF BAIT-FISHING

Why fish with bait?

Unfortunately, there is an unwarranted distinction drawn between bait fishermen and artificial-lure fishermen, a discrimination based on Old World orthodoxy that, in its hypocrisy, attempts to put the bait fisherman beneath the level of other sportsmen. Bait fishermen are every bit the sportsmen that lure anglers purport to be. Anyone who keeps more than the legal limit or who takes fish he doesn't really need is not considered a sportsman, no matter what kind of enticement he uses.

When the accent is put on the sporting aspect of tactics and tricks rather than the goal of catching as many fish as possible, fishing with natural baits is more efficient than fishing with lures. The natural-bait fisherman gives the fish what it wants: the food upon which it feeds. Present this food in the most natural manner and with the most sportsworthy tackle you can buy.

There are many types of natural baits and bait species. Particular waters have resident baits that can be used to entice the bass that ordinarily feed on them. Bass like minnows, lake shiners, and frogs, and will also feed on their own offspring when the nesting season is over and the little ones have grown a bit in size. The stream bass finds insects living in the rocks and gravel of its stream. The fisherman merely needs gather the right bait and present it to the fish in a natural manner.

Baits also fall into certain categories. Natural baits derived specific waters include, in streams, aquatic or water-bred insects that except for a few days in the air spend most of their time in the water. Stonefly larvae, caddis flies in their stick-and-stone cases, mayfly nymph, dobson flies, hellgramites, and other "wormy" looking aquatic insects can be used successfully in both streams and lakes. Lakes and streams off minnows, shellfish, frogs, and worms. Other natural baits include land-bred insects and creatures that live in and about lakes and streams and find their way to the water, such as grasshoppers, crickets, moths, earthworms, and caterpillars. They can be presented in various ways: alive or dead on a hook, or dead on a hook and rigged in special ways, such as when cut into small or large sections. Unnatural baits, made from food materials not found naturally in the water but coming from the human larder, include cheese, corn, and meat, especially pork. Baitfishing offers a broad choice to the angler and permits many ad-libs.

Catching and keeping aquatic insects and fish requires a bit of knowledge and work. First, however, check the local fishing laws, for the collection of some baits is restricted in some areas. When wading or walking along the stream while fishing, deposit your bait storage box or container in the shallow water and return to it for replenishing. Carry your "working supply" in a bait can on your belt. In boat fishing, the main stock can be kept in a bait can and lowered over the side when you are not moving fast. The bait you collect can often be kept overnight for the following day's fishing.

The hellgramite, or nymph of the dragon- or dobson fly, is one of the best and strongest baits for bass. Often called the "perch bug," it is collected from muddy bottoms by digging and screening. It can be kept in screened boxes filled with several inches of mud and submerged in water of about the same temperature as that from which you take it. Hellgramites eat each other unless you feed them chopped worms and small insects. Stonefly nymphs must be kept in water as cool as the stream from which they come. Put the ones you collect in a container with rocks and slime from the same general location in which you capture them. The same treatment applies for caddis fly and mayfly nymphs.

The crawfish is one of the most useful of aquatic baits for all game fish. You can discover them in profusion along lake shores and in slow-flowing rivers. They are best spotted at night. Use a small dip net to catch them, but be quick about it; they can dart right back into the water before you have dumped them into the bucket. Feed them meat or fish or they will devour each other. Keep them in cool water with a few rocks, some gravel, and a good supply of lake grass or pond weeds. Snip off the claws to keep them from pinching you.

The stone catfish is another good bait for bass. It is found under stones and stream-bed debris and grows to about four inches in length. It should be kept in a well-aerated, screened box underwater, or in a bait can.

Catching and keeping live minnows is quite a job. You can catch them in seine nets and baited minnow nets and traps, and by angling for them with tiny hooks. They will survive in a big barrel or a large aquarium with frequent water changes or in a screened box kept underwater. The working supply of these fish is kept in a bait container on your belt and replenished as needed from the main supply.

The land-bred insects you use for bait need not be alive. A big moth taken from beneath the porch light the night before you fish will be attractive bait the next day, cast as you would a fly-rod bug.

Crickets and grasshoppers can be caught easily while the dew is still on the ground in the early morning. They will survive in a jar that has air holes punctured in the tin top.

Earthworms and nightcrawlers can easily be dug up from the ground or collected from manure piles, damp and dark grassy areas in the woods, or fields. Keep them in plenty of fresh, cool, and damp earth, or store them alive in a big box, with frequent dampening. Add lettuce or greenery for them to feed on. Corn meal is also excellent. A corner of your garden can be reserved for their residence. They multiply rapidly, and if kept well a supply will always be available. To prepare them for fishing, put them on moist sand for a few hours before using them. This will clean them out and brighten and toughen their texture so that they will remain on the hook better and offer a more appetizing morsel for the fish.

BASIC BAIT-FISHING TECHNIQUES

Simple Stillfishing

Stillfishing from the bank of a river or the edge of a lake is the simplest form of fishing. It consists merely of casting the bait, usually with its sinker and floater, out into the water and letting nature take its course.

(A)

(B)

(C)

(D)

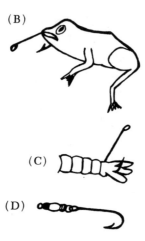

Figure XVI.   (A) The proper manner of hooking a minnow for casting. This is most delicate. The hook goes through the lips only, not through the head, or the minnow will be killed. (B) The frog is hooked in the same manner as the minnow, for the same reasons. (C) The crawfish is best hooked through the tail, in the last "joint." Some anglers hook it through the collar, but the bait will then tend to spin. (D) Don't forget to use a swivel ahead of the hook.

The refinements are many, however. First, the bait (if alive) must be cast in such a way as not to kill it, flick it off the hook, or have it become tangled in its own line or in weedy snags. This requires soft handling of the tackle. The cast, whether it be made with a fly rod, a spinning rod, or a baitcasting rod, must be slow and steady, not jerky or "snappy." Sufficient line, including the rig, should extend from the rod tip before the cast is made. The cast should be either a sidewinder or a lateral cast.

As the line is released it is allowed to slip out in as free a state as possible, with the slack between the floater and the rod tip being gathered in. If no floater is used, the angler must attempt to "keep in touch" with the bait, which calls for a minimum of slack. When the fish takes the bait or the angler feels the bait being mouthed, the strike must be withheld until there is sufficient reason to believe that the fish has the bait securely in its mouth. Sensing this takes much practice.

In many instances, in water three to ten feet deep, it is advisable to fish a live bait without any floater or weights of any kind. Casting this light bait requires an extremely light rod-tip action, much care, and a very slow swing of the rod. The cast will not be a long-distance one. The only way you will know that a fish is interested in devouring your offering is when the line begins to move forcefully in a definite direction as it is towed out by the fish.

As we have seen, bass when not actually hungry or on the feed will quite often take a free bait, mouth it, spit it out, mouth it again, and play with it. On a slack and weightless line you'll be lucky to know that this is happening unless you can actually see the action. But when the fish means business, you'll know it. Let him run a bit and then strike.

Stillfishing from the shore is best done in a deep hole near the shore; from a bank where the water is deeper than it is along the rest of the shoreline; near a collection of snags; or off a point of rocks. How to fish these situations is detailed in various chapters of the book.

Stillfishing in a stream is best done below a falls, in the slack water beside a rapids, or in any stretch of the stream that will allow a free action of the bait without having it whisked off by the faster current. For details on this, refer to the section on river fishing for bass.

Drift Stillfishing

This is a modification of stillfishing that is done from a boat on a lake or in a slow-moving river. The unweighted bait is merely dropped over the side, with the line being fed out by degrees as it is pulled either by the bait or by the drifting motion of the boat. If the boat is drifting with a wind, a slight weight can be added, depending on the speed of the drift. The idea here is to allow the bait as much freedom as possible while maintaining it as deep as is practical in a given situation. When the depth of the stretch of water is known, a bobber can be added for better control. With a bobber you can also know approximately where the bait is at any given moment. The bait can be weighted or unweighted, as desired.

In river drift fishing, the bait can be allowed to drift down-current from the boat by simply holding the progress of the boat below the speed of the current that is carrying the bait. When the boat is allowed to drift more slowly than the bait, the current pulls on the bait, giving it some action and life. If the ratio of the two speeds becomes too great and the current acts too strongly on the bait, it will be dragged to the surface. Correct this by allowing the boat to drift faster or by adding weights to the bait.

Drift stillfishing on a fast-water stream offers somewhat the same conditions as on a river. You can adjust the speed of the drift by the amount of line that is fed from the rod, thereby keeping the bait from snagging the bottom or being brought to the surface by the current. Add more weight if and when necessary.

Deep Stillfishing

The same wide choice of terminal tackle exists for this as for drift stillfishing. The only difference is that more weight is needed to sink the bait down deep until the lead hits the bottom. When it hits, reel in a couple of feet of line promptly so that the rig will not catch on bottom snags and rocks. On a calm lake with no wind to drift the boat to any degree, an anchor is not necessary. When the breeze is sufficient to move the boat and it is desired to fish the boat sideways to the wind, two anchors are needed: one from the bow and the other from the stern. The same thing is required when fishing a slow-moving river or stream.

One of the most effective rigs is the simple monofilament line and single hook with no weight of any kind added. It is stillfished by merely dropping the bait over the side and then feeding out lengths of line as it is absorbed and sinks with the swimming bait. Use as much as a hundred feet if you are drifting slowly. The bait is completely free and will not scare finicky fish. The bass will often take the bait and you will not be aware of it until he takes off in a run. By this time the bait is well down his gullet and all you have to do is snub him.

Midsummer deep-lake stillfishing is best done where there are spring holes, or at least deep water that will be cooler than the shallows. It is also good to deep stillfish along the edges of steep cliffs where the water is of a sufficient depth.

Many such situations are detailed in this book, and you will find that there will be other fish along with the bass in these choice holes. They will steal your bait unmercifully, especially the catfish, but when the bass takes hold, you'll know it.

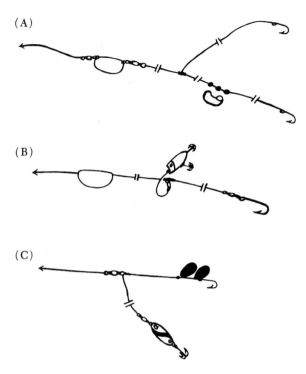

Figure XVII. (A) The jig baited with a worm for bottom bouncing. The alternate would be a minnow hooked this way. (B) A floating-diving plug attached ahead of the jig will aid in activating the jig and also offer an alternative to the fish. (C) The live bait is tied in above the weighted jig. By activating the jig, you'll be activating the bait.

Casting and Retrieving Live Bait

In addition to the need for proper terminal tackle and gentle casting of the bait, as described previously, a sensitive hand must be employed to retrieve the bait so that it will remain natural looking and "alive." This calls for a very slow retrieve, inch-by-inch, all the way to the rod tip, for a bass can and often does follow a bait for a long distance and can surprise you by grabbing it just as it is about to come up to the surface.

Trolling

Trolling requires special terminal tackle, as shown in Figures XVIII and XIX. Either live bait or artificial lures and flies can be used. Trolling can also be done with a bait impaled on the hook of

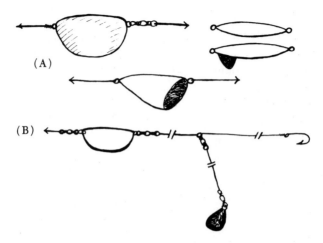

Figure XVIII. Terminal tackle rigged for trolling. (A) Trolling fin, weight, and finned weight. (B) Trolling fin, swiveled sinker, and hook (or lure).

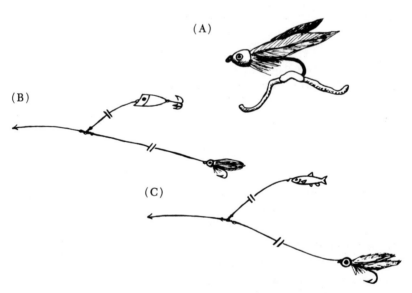

Figure XIX. Three trolling rigs, showing different ways of using terminal tackle. (A) Two hooks, the end one weighted so that it will not tangle with the leading hook. The weight also helps to sink the entire rig. The weights are either splitshot or clamp-on sinkers. (B) A "teaser" plug is attached ahead of the bait on a short line, offering the bass a choice. The action of the plug will affect the bait nicely. (C) A deeper going rig employs a spoon on the first dropper and twin spinners (Indiana-type) ahead of the bait.

a lure such as a spoon or a jig. The use of two or even three terminals can call for a weight, spoon, plug, and bait on separate tippets.

Trolling can be done at all levels, from the surface of the water —with floating plugs, big wet flies, bucktails, and tandem-hooked streamers to which a bait such as pork rind is attached—to deep levels with heavy weights. Jig bouncing while slow trolling is another effective bottom technique and calls for the use of an eel (live or artificial) or a slim piece of pork rind.

Read back over the introductory section of the book with my suggestions on casing the lake for hints as to when, where, and how to troll, and also the various chapters where bass "hunting" is done by trolling. Here in the Appendix we are concerned with rigs and basic techniques as they apply to tackle use.

Throughout the book are many more diagrams of situations where a combination of casting and trolling is used, particularly when two anglers are fishing together.

WADING

In order to go equipped for shoreline and on-the-lake fishing, proper footgear is needed. For casual angling when you will not actually be entering the water, a simple pair of canvas shoes will suffice. You may get them wet once in a while, and muddy for sure. But to better protect your feet from water, snakes, rock bruises, and mud, not to mention cold, a pair of rubber boots is needed. No, you won't have to wear them "full up" all the time, but do fold them down to below your knees and snap them securely so that your leg movement is not impeded. The waterproof cover the boots will give your lower legs will let you enter shallow water in order to unsnag a lure or net a fish. They are good to use in the boat as well, for you will often be landing or embarking from the shore or trudging through shallows. When needed, the extra hip-height of the boots will be available.

For comfort, I recommend a pair of cotton socks next to the skin to absorb perspiration, and over these a pair of lightweight wool socks (the weight depending on the temperature). Fold and tuck your pants legs into the outer pair of socks for ease in getting in and out of the boots.

When the urge comes for deeper going, the best answer is a pair of chest-high waders. They'll be hot and heavy in the bright sun of midsummer, but to cool off, you can bend down occasionally and wet them almost to their tops. The high waders will allow you to wade fairly deep. And while you sink into the mud of the bottom, the extra height will let you wade to the hot spots or to better casting positions.

There will be times when you are boating that you will prefer to leave the boat and wade out into a grass or pad flat. Getting out of a boat or canoe in waders is not the easiest project. If you have been fishing from the boat and wish to don the waders, put them over the side (where they can rest on the bottom solidly), and then, foot by foot, step into them and then pull them up. You can also don them aboard the boat and by lying partly down along the gunwale of the craft (being careful to maintain balance for yourself and the boat), get out of the boat by moving one leg over at a time. With one foot secure on the bottom, the other can follow. In this way you will not be straining the stiff crotch of the waders.

It is a good idea when wading water with doubtful bottom solidarity to carry a wading staff (a stick of wood or old broom handle with a thong attached) to poke at the bottom ahead of you. In this way you'll avoid stepping on bogs and into deep holes and mires.

Don't forget to anchor the boat before you leave!

BOATING

While this subject is detailed in various chapters in the book, I do suggest two forgotten or unknown methods of propulsion that should be used instead of the motor, after you have approached the fishing grounds.

Poling

When you approach a good shallow-water fishing spot, the motor should be stopped. If it is awkward to row or too difficult to paddle easily, the use of the pole is recommended. Proper poling will not disturb the water and will move the boat quietly. A stout, lightweight pole (bamboo can be used) about ten or more feet in length does the job very well. Today, the lost art of poling is remembered only by back-country guides. It is used almost exclusively as a method of boat movement in some sections of the country, such as the Ozarks, the Pacific Northwest and, of course,

Down East. Most moderns have never learned the art. Poling is also a must in proper river travel, since the pole can serve as the motive power for the boat as well as in controlling its drift. With the pole, the boat can be held still in even a fast current. In upriver fishing or travel, the pole must be used when the paddle cannot deliver the power or the control needed (and when the motor would be useless).

Sculling

Another almost unknown way of moving a boat in the fishing grounds is sculling. It is a simple and effective way of propelling a boat effortlessly and quietly. I learned this useful method years ago from commercial fishermen in the Bay of Fundy. A short oar or paddle can be used. A notch to fit the stem of the blade is cut into the transom (stern board) of the boat, away from the motor but not too far toward the corner. The paddle is put into this slot so that the blade is properly submerged in the water and is pushed back and forth or up and down while being feathered or turned in the same manner as you feather or turn a paddle when paddling in the usual way. This allows pressure to be applied in one direction and a pressureless return to the starting point of the paddle push. This is a one-handed operation, and you can hold the fishing rod in the other hand, trolling slowly and entering a good fishing area without spoiling it by too much activity.

For better progress in either poling or sculling, make sure the motor is tilted up and out of the water so that it will not drag in the water and pick up weeds.

INDEX

Page numbers in **boldface** type refer to illustrations.